C0-AOF-746

Israel's Odyssey

Israel's Odyssey

A SURVEY OF ISRAEL'S RENAISSANCE, ACHIEVEMENTS AND PROBLEMS

By Abraham Mayer Heller

FARRAR, STRAUS AND CUDAHY · NEW YORK

Library of Congress catalog card number 59-9176

First Printing: 1959

Published simultaneously in Canada by
Ambassador Books, Ltd., Toronto

Manufactured in the United States of America
By The American Book-Stratford Press, Inc., New York

TO

FRANCES

Preface

Insofar as possible, though a Zionist since my early youth, I have earnestly endeavored in *Israel's Odyssey* to survey Israel's national renaissance, achievements and problems without favor or prejudice.

The thought of writing this book came to me while spending the fall and winter of 1956-57 in Israel. The new state was then practically evacuated of tourists because of her involvement in the Sinai Campaign and the aftermath of United Nations threats of sanctions. Mrs. Heller, who accompanied me to the Holy Land, and our son Zachary, who was then a student at the Hebrew University, and I were among the few visitors who remained in the Holy Land. We were accorded a warm welcome in every section of the land and were cordially received by responsible leaders in every walk of life.

My daily observations, impressions and interviews supplemented by the various governmental reports, as well as other public documents and statistics, form the basis of this work.

Much has been written about Israel, mostly specialized treatises on one phase or another of the life of the people and state. *Israel's Odyssey* is designed to present a comprehensive portrayal of the new state, the historic forces which paved the way for its establishment, the major accomplishments of the Zionist movement since its inception and the countless problems confronting the new republic, with special emphasis on Arab-Jewish relations and the vital links between Israel and world Jewry.

Numerous Hebraic terms have been employed in this book. While their English equivalents are parenthetically defined, the reader will also be aided by a glossary of Hebrew words together with a schedule of Israeli measurements, weights and monetary denominations which appear at the end of the book.

For the purpose of confirming statistical facts and figures, many sources such as histories, encyclopedias, journals, magazines and brochures were consulted. In addition thereto I am very much indebted to my dear friend and colleague Dr. Louis D. Gross, who carefully examined the manuscript and contributed many valuable suggestions which are incorporated in the text. This volume benefited considerably from his intimate knowledge of the story of Israel's rise to nationhood and from his experience as a talented journalist. I am also deeply indebted to my own beloved life companion, whose encouragement persuaded me to undertake this task and whose careful reading of the manuscript proved invaluable.

A. M. H.

Contents

I. Was It a Miracle?

What was in the beginning only an idea, a dream, a pious hope, became ultimately a miraculous achievement.

Even the realists in Israel now believe in miracles. For logic and reason alone can only partially explain the resurrection of the State of Israel after two thousand years of Jewish dispersion.

How the miraculous emerged in terms of human efforts is the purpose of this introductory chapter.

In 70 C.E. the Romans officially proclaimed, "Judea capta est"—Judea is conquered, never to rise again. World history since the catastrophic destruction of Jerusalem under Titus did not favor the re-establishment of the Jewish state in the Holy Land. Yet, like the legendary phoenix, rising out of its own ashes, Israel reappeared on the international horizon in 1948 with the cry of a lusty infant for the right to national independence and the pursuit of a creative life.

The concept of the Jewish Return is as old as the Galut—Jewish Exile. The formula of Dr. Theodor Herzl, founder of Political Zionism—"a publicly secured and legally assured Jewish homeland in Palestine"—some 60 years ago, only articulated long dormant Jewish aspirations. The yearning for Israel's reunion with the Holy Land never ceased during the intervening centuries.

On the very day when Palestine was laid waste by the Romans, the ancient Jewish Temple destroyed and the nation scattered to the four corners of the earth, Zionism was born. At no time since that event have the Jewish people abandoned the Holy Land in thought or sentiment. So deep has been the attachment of the Jew to his Holy Land through the centuries, that in spite of war, plague, famine and exile, that land has never been bereft of Jewish inhabitants from the earliest Bible times to this day.

Jewish folklore relates that Rabbi Akiba, supporter of Bar Cochba's rebellion against Rome, while traveling with a few of his illustrious contemporaries toward the Holy City, heard shouts of joy from the enemy's camp. The saddened companions could find no word of comfort when they beheld their beloved Jerusalem enveloped in mourning as evil Rome celebrated Israel's defeat. Rabbi Akiba was of another mind: "Surely if God does not reject a cruel people, will He not then in His mercy restore righteous Israel to a position of splendor? If we believe in the prophecy of the Holy Land in ruins, shall we ignore the equally prophetic promise: 'For I will cause their captivity to be reversed and will have compassion on them.'" This spirit of faith and hope was translated by Rabbi Johanan ben Zakai into a practical instrument for Jewish survival.

Robbed of political independence and deprived of the Holy Temple, Torah, the study of Jewish law and lore, became the central spiritual force uniting all Israel. The establishment of the little Academy of Jabneh outside of Jerusalem, General Vespasian's concession to Rabbi Johanan, became the foundation stone for the Jewish edifice of the future. Throughout the Jewish dispersion, the academies of Jewish learning throughout the world, in the tradition of Jabneh, nurtured the Jewish spirit and instilled the hope for the ultimate restoration of people and land. Though living under abnormal and adverse circumstances, the Jewish people devotedly adhered to the Psalmist's affirmation: "I shall not die but live and recount the works of the Lord."

The Messianic hope of Israel reborn never became the monopoly of an aristocracy of learning. The entire people, irrespective of station in life, yearned for Zion. Unfalteringly they accepted the dictum of Maimonides: "I believe with perfect faith in the coming of the Messiah, and, though he tarry,

I will wait daily for his coming." This implicit faith, common to most Jews, is well illustrated in the life of an ancient sage who nightly placed his walking cane next to his bed. If perchance the Messiah should arrive in the middle of the night, he would be ready to respond to the call without a moment's delay.

As the Jews prayed throughout the centuries, they turned eastward to symbolize their unbroken fidelity to the Holy Land. When they uttered the benedictions of "Mayest Thou return to Jerusalem with joy" and "May our eyes behold Thy return to Zion" and "Next year in Jerusalem" their faith in Israel reborn was increasingly renewed. When the footsteps of the messenger of hope would someday be heard, they were convinced that not only the living but also the reawakened dead, together with their institutions of the Galut–Exile—would be gathered from all corners of the earth in the Holy Land.

To symbolize the incompleteness of their lives while Zion remained unredeemed, the eastern wall of the Jewish home was left partially undecorated to indicate national bereavement. Special fast days and periods of mourning were incorporated in the Jewish calendar to commemorate the loss of Israel's independence. The breaking of a glass at a wedding ceremony was interpreted as a reminder of the destruction of the Holy Temple. Grains of sand brought from the Holy Land accompanied the dead to the grave and many deemed burial in the sacred soil of Israel itself an especial privilege reserved for the most pious.

What made the Jew through the ages cling so tenaciously to the ideal of Zion reestablished? As he studied the Bible he became more intimately conscious of his ancestral land, the cradle of his religion and nation. He identified himself with the heroic figures of the Jewish past: kings, prophets, scholars, heroes, saints and martyrs. The Oral Law taught him the superior merit of life in the Holy Land over and above the traditional 613 commandments constituting the sum total of Jewish practice.

According to the best accepted religious teaching, no matter what the needs of the local community, aid to the poor in the Land of Israel took precedence over every other act of kindness. There followed the realization that the fullest Jewish religious life would become most feasible and enduring in the Holy Land. Therefore on all appropriate occasions, the Jew renewed the pledge made by his ancestors at the waters of Babylon, "If I forget Thee O Jerusalem, may my right hand forget its cunning..."

Oppression, the inequities and enmities to which the Jew was subjected in the lands of dispersion, gave impetus to his longing for resettlement in the land of his forebears in order to be master of his own destiny. Robbed of his possessions, forced to abandon his faith, expelled from his native or adopted land and driven from pillar to post, the wandering Jew learned to bear his burdens more courageously because of his unfailing faith that God in His mercy would someday reunite him with the land of his fathers where he would live "under his own vine and fig tree with none to make him afraid."

However, hope was long deferred and detoured by the rise of the political and industrial revolutions which signified for the Jew the beginnings of a changing life. The slogan of "Equality, Liberty, Fraternity," resounding through the civilized world, pierced the darkened horizon of the Exile like a ray of light.

Many rejected the new opportunities for cultural enlightenment because they feared the apparent consequences of assimilation. Others, however, cast aside their outer garb of dispersion to welcome every opportunity of equality offered by the new age. Readily they discarded the tradition of the peoplehood of Israel, muffled the dream of a return to Zion and elected to become identified with modern Western culture and civilization.

They were soon disillusioned. The promised equality was only a mirage. Instead of fraternity they found discrimination; in place of liberty they soon learned that the gates to the fuller life were still closed to them. They further realized that while assimilation might negatively solve the problem of the individual Jew, through the loss of his identity, it surely could bring no salvation to the group.

In the backward countries, the Jew was subjected to sporadic pogroms; in the enlightened countries, devices more refined but no less cruel were invented "to keep the Jew in his place." Under these conditions only the decadent Jew deserted his group to save his own skin. The Jew with a consciousness of his heritage preferred to share the hard lot of his brethren. Zionism was his answer to the problem of Jewish survival.

The religious Jew never forsook the hope for Zion redeemed; the persecuted, homeless wanderer continued to yearn for a national Jewish home and the cultural Jew was resolved to advance the cause of Jewish creativity through Zion revived.

Jewish longing for a national homeland became articulate in the Zionist platform adopted in Basle, Switzerland, in 1897, though some practical achievements by the "Lovers of Zion" in Palestine with the aid of Baron Edmond de Rothschild predated Herzl's political program. The Jewish problem, however, in its larger dimensions as the concern of the statesmen of the world, did not make itself felt until the rise of the Herzlian leadership.

The last decades of the 19th century, filled with catastrophic events in Jewish life, brought Palestine into sharp focus on the Jewish horizon in answer to Jewish homelessness. In czarist Russia, a three-pronged program for dealing with its Jewish problem was promulgated: One third of the Jewish population to be exterminated, another third to undergo forced conversion and the last third to be expelled.

Those who sought a haven of refuge found the United States, at the time, the solution of their individual problem. But those who were more concerned with the collective Jewish problem, the building of a homeland for a homeless and landless people, than with their own personal distressing situations, selected the hard road of Zionism.

They proceeded to knock at the gates of Palestine. Using every resource at their command, they finally succeeded in slightly opening the doors of Zion under Turkish Ottoman rule to admit a few daring souls to establish a Jewish base in their ancestral land. Between the Russian pogroms in the 1880's and World War I in 1914, Jewish settlement in Palestine increased more than threefold, from 24,000 to 85,000 pioneers, and though substantially reduced during the world conflict, they could not be dislodged as the bastion of the eventual national Jewish home.

Herzl (1860-1904), the founder of Political Zionism, sought aid from all quarters. He negotiated with Turkey. He looked for encouragement from the German Empire. He visited Russia and interviewed many European statesmen. But he reposed his strongest hope in Great Britain. Herzl saw the Promised Land; but his supreme ambition, the world charter recognizing Jewish claims to Palestine, was not attained until four decades after his troubled soul was linked with eternity.

As the conquest of Palestine by General Allenby became one of the military goals of the Western Allies, Dr. Chaim Weizmann (1874-1952), a celebrated scientist and citizen of Great Britain, disciple as well as critic of Dr. Herzl, founder of Political Zionism, used his persuasive influence with the political leadership of his country to endorse the Zionist program and to promise its aid in the realization of its aims.

After long negotiations and consultations with the Allied nations including the United States, the British government on November 2, 1917, issued the Balfour Declaration, which in essence gave fulfillment to the Herzlian Zionist platform of 20 years earlier: "His Majesty's government view with favor the establishment of a national home for the Jewish people in Palestine, and will use their best endeavors to facilitate the achievement of this object, it being clearly understood that nothing shall be done which may prejudice the civil and religious rights of existing non-Jewish communities in Palestine, or the rights and political status enjoyed by Jews in any other country."

This Declaration was hailed by Jews everywhere as of great historic significance, equal in importance to the Proclamation issued by Cyrus, King of Persia, permitting the Jewish exiles in Babylon to return to their ancestral homeland. (The first contingent returned from Babylon in 538, and the Temple rebuilt in 515 B.C.E.) "Whosoever is among you of all His people, his God be with him, let him go up to Jerusalem, which is in Judah, and there build the House of the Lord, the God of Israel, He is the God who is in Jerusalem. And whosoever is left in any place where he sojourneth, let the men of his place help with silver and gold, and with goods, and with beasts, besides the free will offering, for the House of God which is in Jerusalem."

The Babylonian returnees had to face resistance from the new occupants of their ancestral land. The Jewish pioneers of the 20th century in the Holy Land likewise were hampered by Arab threats of extinction. No less ominous was the gradual nullification of Britain's pledge to aid the reestablishment of a national Jewish homeland in Palestine.

"Zion will be rebuilt in justice" has been the prophetic ideal of Israel's drive for a renewed nationhood. Zionist opponents questioned the justice of Jewish claims to a national home in Palestine. Their sympathy was with the Arabs. Haven't they lived there for centuries? On what moral grounds should the displaced Jews, victims of modern anti-Semitism, displace the impoverished native population of that land?

The founders of the Zionist movement were never insensible to the moral issues involved. Their claims to Palestine were not predicated solely on Jewish need, an asylum for the oppressed and persecuted. The Jewish charter to the Holy Land is indelibly inscribed in the Bible and in all of Jewish history up to and through the modern era. The claim to the charter was never renounced or relinquished. Neither in law nor in sentiment have the Jews ever abandoned the land. They were robbed of it. Its illegal possession by others in no way violates the Jewish title thereto through the passage of time. Those who work the land, who enrich it by toil and sweat, may acquire some vested interest in it, a principle well recognized in the law of equity. But for centuries Palestine by reason of Arab sloth and incompetence had been sorely neglected, its soil corroded, its forests cut down, mother earth bereft of her children. The Jewish returnees, on the other hand, brought with them willing hearts and dynamic hands, restoring to the land its ancient character: "A land flowing with milk and honey."

With legal and moral rights to Palestine as well as by historic and international recognition, Jews went back there armed with the plow and not with the sword, not to displace Arabs but to make room for both. Arab leadership feared not the alleged aggressive intent of the Jewish pioneers but their higher standards of living which might influence the fellahin, the poor landless Arab population, to demand from their overlords, the effendis, improved economic conditions. Jewish settlement in Palestine, they assumed, might give new and "dangerous" ideas to their enslaved subjects. The Arab mass population had no reason for apprehension from an increased Jewish population which could and did provide them with additional opportunities for employment and a greater demand for their produce.

Colonial political indecision prompted by Arab resistance impeded the Jewish movement toward Palestine but could not stop it completely. Britain, placed in the unenviable role of fulfilling her pledge of aid to the Jewish people in the face of Arab opposition, chose to reinterpret her Balfour Declaration in order to retain her influence in the Middle East. Entrusted by the League of Nations to administer the Holy Land in the spirit of the Declaration, Great Britain resorted to legal quibbling, subordinating the pledge itself to the clause, "safeguarding Arab civil and religious rights."

The Declaration omits every mention of political rights for the existing non-Jewish communities in Palestine, but the mandatory government has, with sinister design, made them its primary concern. However, neither Arab intransigence nor British intrigue could halt the onrushing historic events which by their very weight forced open the barred doors of Palestine to admit ever-growing numbers of Jews fleeing for their lives from their deadly tormentors. Many untold additional thousands might have escaped certain death were British conscience attuned to the cry of human souls in anguish rather than to political voices of questionable integrity.

The first Jewish Exodus was shrouded in the supernatural not only because of the havoc inflicted on Egypt but also because of the united yearning for freedom which Moses succeeded in instilling into the life of the divided Children of Israel. No less miraculous was the Zionist achievement in making the goal of a redeemed Holy Land the common cause of world Jewry. With the rebirth of Israel, excepting for a few strident voices, Jews everywhere have become united in their support of the reconstituted nation.

In the early Zionist days, the goal of Jewish nationhood was a divisive force. In the main, the opposition came from four distinct segments in Jewish life.

1) The Orthodox Jews argued: "Except the Lord build the house, they labor in vain that build it." They sincerely believed in the coming of the Messiah as a prerequisite for the establishment of the Jewish state. Today, only a small faction of the orthodox elements abstain from cooperation with the State of Israel.

2) Organized labor, primarily concerned with economic betterment, at first demurred because it saw no advantage in a Palestine sweat shop over its counterpart in the lands of dispersion. Today Jewish labor everywhere proudly endorses labor's achievement in Israel with grants in aid for an improved social order there.

3) The followers of Reform Judaism opposed Zionism because of their negation of the concept of Jewish nationhood. They feared suspicion of dual allegiance. With a greater sense of security in their native lands, they abandoned their old theories in support of Israel and in recognition of their spiritual ties with their Jewish brethren everywhere.

4) Jews of practical affairs in the world of finance and industry considered Zionism a mere dream and Zionists hopeless visionaries. They used to argue: The Turkish Ottoman Empire will never sanction Jewish immigration to Palestine; the native Arabs will crush every attempt of Jewish settlement; the land is too unproductive to support a sizable Jewish community; the Jews will not choose to go to Palestine, preferring migration to other lands; the Jews can never adjust themselves to an agricultural economy and, should they ever succeed in forming a sovereign state, it will soon fall apart because they are incapable of self-rule. All the seemingly insuperable obstacles have been overcome.

The religious found their place within the framework of Zionism; the social idealists were converted to the movement; the Reform group adopted a policy of cooperation; the Political Zionist found common ground with the culturalist; manual labor was clothed with dignity, and Israel became the most stable government in the entire Middle East with material achievements bordering on the miraculous.

Jews are "rumored" to be wealthy. Individually, some Jews have acquired important financial standing. Their reputedly excessive collective wealth, however, in proportion to other groups of comparative numerical strength is mythical. But whatever be the material position of individual Jews, the Zionist movement never possessed the power of taxation with which to finance Jewish settlement in Palestine. The countless small voluntary contributions in aid of the Zionist cause are symbolic of the strong Jewish will for nationhood. Dr. Herzl in his diaries records his disappointment in the London branch of the Rothschild family for refusing financial aid to the Zionist movement on the ground that it was visionary and impractical.

The Zionist leader comforted himself with the thought that a national song or flag symbolizing Jewish unity and hope could be far more important to the cause of Zion than all the money of the House of Rothschild. This proved to be no legend. The various congresses created voluntary financial instruments for the realization of Zionist aims. The leadership assumed the dual responsibility of political organization and solicitation of funds wherever Jews could be found.

The small voluntary gifts of the masses, followed in later years by the larger contributions of wealthier Jews, became the foundation stone of the Third Jewish Commonwealth structure. In the history of philanthropy there has never been a more full-hearted response than the outpouring of aid to Israel from every segment of Jewry.

This unprecedented generosity in behalf of Israel's cause was authentically reported in one of the best known U.S. weeklies: "In the eight years of Israel's independence, American Jewish organizations alone raised 700 million dollars. . . . Beyond United Jewish Appeal other organizations raise about 15 million dollars a year for specialized projects. And beyond all the charity activity, the Bonds for Israel drive . . . has raised since 1951 the staggering sum of 275 million dollars . . . an outpouring that is the number one phenomenon of U.S. philanthropy. . . . In America, for example, the American Red Cross raised about 42 million dollars from about 41 million members, while the U.J.A. raised 65 million from about 2 million Jews and 500,000 non-Jews." This consistently munificent financial aid well symbolizes the magnitude of appeal Israel reborn makes to world Jewry.

The solution of the problem of consolidation is an intrinsic part of the miracle of Israel's re-creation. America has become known as the melting pot for its ability to merge all its variegated elements into a cohesive unity. Literally overnight, Israel's pressure-cooker process has homogenized its diversified population into nationhood.

Jewry in Israel is made up of the ingathering from every corner of the globe, from the pale-faced European Jew to black-skinned Ethiopian (Falasha) who only in recent years discovered his kinship with the Jewish people.

There is no color line nor racial segregation in Israel. At school and play, in shop and factory, in synagogue and health center, in housing and hotel, everywhere, there is a cooperative living together based on kinship of historic memories, a common fate and faith and the hope of Israel securely founded in a world of peace.

The predominance of the youth population in Israel is an added factor for the fusing together of the various national origins. They are less contaminated by unworthy prejudices than their elders. The average age in Israel is 28. Forty-one per cent of the population are 20 years of age and under and only 7 per cent are above 60 years of age. This youthful population spells for Israel both the necessary physical vigor and open-mindedness to recognize each citizen as a brother despite all outward differences.

In Palestine, particularly at the blossoming of Israel to statehood, the Jew amazingly was transformed from fugitive to guardian of his own destiny. He learned to face his adversaries unitedly with self-discipline and tenacity. What he lacked in arms he made up in courage. Perhaps, as some would have it, it was because of "General Ain B'rerah"—no alternative to survival—but this is not entirely correct. For, were the pioneers constituted of different fiber, they could with easy justification have declared to the world: Our numbers are all too few and our strength too insignificant to engage both the Arabs and the British in mortal combat.

This indeed is the wonder of the ages. A people, civilian in philosophy and character, but with stout hearts, outnumbered twenty to one, fought their enemies victoriously. Even the "non-believers" in Israel speak of the "miracles" in their War for Independence and in the Sinai Campaign.

In the lands of their dispersion, Jews suffered from the curse of fear described in the Bible: "I will send a faintness into their hearts in the lands of their enemies, and the sound of a driven leaf shall chase them and they shall flee. . . ." But in Israel, captains of their own souls, they found the prophetic blessing of courage: "And ye shall pursue your enemies . . . And five of you shall pursue a hundred. . . ."

By force of historic circumstance the Jew was characterized as the "middleman" of the world. It took the romance, the magnetism of nation building to reconvert him to manual labor and land cultivation. The new pioneers, many university trained, without divesting themselves of their intellectual interests learned to build roads and houses, to construct factories and schools, to dry marshes and clear fields.

The Hebrew word adam—man—is derived from adamah—earth. Neither is complete without the other. Their interdependence has been made self-evident by the new builders of Zion. They became rooted in the soil of Palestine which in their devoted hands has been transformed from a languishing desert to a flourishing garden. Perhaps, adom, meaning red, and dom, blood, are interlinked with concepts of man and earth. Much of Israel's soil is not only naturally red, but metaphorically as well. Today as in the past, the title to the land of Israel is sealed with Jewish sweat, tears and blood.

The realists in Israel have come to believe in their miracles of achievement but not to rely on them. Every advance in the fulfillment of Zionist aims was the result of sacrificial labors of love. On August 29, 1897, the Basel Program was announced to the world: "Zionism aims to establish for the Jewish people a publicly secured and legally assured home in Palestine." Fifty years later, on November 29, 1947, the United Nations after much study, debate and searching of soul adopted the Palestine Resolution favoring the establishment of a Jewish national home in Palestine.

"What hath God wrought" in only half a century?

II. The Infant State

In time and space Israel's rebirth is unique in the history of man. Other nations, too, regained their political independence, particularly in consequence of the two world wars, but none was uprooted from its native soil and none was denied its right to nationhood for 19 centuries.

More than half of its lifetime as a people, Israel existed in the uneasy realm of suspended nationalism, an unassimilated minority everywhere without a majority status anywhere. What other nation in history survived the corroding onslaught of time through 19 centuries of an uncertain morrow?

In space, too, Israel's position is incomparable to all other reconstituted states which regained their political sovereignty on the same land they previously occupied and over which they claimed dominion.

Israel remained by force of history a spiritual nation as well as a unified people scattered throughout the world when on November 29, 1947, the United Nations finally performed the Caesarian operation giving birth to a Jewish republic in Palestine. There was unsuppressed rejoicing in every Jewish community, best portrayed in the words of the Psalmist: "When the Lord returned the captives of Zion, we were as in a dream. Our mouth was filled with laughter, and a song of exultation was on our tongue."

The hard realities of commonwealth-building under unprecedented historic circumstances dampened the joy of world Jewry when Great Britain, in an about-face betrayal of her solemn commitment, announced her unwillingness to implement the United Nations Resolution and the Arabs threatened to annihilate the infant state.

The United States, the most influential member of the United Nations with respect to the adoption of the Palestine Resolution, alarmed by the opposition, offered in the Security Council a trusteeship proposal for the solution of the Palestine problem which for all practical purposes would have nullified the General Assembly's decision. Great Britain set May 15, 1948, as the date for terminating her mandate over Palestine with a malevolent design to enable the Arabs to fall heir to her military position for the purpose of extinguishing all Zionist hopes for Jewish statehood.

Destiny ordained otherwise. The 50,000 Jews in Palestine in 1897, at the time of the proclamation of the Basle Zionist program, had grown to more than half a million a half-century later, to become masters instead of interlopers in their own historic household. Egypt, Iraq, Jordan, Lebanon, Saudi Arabia, Syria and Yemen carried out the threat they had made in the U.N. when the Palestine question was under discussion. No sooner did the British withdraw and the Jews in Palestine proclaimed themselves as the Republic of Israel, when the seven Arab states swooped down from all sides upon the newly created commonwealth to throttle the breath of its life before it could grow strong enough to resist or call for help.

The British must have been sorely disappointed with their Arab protégés, who proved more formidable with threats than with acts. Neither superior weight of manpower nor armaments availed them. At the time of the War for Independence, Egypt counted 150,000 armed forces, Syria 60,000, Iraq 50,000, Yemen 40,000, Jordan 30,000, Lebanon 8,000 and Saudi Arabia an insignificant number. While they did inflict tragic and serious loss of life and property on hard pressed, poorly equipped Israel, they were no match for the intelligent, heroic, self-disciplined Jewish military and civil population, which was limited in numbers and resources. Untrained in warfare, the Jews fought with incredible skill and lionlike courage against the threefold threat of being expelled from the land, pushed into the sea or having their remnants remain as a minority of second-class citizens under the rule of their victors in their own homeland.

So confident were the Arab leaders of their power to render the Jewish state stillborn that they urged the native Arab population to abandon Palestine temporarily to keep the roads and other strategic places free for their armies to engage Israel in open battle. The assurance of Israel's defeat and the certain seizure of her property held out as tempting bait persuaded hundreds of thousands of Arabs to flee from their own land to become refugees in the lands of their kinsmen. The Israelis accepted the challenge soberly and prayerfully. They had to fight or perish. They fought and won. It was a victory which overwhelmed their foes and stunned themselves. To this day many devoutly believe it was a divine miracle.

President Truman's noble impulse to give to Israel de facto recognition on the day of her Declaration of Independence, despite, to put it mildly, the reluctance of the State Department, rallied the needed favorable world public opinion and strengthened the Jewish will everywhere to support the new state in its struggle for survival.

The Jewish state carved out by the United Nations Resolution of November 29, 1947, was inadequate in size and difficult of defense. These hazardous defects troubled the Zionist leadership at the U.N., but considering the seemingly insurmountable difficulty of persuading two-thirds of the membership of the General Assembly to vote in favor of any kind of a Jewish national home, the Jewish leadership reluctantly accepted the minimum that was offered in the hope of eventually developing it into a viable state. Also, aware of Arab threats, the Jews preferred territorial limitations to bloodshed.

The War for Independence gained for Israel a greater share of Palestine territory than that contemplated by the U.N. Resolution which also provided an Arab state in the remainder of Palestine with a proposed economic union for both states. Israel's heroic defense, if not for the premature U.N. cease-fire command, would certainly have resulted in still further gains, but above all, its borders would have been less dangerously contiguous with the Arab states.

As a result of the armistice Israel, comprising 8,000 square miles, was left with abnormally long borders, 750 miles of combined land and water frontiers: 329 miles of span with Jordan, 164 miles with Egypt, 49 miles with Lebanon and 47 miles with Syria, plus 158 miles of water borders. This led to infiltrations, to friction and even to sporadic military clashes. The real threat to Israel came from the Fedayeen intruders, suicide squads organized by Egypt in cooperation with other Arab governments, thus diverting creative Jewish energies from constructive efforts to military defense.

With sword in one hand and plowshare in the other, Israel began her career as a state, dedicated to territorial integrity and a constructive national life even in her truncated land. Zionist ideology envisioned an ideal republic in which the individual would find untrammeled opportunity for fulfillment and the nation an active participation in world affairs.

To give reality to the lofty concepts on which the new sovereign state was to be based required a written constitution embodying the highest principles of government.

After a decade of national sovereignty, such an instrument has not as yet been consummated in the life of Israel. While a commission of recognized experts was designated to make a study of recommendations for presentation before a constitutional assembly, no such body was convened and no official action taken for two reasons: the general atmosphere created by Arab threats and world conflicts was not conducive to calm deliberation or to the formulation of principles of enduring significance. Secondly, the leadership feared internal dissension resulting from sharp differences of opinions on religious, economic and social issues. In the face of threats of war, Israel could not afford strife from within which might sap her strength sorely needed for a common defense. Since internal dissention and conflict might threaten the very life of Israel, deliberations for the adoption of a constitution were postponed for a more opportune time, when Israel should have become more stabilized and the danger of war minimized.

In lieu of a constitution, the Provisional Council adopted a preamble embodying in general terms the principles of human equality and citizenship rights, declaring the statutes of the British mandatory power as the provisional or temporary law of the land, voiding only two ordinances: 1) the immigration measure which restricted to a trickle the number of new Jewish settlers and 2) the land purchase decree which prohibited sale of Arab land to Jews. The new constitution is yet to be written and promulgated, but at the birth of the new state, a "little constitution" officially known as Transitional Statutes was proclaimed.

On May 15, 1948, as the British terminated the mandate over Palestine, the Yishuv—Jewish settlement—declared its independence and fully justified its act in proclaiming itself the State of Israel. In essence, the following general principles were enunciated in support of the proclamation of the State:

(1) *Historic Association.* The Jewish people began its career in Palestine. The Bible documents its birthplace. The Children of Israel received the mandate and title to the land from God Himself. After a sojourn in Egypt, they returned to Palestine, establishing it as the Holy Land through the sanctified and dedicated labors of their saints, scholars, prophets, leaders and martyrs.

They were forcibly expelled from the Holy Land by the Babylonians in 586 B.C.E. to return within seven decades. They reestablished themselves as a nation marked by renewed spiritual rebirth. With their blood, the Maccabees sealed and confirmed Jewish identification with the land in 168 B.C.E. Again the Jewish people heroically fought Roman aggression only to be defeated in 70 C.E. Complete loss of independence came in 135 C.E. with the unsuccessful Bar Cochba rebellion.

But there was no abandonment of the hope to return. In token of Israel's everlasting association with and title to her ancestral country, there was never a time when some remnants of Jewish communities did not reside in the Holy Land.

(2) *Zionism.* Since the Jewish people, homeless and landless for centuries, remained faithful to the memory of Zion, it became a natural historical process as well as an imperative necessity for people and land to be reunited. Discrimination against Jews in many lands and the fear of loss of Jewish identity through assimilation in the more enlightened countries brought forth a reawakened Jewish nationalism. This was made manifest at the First Zionist Congress in 1897, proclaiming to the world the Jewish needs and rights to "a legally secured and publicly established homeland for the Jewish people in Palestine." Within two decades this proclamation, characterized as an impractical dream by world statesmen, became the accepted policy of the Western Powers through the Balfour Declaration in 1917, approved by the League of Nations shortly thereafter.

(3) *The Nazi Holocaust.* In *Mein Kampf* Hitler presented a blueprint of his plans to exterminate the whole Jewish people. Some considered him a madman, others a windbag. Upon assuming governmental authority they predicted for him a more subdued sense of responsibility in word and act. Precisely the opposite happened. The world stood by as one-third of world Jewry suffered annihilation, not as casualties of war but victims of hate. There was profound mourning and there was ineffectual diplomatic intercession, but the doors to the free world remained closed in the face of millions who sought escape from the fate of the crematoria. That ghastly spectacle was an unforgettable indictment of the civilized world, which scarcely lifted a finger to help those agonizing millions whose only sin was the religious faith they professed.

(4) *United Nations.* On November 29, 1947, the United Nations voted for the Palestine Resolution favoring the creation

of the Jewish state in the Holy Land. If the vote had depended on national political considerations, Zionist aspirations might have been doomed then and there. Fortunately many of the member nations for the moment forgot the scramble for political advantages. They remembered the frightful wounds inflicted on world Jewry between 1939 and 1945. As if conscience-stricken and as a gesture of sympathy they voted in favor of the Jewish state. The six million dead thus did not perish in vain. Their sacrifice inspired the necessary two-thirds vote plus two at the United Nations. Was the price paid for Israel too great? History will give us the answer, tomorrow.

(5) *Citizenship Rights and Obligations to the U.N.* The Transitional Statutes proclaimed in no uncertain terms the State's duties toward its citizenry and toward mankind: "The State of Israel will be open to the immigration of Jews from all countries of dispersion; will promote the development of the country for the benefit of all of its inhabitants; will be based on the principles of liberty, justice and peace as conceived by the prophets of Israel; will uphold the full social and political equality of its citizens, without distinction of religious conscience, education and culture; will safeguard the holy places of all religions and will loyally uphold the principles of the United Nations.

"With trust in the Almighty, we set our hands to this Declaration at this session of the Provisional State Council on the soil of the Homeland in the City of Tel Aviv on the Sabbath Eve of the fifth of Iyar 5708, the fourteenth of May 1948." (The official date of declaration is the 15th of May to coincide with the date of the termination of the British mandate. But since the 15th fell on the Sabbath, the proclamation was issued on the day preceding.)

Israel, the newly adopted name of the Jewish homeland in Palestine, is derived from the Biblical account of Jacob's battle with a hostile and mysterious stranger in the dark of night, winning from him the blessing: "Thy name shall be called no more Jacob, but Israel, for thou hast striven with God and with man, and hast prevailed." This has been the story of the Zionist movement: A struggle against hostile forces through the long dark night of the Exile, the dawn of the morning star, the new State of Israel, Israel, "Plenipotentiary of God." The name symbolizing the collective Jew has undergone a number of variations, each connoting a different circumstance in Jewish history.

During their sojourn in Egypt, the Jews were known as B'nai Israel—the Children of Israel. In Biblical history their name varied. Most frequently they were called the Children of Israel with the additional variations of Israel-Bet Israel—The House of Israel, K'hal or Adat Israel—The Congregation of Israel and Am Israel—The People of Israel.

After the division of the kingdom in 930 B.C.E., the Ten Tribes in the North assumed the name of Israel, while the tribe of Judah in the South continued to be known as Judah or the Kingdom of Judea. The former, though destroyed as a nation by Assyria in 721 B.C.E., never lost its name in Jewish history, with prophets and psalmists continuing to refer to the Jewish people, past and present, as Israel. On the other hand, Judea, from which the name Jew is derived, gradually became dispossessed of the name after her final loss of political independence in the revolt against the Romans.

Thereafter, Knesset Israel—the Community of Israel—descriptive of the religious character of Jewish peoplehood began to be emphasized. At the reawakening of Jewish nationalism in the 19th century, Am Israel—the People of Israel—gained favor among large communities of Jews. At the birth of the Third Jewish Commonwealth, the new republic assumed the name of the State of Israel.

To the question, what constitutes an Israeli?—the answer is clear and concise. Those born in the land, those residing there before the declaration of statehood, or immigrants upon declaring their intent to assume the responsibilities of citizenship.

The Law of Return opens the door to Jewish immigrants

from the world over, but with no implication concerning their allegiance to their respective native lands. Israel disclaims any political jurisdiction over Jews outside her borders. Even those who enter the land do not ipso facto gain citizenship status until the intent has been formulated and declared. The interrelationship between world Jewry and Israel has never been envisioned as political in nature. Both Zionist philosophy and Israeli practice consider spiritual and cultural bonds as the only cementing elements between the nation in the Holy Land and Jews in the Diaspora.

The Jewish people, heir to the prophetic teachings of the dignity and worth of man, also brought to Palestine the Western concepts of political democracy. Therefore the Transitional Statutes and the legislation enacted since the establishment of the state concerned themselves with democratic principles reflected in the Bible and practiced in the free civilized world. Except for the precautionary measures, such as restriction of Arab movements and exemption of their military service to insure the security of the land, Israel's democratic processes have applied to Jew and Arab alike. Because of the urgent problem of security, universal military service of two and one-half years for men and two years for women, had to be adopted, calling on men between the ages of 18 and 49, and single women between 18 and 39 to give their all if need be in defense of their country. Young people upon reaching the age of 18 are called into military training with the opportunity to acquire proficiency not only in the art of defense but also in other academic and practical subjects in preparation for a more useful civilian life after completing their period of military service.

The law requiring the draft of women into military duties stirred considerable debate. The religious elements maintained on moral and religious grounds that a law requiring military service from women was inconsistent with Jewish tradition. As a concession to the opposition, the law as finally adopted granted exemption to those who on religious grounds could not square their conscience with military activity. Instead they are obliged to render service to the country in the field of education and welfare.

When the Israeli Arabs are fully consolidated into the state, the universal military draft law will apply to them as well as to the rest of the population, including the Druze Arabs who constitute approximately 10 per cent of the Arab population in Israel, and who during the War for Independence fought together with the Jewish forces and have since then consistently and loyally supported the State of Israel.

For nigh two millennia, the Jewish people under pressure excelled in commerce and learning but of necessity had neither heart nor talent for military life. They were excluded or for obvious reasons sought exemption from armed service. When they finally achieved equality of citizenship in the Western World, individual Jews did gain distinction in organized military forces and on the battlefield, but Jews generally were not concerned with making a profession of army life.

Reconstituted Israel transformed that lack of interest into a proud national accomplishment both for defense as well as for creative civilian life. The armed forces have become a cementing influence in the land, drawing the youth of various national origins into a closer fellowship. It is noteworthy that since so many of the Oriental members of the military forces came to Israel after the War for Independence, they did not feel on a par with their comrades in arms of European derivation who were responsible for the victory in 1948. However, the active and devoted service of the newcomers in the Sinai Campaign of 1956 relieved them of their self-consciousness and gained for them warm public recognition. A major reason for the high quality of the armed forces is the youth of their officers, energetic, intelligent and democratic. With no political interference and under civilian control, these services have successfully avoided any taint of the militaristic spirit. In the program of defense, they have amply demonstrated their striking power; in their ambition to build useful citizens they have attained a goal of distinction.

They gained added stature in the phenomenal success of the Sinai Campaign. They scored in five days the operation which took General Allenby in World War I one and a half years. They captured over 5,000 Egyptian prisoners while only four Israelis fell into the enemy's hands. They destroyed Fedayeen bases and seized a vast store of valuable arms and equipment. They cleared the Gulf of Aqaba for Israeli shipping. They dramatized before the world Israel's precarious position resulting from Arab provocative acts and at the same time dampened Arab enthusiasm for a "second round." They inspired the people with confidence in the nation's ability to defend itself.

Israel has also gained France as a dependable ally. And, despite the condemnation proceedings at the U.N., the aroused world grudgingly but openly expressed admiration for Israel as a brave people and for its heroic army on land, sea and in the air.

There were skeptics before and since the birth of the state regarding the ability of her people to function unitedly. Besides the religious divisions, there were differences on economic policies as well as on strategy toward the Arab world. But despite the characteristic individualism of the Jew and the multiplicity of conflicting political, economic, religious and social divisions, Israel has maintained in the past decade the most stable government in the Middle East. Democracy has become not a boasted ideal in Israel but a practical accomplishment essential to national survival.

The voice of the people is fully heard in Israel. Representative government is well established. Israel's authorized spokesmen numbering 120 are members of a unicameral body known as the Knesset—Parliament. They are elected for a four-year term on the basis of a proportional vote. Theoretically, this method of election assures the greatest measure of democracy, but in practice it creates a labyrinth of political parties making it nigh impossible for any party to win a majority with which to form a responsible centralized government.

The second inherent disadvantage in the proportional system of voting is that the electorate is deprived of the opportunity to select the candidates. The voters place their confidence in the party and its platform and not necessarily in the men who are designated by the party.

Responsible political leadership has become aware of these shortcomings but for the present at least, those benefiting from the proportional voting system, will not permit the adoption of a new plan which might curtail their power. However, even if the will were there, some of the minor parties could not be eliminated, making it improbable for the two major party system in vogue in the U.S. to prevail in Israel. The natural affinity between geography and ideology would prevent such a radical innovation. The rural area, predominantly Socialist, would vote for the leftist parties; the middle class, more numerous in the urban sections, would give its support to the center or to rightists and the religious elements, concentrated as they are in given geographic areas, would be assured of considerable political strength. However, despite the multiple party system, the government has proved to be both stable and truly representative.

That political democracy is a dynamic force in the land may be judged from these facts: In 1955 there were in Israel 1,057,-795 eligible voters, 971,066 Jews and 86,279 non-Jews. Of these, 876,085 voted in 2,073 ballot boxes throughout the land. Over 80 per cent of the eligible voters cast their ballots. There were no single party candidates, no government compulsion, only the citizens' voluntary, intelligent exercise of the right to democratic self-rule through proportional representation.

The people's intense interest in the political life of the country is further evidenced by extraordinary demands at all times for public discussion on government policies and issues. In 1956-57, a non-election year, members of the Cabinet, Knesset and others prominent in public affairs addressed 2,200 open meetings and forums with an audience participation of 350,000. Politically Israel symbolizes democracy in action.

The instruments for democratic government are:

A. The Knesset as the supreme legislative body with superior authority over the Executive and Judicial branches of government. No single political party in Israel has as yet succeeded in persuading the electorate to give it the necessary majority to form a government. Therefore Israel has been ruled by a coalition on a quid pro quo basis with concessions and compromises holding the government together.

1. The largest and most representative party is the Mapai (Mifleget Poalai Eretz Israel)—the Workers' Party of Israel, numbering 40 out of the 120 members in the Knesset. In its foreign policy it is oriented toward the West. Economically the Mapai program looks to "Socialism in our day." While Mapai, Ben Gurion's party, adheres to Socialism as a philosophy, it is non-Marxist in party structure and economic program, permitting "free enterprise" considerable latitude to prove its worth. Were it not for a disinclination to offend the parties further to the left, the Mapai might even be favorably disposed toward greater private initiative in certain economic fields.

2. The major "Majesty's Opposition" party is Herut—Freedom—numbering 15 members in the Knesset. In theory and action, Herut's major thesis is fervent nationalism, a strong and powerful nation, militarily adequate to cope with the Arab threat and to maintain the respect of the Western Powers. It favors private enterprise and vigorously opposes the Federation of Labor known as Histadrut. While it speaks of an expanded territory covering both sides of the Jordan, Herut does not advocate aggressive measures for the fulfillment of that goal. Like Mapai, it rejects Communism as a political philosophy of government but unlike Mapai it disapproves of a Socialist economy. While in economics it is inclined toward the right of center, fairly close to the General Zionists, this phase has not

become a central party issue. Its real concern is security, an aggressive policy of defense, if need be, even in defiance of East and West combined.

3. The third parliamentary party in numerical strength is the General Zionist with 13 members. Oriented toward the West, moderate in dealing with the Arab world, the General Zionists emphasize the economic issues of their program. They represent the upper middle class, such as grove owners and bigger business, convinced that a new and young pioneering country can not afford the luxury of economic experimentation. They strongly adhere to the principle of private initiative and reject restrictions on legitimate profits derived from sound investments.

4. In foreign relations the Progressive Zionists who number five members in the Knesset have a kinship with the General Zionists. In their economic views they are slightly less critical of the party in power but the justification for separate party existence lies rather in their greater appeal to the lower middle class and intellectual elements while the General Zionist support is derived from the mercantile economic upper middle class. When compared to their counterparts on the British political arena the General Zionists may be categorized as the "Conservatives" and the Progressive Zionists as the "Liberals." The attempts to weld them into a united political organization thus far have failed not only because of the issues on which they are divided but also because of the added opportunity for fulfillment of individual ambitions, submerging the greater good for personal advancement.

5. Political religious parties, though unknown in the Western Hemisphere, are common on the European continent. The religious elements in Israel have followed the European pattern. Organized in two parties, they differ from each other primarily in the degree of strictness of Orthodox interpretation of Judaism and emphasis on labor. The Hapoel Hamizrachi-Mizrachi, numbering 11 members in the Knesset, is a union of the reli-

gious labor members and the religious middle class elements who had occupied an important position in the World Zionist Organization before the rise of the state. With labor elements predominating, this religious party stresses the togetherness of Torah and labor and accents a program of social justice and cooperative enterprises. The Mizrachi as a party was founded under the leadership of Rabbi Isaac J. Reines in cooperation with the distinguished rabbis Samuel Mohilever, Jonathan Eliasberg and Naphtali Z. Berlin. Though they differed with the secular nationalists on matters of religion, nevertheless they found it possible to work with them in the cause of Zion rebuilt. Rabbi Meyer (Berlin) Bar Ilan gave the movement its longest and most active leadership.

6. The second religious party, with 6 Knesset members goes under the combined name of Agudat Israel-Poalai Agudat Israel. Originally it looked with disfavor on political Zionism but became reconciled to the state after her establishment. The majority of the second religious party is made up of right-wing members whose economic and social philosophy resembles that of the General Zionists. It is more to the right than the Hapoel Hamizrachi-Mizrachi on religious matters, approximating the concept of a theocratic state. Though not always in agreement on policy and method, the two religious parties, numbering 17 members in Parliament, in the main strive together for legislation to advance the cause of religious life in Israel.

7. To the left of the center is the Achdut Ho-Avodah-Poalai Zion—United Workers and Left Labor Zionists—with 10 Knesset members. Though adhering to the Marxian philosophy, they have been for some time critical of Russia and the Eastern Bloc on the ground of the bureaucratic nature and practices of the Soviet State. The Achdut Ho-Avodah-Poalai Zionists, deriving their strength from kibbutzim, are essentially democratic in character. Russian anti-Israel policy and her brutality in the suppression of the 1956 Hungarian uprising have further dissipated the glamor of the Communist philosophy in action.

8. Even further to the left is Mapam (Mifleget Poalim Meuchadim)—United Labor Party—with 9 parliamentary members. Rigid in its Marxian ideology, Mapam has not completely abandoned its pro-Russian sympathies and advocates a neutral position in foreign affairs. However, in recent years Mapam, too, has been critical of Russia and the Eastern Bloc because of their opposition to Israel, to Zionism—home and abroad—and for their pro-Nasser position in the Middle East. The imprisonment of M. Orenstein, one of their party leaders in Prague, disillusioned the Mapam Party, but they still hope for a more favorable Russian attitude to Israel and Zionism.

9. Were it not for the proportional voting system, the Maqi —Communists—might not be represented in the Knesset, surely not by as many as six elected members. Israel being a democracy is receptive to every form of political philosophy but there is a widespread antagonism to Communism. From left to right, the Communists are considered traitors to Israel's cause. Small in number, the Jewish Communists sentimentally cling to their ideology of favoring Nasser and Russia. The Arab Communists, however, employ the party not to further a Communist philosophy but as a political instrument for the purpose of embarrassing the state.

10. The two Arab parties, the Agricultural and Development, and the Progress and Work, are represented by five members. In addition to specific demands for the Arab community in Israel, the former stands for organization of Arab labor in cooperation with Histadrut, National Labor Union, while the latter advocates the resettlement of Arab refugees in Israel plus the development of Arab towns, villages and cooperatives. They enjoy equal rights in the Knesset with the privilege of addressing the Parliament in their own language.

With no majority party, Israel is thus ruled by a coalition Government consisting of Mapai with 40 members, Hapoel Hamizrachi-Mizrachi 11, Achdut Ho-Avodah 10, Mapam 9, and Progressive Zionists 5, a total of 75 of the 120 members constituting the Knesset. The parties comprising the coalition are not constant, since differences on vital questions may break up party alliances and necessitate a reshuffling of the Cabinet, as it has been recently demonstrated in the differences between the religous faction and the government on a definition of what constitutes a Jew.

B. The President: He is elected by the Knesset for a five-year term, there being no direct popular vote for the official head of the state. Ten or more members of Parliament may name a candidate for the presidency by presenting his name to the speaker of the Knesset, a majority vote determining his election.

The Israeli president is only the nominal head of the government, exercizing such influence as his own personality can command. His office is vested with prestige rather than with power. His formal functions are beyond political maneuvering, incriminations and decisions. The president offers the formation of the government to a leading member of the Knesset whose party commands the largest number of elected representatives. He also accepts the voluntary or forced resignation of governments. He attaches his signature to all laws adopted by the Knesset. He grants formal approval to recommendations for appointment of judges and ambassadors. He receives the credentials of foreign representatives. He welcomes dignitaries. He accords receptions on the occasion of the New Moon ceremonial to delegations of immigrants, grouped according to countries of origin. In sum, the president's official residence is the rendezvous of the statesmen, the wise and the cultured, as well as of distinguished visitors from many lands.

Isaac Ben-Zvi, the second president, was elected to office on December 8, 1952. He did not bring with him the international reputation of Chaim Weizmann, first president, widely known as scientist and statesman, who pleaded the cause of Zion before the leaders of the world. But Ben-Zvi was no less known and equally beloved in the land of Israel, where he settled as a pioneer in 1907. Born in Russia in 1884, he became a Socialist

Zionist leader at a very early age, organizing the movement abroad and in Palestine while contributing to Hebrew letters both as a journalist and scholar. He came to the U.S. as an exile from Palestine in the early stages of World War I and, together with Ben Gurion, organized the Jewish Legion, returning to Palestine in 1918. From 1931 onward he served as president of the Vaad Leumi—National Jewish Council in Palestine.

While consistently maintaining an active interest in his party, he is the least partisan of the political leaders of the land, devoting much of his time to scholarly research and authorship. At 74, after 50 years of creative effort and leadership in Israel, he is one of the most trusted and beloved figures in the land. Because of his genial personality, his indifference to partisan politics and his deep concern for the welfare of the whole people, he has brought distinct prestige to the office of president.

C. Prime Minister: The government's executive power is entrusted to the prime minister. His power and influence rest on two factors, legal and personal. The framers of the Provisional Statutes designated the president as nominal head of state while the prime minister was vested with the responsibility of government. They gave preference to the French and British forms over that of the United States presidential authority in order to make the government more responsive between elections to changing conditions as expressed through the popular will. But merely legal power vested in the prime minister could not for long hold the coalition government together were it not for the personal prestige and influence of Ben Gurion, the incumbent. He enjoys extreme confidence throughout the land and is trusted for his proven vision, daring and sincerity.

Ben Gurion began his Zionist career at the youthful age of 17 in Poland, where he was born in 1886. Three years after organizing the Poale Zion movement in his native city, he migrated to Palestine in 1906. Immediately he rose to leadership, from worker and guard to labor organizer, journalist and editor. He became a founder of the Jewish Legion in World War I in whose ranks he served for two years, after which he returned to Palestine to assume positions of importance in his own party, World Zionist Organization, and Jewish Agency. With breadth of vision and dynamic energy he opposed partition of Palestine and led the Yishuv into statehood in 1948. He cherishes strong convictions and has the will to fight for his views and the courage to admit mistakes. He more than any other single Jew is responsible for the birth of the state, and during the first decade of Israel's existence proved himself to be her most brilliant and valiant statesman.

D. Cabinet: The government is not limited by law as to the number of cabinet members or ministries. The first provisional government had 13 cabinet members, presiding over 17 ministries. The second government, regularly elected for a full term, had a Cabinet of 12 in charge of 18 ministries and the third, which is the current government, has 16 members in its Cabinet with 18 posts. Each cabinet member may appoint a vice chairman who is a member of the Knesset to represent the ministry in parliamentary debates or recommended legislation.

How is law made in Israel?

The democratic processes of government have in no way been affected by the prime minister's power and practice. The Knesset remains the supreme ruling body. The government, through its ministries, proposes new legislation requiring three readings at regular or special sessions of Parliament before it can be enacted into law. Each recommendation is "laid on the table," *i.e.*, required to wait at least two days for its first reading in the Knesset.

If it be an emergency law, the speaker of the House may consent to dispense with the waiting time. At the first reading, the ministry proposes the new legislation and explains its need. After discussion, with time equally divided between proponents and opponents, the proposal is either sent to a proper committee or, on failing to receive a majority, it is returned to the government for restudy. The committee's recommendations are presented to the Knesset with the privilege of offering amendments on each paragraph of any proposal. After the third reading, if approved by the majority, it is enacted into law and becomes enforcible with the consent of the prime minister and the president's signature.

Bureaucracy is a natural enemy of democracy. There are those who accuse the government of being overmanned with budgets beyond the fiscal capacities of the country. The facts do not fully support that severe indictment, though all agree that a better balance between income and expense is most essential and will in time have to be achieved.

In March 1956, the government machinery, ministries and civil servants, consisted of 40,097 personnel. In the brief span of eight years of sovereignty, the State of Israel succeeded in creating the various functions of government with an efficiency worthy of a long and well established nation.

To the office of the president are assigned 13 employees; the Knesset secretariat consists of 100; the controller's department is handled by 356; the prime minister's office by 837; Ministry of Finance employs 5,720; Defense, 1,044; Health, 4,716; Religious Affairs, 283, which includes the chief rabbinate and rabbinical courts; the Ministry of Foreign Affairs 880, including a Jerusalem staff of 310 and 570 in 44 countries, of whom 260 were sent out from Israel; Education and Culture, 807; Agriculture, 1,891; Commerce and Industry, 1,186; Ministry of Police, including the head office, policemen and prison guards, 7,456; Labor, 2,204; Justice, 867, including 98 judges and 769 staff-workers at the head office; Social Welfare, 837; Development, 117; Interior, 677; Posts, 5,822; Communications, 3,560 and miscellaneous, 1,260.

Two categories not included in the 40,000 civil servants are teachers and the armed services, the former numbering over

27,000, while information on the latter, for obvious reasons, is not made public.

The 1957 plans for a slight increase over the previous year in Civil Service personnel did not materialize due to the extra financial burden resulting from the Sinai Campaign and the temporary withdrawal of U.S. financial aid.

Civil Service compensation is commensurate with the general wage standards. There are 15 wage categories ranging from 61 IL to 580 IL per month plus cost of living increase, in some instances almost the equal of the basic pay. The Civil Service organization maintains disciplinary courts to try all cases of inefficiency, indolence and insubordination. The severest criticism voiced against the government is expressed in the single word "Protectzia"—political favoritism.

Each party is very zealous of the proportionate share of its members appointed as employees of the government or semi-governmental agencies. Loyalty to party often carries greater weight than fitness or efficiency. Critics of Mapai, the largest party in the coalition government, claim that its voting strength would be considerably reduced, if it were shorn of its power of patronage distributed among employees of government, labor union and sick fund benefits. In all fairness, it must be stated however, that the government with Mapai as the dominant party has taken measures to eliminate political favoritism. Appointments to Civil Service now require competitive examinations and a law prohibiting political activities on the part of Civil Servants is under legislative consideration.

To maintain all government functions the State of Israel for the year 1957-58 proposed a budget of 849,750,000 IL. Although budgets vary from year to year, the 1957-58 budget, shown on the following page, gives a fair and general picture of the revenues and expenditures of the Israeli government.

INCOME

I—ORDINARY REVENUE . . . . . . Consisting of taxes from income, property, inheritance, customs, excise duty, license fees, etc.		461,450,000
II—TRANSFERRED REVENUE . . Taxes to local councils consisting of purchase, amusement and vehicle licenses.		6,550,000
III—REVENUES FROM POSTS AND TRANSPORTS . . . . Post Office, ports, airfields, navigation, aviation and railways.		56,250,000
IV—REVENUES FROM COUNTERPART FUNDS, etc.		325,500,000
German Reparations,	73,000,000	
U.S. grant in aid & agricultural surplus . .	76,500,000	
External loan	43,500,000	
Collections on account of loans	27,500,000	
Collections on account of posts, transports. . .	5,000,000	
Sale of property.	8,500,000	
Internal loans from insurance, provident and pension institutions	29,000,000	
Telephone install. . . .	1,500,000	
Transfer of taxes from ordinary budget	12,000,000	
Total		849,750,000 IL

EXPENSE

I—ORDINARY EXPENSES . . . . Consisting of president, and his office, Knesset, members of Cabinet, prime minister's office and ministries and pensions for their families.	293,950,000
II—GENERAL AND IMMIGRATION RESERVE	12,500,000
III—SUBSIDIES AND ENCOURAGEMENT OF EXPORTS. . .	42,000,000
IV—DEFENSE AND SPECIAL EXPENDITURES	68,000,000
V—INTEREST PAYMENT	45,000,000
VI—TRANSFERRED EXPENDITURES	6,550,000
VII—EXPENDITURES ON POSTS AND TRANSPORTS	56,250,000
VIII—DEVELOPMENT BUDGET. .	234,500,000
IX—DEBT PAYMENT	56,000,000
X—WORKING CAPITAL FOR FINANCIAL OPERATIONS.	35,000,000
TOTAL	849,750,000 IL

Summary of income from the four categories in brief:

I. Ordinary Revenue	461,450,000
II. Transferred Revenue	6,550,000
III. Posts & Transport Revenue.....	56,250,000
IV. Counterpart Fund Revenue.....	325,500,000
Total	849,750,000 IL

After its first decade, what is the condition of the government of Israel? The constitution is still in the process of formulation, not by formal deliberating bodies but by the experimental and cumulative effect of dealing with current problems and through legislation enacted by Parliament.

Israel has not come as yet to grips with conflicts of opinions that tend to retard the attainment of national unity and disrupt orderly government. Perhaps such a crisis may be averted through the government's policy of gradual development expressed in Israel's basic democratic principles: "The third Knesset shall carry on and complete the enactment of fundamental laws which will together form the state's constitution based on democratic principles. These laws will implement and safeguard complete equality of rights and duties of all residents of the state regardless of sex, race, status, and nationality; freedom of religion will be maintained; the powers of the president, Knesset and the government and of the courts as well as the rights and duties of Knesset members will be determined; the rights of the individual will be protected; freedom of association, speech and written expression will be assured, subject to the state's security and independence; the democratic regime will be upheld against violence and dictatorship; state and military secrets will be guarded, and emergency powers for the security of the state will be laid down."

How soon these principles will be incorporated into a written constitution will largely depend on the pace of consolidation of the differing elements constituting Israel. When religious convictions are tempered by tolerance, economic philosophies become less dogmatic and distinction of origins is obliterated, then Israel will be sufficiently mature and secure to fashion a permanent instrument for the nation and the wellbeing of its people.

The multiplicity of parties and the problem of a balanced budget will trouble the state for some time to come, but unification remains the major problem requiring concerted effort. In the words of Ben Gurion: "Nevertheless, the social and cultural differences between a great part of the immigrants and the newer settlers have not yet been obliterated. . . . This [integration] will not be accomplished unless the government makes incessant efforts to improve the material and spiritual welfare of those immigrants who have been denied education, and unless there are voluntary efforts on the part of the younger generation, men of letters, educators and instructors to assist the immigrants." The process of solidarity must be quickened for the greater good of Israel and for her national fulfillment.

III. Growing Pains

In the first decade of Israel's independence the Jewish population leaped from 650,000 to 1,800,000.

If this increment were theoretically applied to the United States resulting in a phenomenal proportionate increase from about 170,000,000 to 465,000,000, it would involve insuperable absorptive problems despite the enormous size of the land, its limitless natural resources and the American know-how in organization, industry and commerce. How to solve the problems of housing, education, employment, health, interracial and intercultural relations would stagger the imagination even of the experts in their respective fields. Minus the natural resources, the land area, experience and skills of America, Israel tripled its population, literally overnight. This was accomplished in the face of military threats against her very existence. She forged ahead unafraid of her mortal enemies and undismayed by the economic, cultural and social dislocation which the new mass immigration was sure to impose on the infant state.

To this incredible accomplishment must be added the solution of two additional burdens. Unlike the United States, Israel provided the transportation costs for most of the new immigrants and did not employ the device of selectivity in the admission of the newcomers. There were no distinctions or exclusions. The Law of the Return, enacted in 1949, gave every Jew in the world the right to settle in Israel as if in fulfillment of Jeremiah's prophecy: "And the Children shall return to their own borders."

Yet, with all the seeming insurmountable difficulties, the task of transplanting over a million souls in one decade was masterfully achieved. During the mandate period (1919-1947), with Great Britain as the most skilled and extensive colonizer on earth, 400,000 new immigrants, averaging only 14,300 annually, settled in the Holy Land, while during Israel's first decade the average exceeded 100,000 per annum, and this was accomplished by a people without experience and without substantial material resources.

Palestine was never without Jewish inhabitants, a considerable number of whom remained there after the fall of Jerusalem in 70 C.E. under the military conquest of Titus. Even the crushing defeat of the Bar Cochba rebellion by Hadrian in 135 C.E. did not succeed in eliminating all Jews from the Holy Land. The surviving remnant, occasionally joined by other religiously inspired Jews from the Exile, braved the wars between the Christian and Moslem worlds, suffering persecution and massacre, but retaining a foothold, if precarious, in the Holy Land.

For the next millennium and a half, motivated by religious fervor, individual Jews or small contingents from different lands, at the risk of life, gradually infiltrated into the Holy Land. They were primarily concerned with personal spiritual salvation by virtue of residence, study and burial in their ancestral land.

Organized efforts for the creation of a home for the Jewish homeless and a national homeland for the Jewish people in Palestine began in the eighteen-eighties when evil days fell upon Russian Jewry. The movement gained momentum with the rise of Political Zionism in 1897. It was accelerated by the issuance of the Balfour Declaration in 1917 and was realized in 1948 on the declaration of Israel's independence.

In 1882 Palestine numbered about 24,000 Jews supported mainly by halukah—charity funds—considered a pious duty and contributed by world Jewry. The assassination of Alexander II, czar of Russia, with evil repercussions engulfing Russian Jewry, provided the spur to Jewish aspirations for a reconstituted Jewish nationhood in the Holy Land.

The spectacle of Jewish suffering and homelessness gripped the attention of the sensitive and thinking Jew everywhere. There were those who ascribed this acute problem, a matter of life and death in Eastern Europe, to a decaying political and economic system devoid of all human instincts of justice and fairness. Therefore, support of the underground socialist revolutionary movement, they were convinced, would eventually bring to the Russian Jews freedom and equality. Others, equally convinced of the need to overthrow the dictatorship of the czars and to establish a Socialist society, hesitated to merge the Jewish problem with Russian destiny.

The revolution was too slow in coming and the pogroms too hard to bear. They, the followers of Am Olam—the Everlasting People, sought a more immediate and realistic amelioration of the Jewish position through emigration to the U.S. and other lands of liberty and opportunity.

In opposition to the Jewish revolutionary plan of solving the Jewish problem as well as to the Am Olam advocates of a new Diaspora, the Hibat Zion—Love of Zion—movement made its appeal to world Jewry. The Bilu(s) (Hebrew word consisting of initial letters of Prophet Isaiah's exhortation, "House of Jacob, come let us go . . .") provided the early pioneers for settlement in the Holy Land.

On the one hand, Palestine had become a relentless land, barren and backward, with a hostile native population and an unfriendly political situation. On the other hand, America was to all a land flowing with milk and honey. When the Lovers of Zion had to decide between a comfortable personal haven of refuge in America and the rebuilding of their national life in Palestine, they chose the latter despite the privations awaiting them. If larger numbers did not emigrate from Russia to Palestine, it was not for lack of will but because of Turkish restrictions and Arab hostility. Between the Bilu(s) and Political Zionism, a period of about a decade and a half, the Jewish population in Palestine increased fivefold, from 10,000 to

50,000. The dreamers of Zion reborn thus established a Jewish beachhead in Palestine.

Since Palestine was unprepared during the Hibat Zion movement and the first two decades of Political Zionism to provide a haven of refuge for the large number of Jews fleeing from persecution and oppression, numerous other settlement plans in South America, Asia and Africa were projected by well-meaning and good-hearted people. Baron Maurice de Hirsch in 1891 proposed to the Russian government a plan for the transplantation of 3,000,000 Jews within a quarter of a century to South America, particularly to Argentina. No philanthropic endeavor could solve the national problem of the Jew. In the first decade hardly 10,000 were transplanted to Argentina.

In 1892 Paul Haupt, professor of Semitic languages at Johns Hopkins University, proposed an ambitious plan to settle the Russian Jews in Mesopotamia, a territory covering present Iraq and part of Syria. His proposal, endorsed by such prominent American Jews as Cyrus Adler, Mayer Sulzberger, Jacob Schiff and Oscar Straus, was transmitted to Dr. Herzl for his serious consideration in place of the Zionist program in Palestine. The proponents of this projected settlement argued that Mesopotamia was a more productive land and free from the complicated problems associated with Christianity's aspirations for the possession of the Holy Land. As to Jewish sentimental and historic attachment to Palestine, they maintained that Mesopotomia was equally sacred, since Abraham was born there, in Ur of the Chaldees.

Israel Zangwill in 1905, in response to continued and intensified Jewish persecution, organized the Territorialist Movement with the object of finding a haven of refuge wherever feasible, since the prospect of the realization of a Jewish national home in the Holy Land seemed remote.

All other schemes to create a Jewish homeland outside of Palestine failed because they lacked the major ingredient, a reawakened Jewish nationalism.

Dr. Herzl, leader of Political Zionism was not unconcerned with the enormity of the problem of the continuing oppression of the Jews, but he was the first to see the need of world political recognition and legal guarantees of Jewish rights to Palestine. These rights would enable the gates of Jewish immigration to that land to be opened wider and would give assurance that the corrupt Turkish rule and Arab animosity would not destroy the settlements already created by the Lovers of Zion.

In 1914, the beginning of World War I, the Jewish population in Palestine suffered a serious setback. The Turkish government, having joined the Central Powers, was bent on destroying the Jewish community in Zion, suspecting it of pro-Allied sympathies. Many of the Jewish settlers (approximately 28,000) were dispersed or imprisoned, and some died of famine and disease, leaving a net Jewish population of 57,000 in 1918 at the end of World War I.

The Balfour Declaration in 1917 opened a new chapter in the historic struggle for the realization of Zionist aims, with new hopes and new frustrations.

The three decades of British rule, punctuated by Arab resistance against Jewish immigration, alternated from a friendly attitude toward the Zionist program to acts tantamount to liquidation of the Declaration.

Sir Herbert Samuel's appointment as first high commissioner of Palestine inflated Jewish hopes. When upon arrival he attended Sabbath service, reciting publicly the prayer, "May the anointed of the House of David soon come to gladden our hearts," . . . there was rejoicing throughout the Jewish world. He was hailed as a herald of the eventual establishment of the Jewish state. But as Arab resistance stiffened, with the British government sensitive to their complaints, the first and only Jewish high commissioner bent backward to placate the Arab opposition, and thus ironically a Jew fostered a spineless and even inimical policy toward the promise of a Jewish national home in Palestine. There is no doubt that he acted under orders from Ten Downing Street, but he earned for himself the vigorous and lasting hostility of the Yishuv and of Zionists everywhere.

Max Nordau, Herzl's Zionist collaborator, with farseeing vision, on the issuance of the Balfour Declaration counseled a general exodus of Jews from all lands of oppression for the purpose of settlement in Palestine, irrespective of the lack of economic preparedness for a mass migration movement. He sensed a limited "honeymoon" period with the British mandatory government and therefore advocated an unprecedented scale of colonization before the ardor could cool. Dr. Nordau was not overconcerned with the problem of difficult adjustments resulting from a mass migration unsupported by correspondingly large financial resources. Together with Israel's ancient sages he maintained that Jews could sustain themselves through mutual cooperative efforts with limited outside aid.

Somewhat later Vladmir Jabotinsky, severest critic of Weizmann's confidence in the British promise to facilitate the establishment of a Jewish national home, in order to further the cause of a larger Jewish immigration to Palestine, reluctantly accepted the verdict of the authorities in Poland that anti-Semitism in that country was inevitable as long as Jews continued to live there.

Who knows? Perhaps if Jabotinsky's counsel to cooperate with the Polish government to help transplant Polish Jewry to Palestine had been accepted, they might have been saved from the Hitler gas chambers. The Zionist organization, however, in no position to foresee the tragic Hitler events, could not agree to a country's anti-Semitic policy—the denial of elementary citizenship rights—as the basis for Jewish settlement in Palestine.

With the passing of each year Arab hostility mounted, giving the British a flimsy pretext for curtailing Jewish immigration to Palestine and in essence gradually nullifying the Balfour Declaration.

However, despite all the impediments, the frequent local government obstacles set up by unfriendly British foreign and colonial policy as well as Arab intransigence and the limited Jewish material resources, the British mandatory rule in Palestine coincided with a considerable increase in Jewish population.

In the first decade of that period over 100,000 Jews entered Palestine, with 34,000 the highest in any one of those years and 2,000 the lowest.

The formation of the Jewish Agency in 1929 announcing an agreement between the Zionists, with Weizmann as their spokesman, and non-Zionists, with Louis Marshall at their head, aroused the Arabs to violent pogroms against the Palestine Yishuv—Jewish community—and tended to discourage further effort toward the fulfillment of the Zionist program and to dissuade Great Britain from giving any aid to the cause of Jewish nationhood. Neither the Jewish settlers in the Yishuv nor their fellow Jews the world over were paralyzed into inaction by the bloody riots of 1929, as they earlier refused to be terrorized in 1921 by Arab savagery. The demand for more visas to the Holy Land increased despite the ferocious Arab outbreaks against the Jewish community and the non-cooperation of the mandatory government.

What forces impelled the Jewish movement eastward? Reawakened Jewish nationalism was a contributing factor, but two more immediate and pressing developments forced the gates of Palestine to be opened to new immigrants: The Polish excesses and Hitler's assumption of power. Some of the escapees from the onrushing tide of an all-consuming war of hate might have preferred more secure havens of refuge in the Western World, but history conspired against them in favor of a Jewish national home. Few lands of opportunity welcomed them. Elsewhere they could plead for asylum for pity's sake only, but in the Holy Land the Jews could claim the right of historic association confirmed by the Balfour Declaration and concurred in by the League of Nations. The Zionists did not cause this state of world Jewish emergency, but they advantageously utilized the catastrophe for the saving of lives and the building of the Jewish nation and homeland. They successfully transformed a world tragedy into an unprecedented national achievement.

The peace treaty following World War I reshaped Polish nationhood and conditioned it on the equality of citizenship for all, including religious and cultural rights for minority groups. But before the peace treaty signatures were dry, Polish traditional anti-Semitism ruthlessly stripped the Jews of all equality rights. In deference to public opinion, the inhuman pogroms were called "excesses" by the Polish government in answer to the great volume of protests.

The unwanted Jewish population in Poland sought refuge in Palestine, but only small numbers were able to reach the shores of their ancestral land. The gates of Palestine were closed partly by English Tommies and partly by limited Zionist financial resources.

The once Zionistically minded large Jewish community in Russia was cut off from world Jewry by Bolshevik decree. In America an economic depression plus a divided Zionist leadership resulted in conflict between the Weizmann forces and the followers of the leading American Zionist, Louis D. Brandeis.

The optimistic view that governmental responsibility would sober Hitler's "kampf" against the Jews did not materialize. Some clung to the legend: "It cannot happen here in civilized Germany, the land of Goethe and Heine," but many German Jews recognized the handwriting on the wall. In 1932 10,000 emigrated to Palestine; the following year the numbers increased to 30,000, reaching 42,000 in 1934, 62,000 in 1935 and 30,000 in 1936, a total of 174,000 German-Jewish settlers in Palestine.

In answer to diplomatic protests of some of the Western democracies, including the U.S., against the butchery inflicted upon the Jewish minority, Hitler in essence replied: "If you like the Jews better than we, you can have them." But no country opened its doors to them.

International conferences on the plight of the refugees did not result in any bold or heroic measures. The U.S. was passing through an economic depression, making it politically unwise for the government to effect a change in immigration laws to enable larger numbers of the 500,000 doomed German Jews and 3,000,000 potential victims in Poland to enter "the land of the free."

Even the Jewish leadership in America, fearful of anti-Semitic consequences, was wary of advocating a new immigration policy. All they asked was a more liberal interpretation of the prevailing laws in favor of the most distressed applicants. The well-publicized Avion Conference on Refugees proved unresultful, since the participating nations had agreed in advance that no solution of the problem would require them to modify or abrogate their respective existing immigration laws.

When in 1932 Palestine admitted 10,000 refugees, the U.S. permitted entry of 2,755; in 1933 the comparative figures were 30,000 to 2,372; in 1934, 42,000 to 4,137; in 1935 the proportion was 62,000 to 4,837. Even the 1939 bill for the admission of 20,000 refugee children in two years, to be deducted from future quotas, was vigorously opposed on the ground that the new immigrants would eventually add to the stress of unemployment. While the civilized world declared a moratorium on its conscience, closing its eyes and hearts to the cries of despair from fleeing refugees, the Yishuv in Palestine, with the aid of world Jewry, compelled the mandatory government to keep the doors open to them for several years.

The sizable increase of the Jewish population of Palestine resulting from the wave of German immigration produced two severe crises: internal adjustment and Arab flare-up. Only a small proportion of the newcomers were Zionist by conviction; the majority, uninspired by nationalist idealism, came only out of dire necessity. Lower standards of living, linguistic and cultural differences complicated the situation. However, with remarkable alacrity they did, before long, become a constructive element in the Yishuv, contributing immeasurably to its growing strength.

The swelling of the numbers of Jewish immigrants aroused further Arab aggression and induced the willing British to restrict immigration to 10,000 in 1937, 13,000 in 1938 and in the critical year of 1939 to 27,000.

In the struggle to keep the doors of Palestine at least partially open to the unfortunate defenseless Jews, the Yishuv adopted the policy of havlagah—self-restraint— toward the Arabs, while English authority was defied by aiding "illegal" immigrants to enter the country.

Before, during and immediately following World War II, the mandatory government kept her eagle eyes closed as Arabs of neighboring lands entered Palestine where the economic opportunities created by Jewish pioneering efforts were superior to their own. But Jewish "illegal" immigrants were detected by the English navy and frequently forced back to the certain death awaiting them. The *Patria,* the *Struma* and the *Exodus,* ships jam-packed with Jewish refugees from Hitler's hell, were brutally forced to return to their respective ports of origin, only to demonstrate how void of content the Balfour Declaration had become in the hands of the British.

In World War II the Jews of Europe were callously left to their fate. Consigned en masse to huge concentration camps for wholesale slaughter, some of them died heroically like the valiant souls of the Warsaw ghetto, others most pitifully suffered martyrdom with not a finger raised to help them from any quarter.

Only in Palestine the Jews refused to take it supinely. Their bid for a Jewish army rejected, they served the Allied cause in a less conspicuous manner until their military unit received official recognition. But even in this precarious period when the German invading armies were approaching the gates of the

Middle East, with the Arabs on the fence or in open sympathy with Nazism, the Yishuv clandestinely managed during the war years to smuggle an average of 6,000 new immigrants into Palestine per annum.

With the Allied victory in sight, even in the face of stern British opposition and Arab hostility, the numbers increased to 15,000 in 1944 and 13,000 in 1945. On the defeat of the Nazi armies 18,000 entered in 1946, 23,000 in 1947 and 17,000 in the first half of 1948 when the Yishuv proclaimed its independence. In all, under the most adverse conditions of British connivery and double dealing, Arab resistance and limited financial resources, 57,000 Jewish settlers at the issuance of the Balfour Declaration rose to 650,000 three decades later at the declaration of Israel's independence.

The Provisional Council which proclaimed the State of Israel accepted all the British mandatory laws as binding until such time as a duly elected legislative body could adopt new laws or modify the old ones, declaring, however, as immediately null and void British restrictions on immigration and the purchase of Arab land.

The Law of Return made it possible for every Jew to enter the land as a matter of right and not of favor or pity. But from where were the new Jewish immigrants to come? Of the 17 or 18 million Jews prior to World War II, six million were lost in the Hitler holocaust, between two and three million were isolated in Russia, another million were behind the iron curtain of Russian satellite states and about five and a half million lived in the United States, in great sympathy with Zionist aims but with no desire to abandon their privilege of citizenship and the opportunities it afforded. Jews in the rest of the free world were similarly minded. Thus it appeared for the first time that the order was reversed: the gates of Israel wide open but there were now few to enter the land.

New historic forces ordained otherwise. In the first decade of

Israel's independence the Jewish population increased by approximately 1,150,000, of whom 900,000 were new immigrants and 250,000 were gained through natural increment. In the first seven and a half months following her realization of statehood on May 15, 1948, 102,000 entered Israel; 239,000 in 1949; 170,000 in 1950 and 175,000 in 1951. Eastern European and mainly Oriental countries provided the bulk of these new immigrants to Israel.

The very Arab states which vehemently obstructed Jewish statehood, unwittingly helped its progress by the ill-treatment of their citizens of Jewish faith, forcing them to seek a haven of refuge in Israel. Through political pressure, however, the gates of exit in Africa and Eastern Europe were closed, considerably reducing the number of new immigrants during the next few years: 25,000 in 1952; 12,000 in 1953; 18,000 in 1954 and 37,000 in 1955.

The slower tempo of immigration was not without advantage as it gave Israel and the Jewish Agency a breathing spell to catch up with the essential housing, employment, educational and health facilities for the newcomers. The Hungarian revolt, Egyptian expulsions following the Sinai Campaign and the new wave of Polish anti-Semitism are reflected in the number of Jewish immigrants to Israel: 56,000 in 1956, 71,000 in 1957 and 26,000 in 1958.

The following concise dates and figures tell the unembellished story of the phenomenal growth of Jewish immigration to the Holy Land since the national reawakening of the Jewish people.

In the first aliyah—ascent to the Holy Land—between 1882 and 1904, approximately 25,000 Jews settled in the land.

In the second aliyah, between 1904 and 1914, about 35,000 Jews entered Palestine. Following World War I Jewish gravitation toward the ancient homeland was constant and often intense.

Year	*Number of new immigrants*	*Year*	*Number of new immigrants*
1919	1,806	1939	27,561
1920	8,223	1940	8,398
1921	8,294	1941	5,886
1922	8,685	1942	3,733
1923	8,175	1943	8,507
1924	13,892	1944	14,464
1925	34,386	1945	13,121
1926	13,855	1946	17,761
1927	3,034	1947	21,542
1928	2,178	1948	101,828
1929	5,249	1949	239,576
1930	4,944	1950	170,249
1931	4,175	1951	175,095
1932	9,553	1952	24,369
1933	30,437	1953	11,326
1934	42,349	1954	18,370
1935	61,854	1955	37,348
1936	29,727	1956	56,234
1937	10,536	1957	71,130
1938	12,868	1958	(approx.) 27,000

Because of Rumania's recently reversed policy, permitting her Jewish citizens to leave the country, 100,000 new immigrants are expected to enter Israel in 1959.

Of additional interest is the Jewish population in Palestine at the various stages of Zionist efforts.

Year	*Jewish population*	*Year*	*Jewish population*
1882	24,000	1940	468,000
1890	47,000	1945	564,000
1900	50,000	1946	594,000
1914	85,000	1947	630,000
1916-1918	57,000	1948 (May)	650,000
1922	84,000	1948 (Dec.)	717,000
1927	150,000	1958	1,800,000
1935	355,000		

Israel's Jewish population originating from over 70 countries is 60 per cent European and 40 per cent Oriental. Until the birth of the state in 1948, Europe supplied 76.6 per cent of the

Jewish immigrants and the Middle East including Egypt, Yemen, Turkey, North Africa, etc., 20.4 per cent.

The European portion came from:

Poland	36.7%
Russia, including Lithuania and Latvia	11.3%
Bulgaria, Yugoslavia and Greece	3.9%
Rumania	8.8%
Hungary, Austria and Czechoslovakia	6.6%
Germany	12.3%

From the Oriental countries:

Egypt, Yemen, Turkey, Iraq	8.7%
North Africa	0.3%
Not classified	11.4%

The sources of Jewish immigrants have been very much reversed since 1950. In the past seven years only 30 per cent came from Europe, 36.9 per cent from Asia, 31.6 per cent from Africa and 1.5 per cent from the Americas.

The gigantic task of the ingathering of such large numbers of immigrants from all the four corners of the earth into a country which had remained fallow for so many centuries was made even more onerous by the problem of youth aliyah. The movement to save the Jewish youth from Hitler's hell was initiated in 1933 under the inspired leadership of Henrietta Szold, founder of Hadassah and most outstanding Jewish woman in the entire Zionist enterprise. In the first 14 years over 21,000 boys and girls were transplanted from their respective lands of persecution to the Holy Land. By 1956 the numbers grew to 81,000 boys and girls homeless and aimless, without kith and kin, restored to their ancestral land and raised to creative life and useful citizenship. Of these youths 14,000 are still the charges of the Jewish Agency for Israel in various camps, institutions, schools and kibbutzim—communal farm villages.

The integration of the very newest immigrants, most of whom had not previously been included in the Zionist program, added to Israel's growing pains. Expelled Egyptian Jews, though geographically nearest to the Jewish state, were Zionistically remote. For years they refused to see the writing on the wall, indicating that their days in their native lands were numbered, because they were blinded by "the flesh pots" of Egypt. They came because they had no alternative. They could not remain in the land of the Nile and no other country would have them.

Of the Hungarian refugees, some were Zionist in their youth, but the majority were either assimilationists to whom the Jewish heritage was a burden or ultra-orthodox who by conviction would not recognize the religious validity of Israel as a state since it had come about without prior benefit of the traditionally envisaged Messiah.

The immigrants from Poland had suffered a rude awakening. They almost believed that Communism had brought them salvation when Polish anti-Semitism, deemed dead, was resurrected to plague the small Jewish remnant, numbering approximately 50 to 60 thousand. The reason for their migration to Israel was best expressed by a former Polish Jewish Communist. "My son was rejected by his playmates because he was a little 'Moishe.' To grow up as a normal happy person he must live with other 'Moishes,' fully accepted by them. There is this natural acceptance in Israel."

The three above described categories of immigrants, plus the smaller numbers of repatriated Polish Jews from Russia, when they landed in Israel required not only the usual aid in terms of shelter and food but sympathy and understanding in the adjustment of their philosophy to make them feel at home in their ancestral land.

Not all who entered Israel remained there. Some, not sufficently inspired by the ideal of a reconstituted Jewish nation to bear the hardships of a pioneering life, found the new life too much for them. They left for better economic opportunities elsewhere, particularly in the Americas. The number of émigrés might have been considerably larger if not for adverse public opinion, discouragement by foreign governments and the limited quota systems for new immigrants the world over.

In 1955-56, 50,000 new settlers came to Israel and 7,000 left the country. This is approximately 10 per cent, seemingly a large proportion. The average number of émigrés during the entire period of mass migration to the Holy Land, since and prior to the beginning of Israel's statehood, has been approximately between 7 and 8 per cent. However, when compared to the number of British returnees from Canada, Australia, New Zealand, etc. who left their native land to start life anew in one of the British commonwealths, the Israeli figures are encouraging. Of those who emigrated from Israel for greater economic opportunities, only a very negligible number were native Israelis. Though conscious of the attractive personal advantages in more advanced countries, they would not leave their own country in its hour of need. No personal sacrifice was considered too great to make the homeland secure. To this they were pledged. They refused to be lured away from Israel for personal gain. A case in point is the story of a newcomer who was invited by his wealthy relative in America to leave Israel for greater financial opportunities which would be afforded him in the U.S. The Zionist pioneer was called "crazy" for rejecting the offer but he refused to dissociate his destiny from that of Israel. This indomitable spirit, zealous fidelity to the land, is the vital force now building Israel.

Israel faced many difficulties, internal and external, to become established as a state, de facto as well as de jure. Among the growing pains of nationhood the following gave Israel great concern:

Integration: Lack of homogeneity among the new immigrants aggravated Israel's growing pains. After she won her independence, the majority of newcomers who originated in Asia and Africa differed from their European brethren of the 1948 days in physical appearance, background, the amenities, culture, language, economic philosophy as well as adherence to religious views and practices.

The problem of amalgamation of the new immigrants in Israel can be assessed by the fact that by 1958 only one out of every three residents was native born, *i.e.,* out of a Jewish population of 1,800,000 approximately 1,200,000 were immigrants of recent years. Israel has not as yet recognized, and may never tolerate, marked distinctions based on economic status, but national origins have created in the public mind supposedly superior and inferior types of population. The Sabra—the native born—considers himself and is frequently regarded as, the national aristocrat; those of the more recent European stock take pride in their cultural background; while the Asian-African immigrants are considered to be at a lower level of the social structure of Israel. Such attitudes, fortunately, are not held by government authorities, the older pioneers and the intellectual elements in the land.

Israel's returnees represent 74 national origins with a babel of languages hampering the process of national fusion so essential to strengthening the common bonds of understanding.

Language: Hebrew, until the rise of the Zionist movement was the language of religion and scholarship only, inadequate as a conversational vehicle and too limited for scientific use. Yet, as if by magic, it has been remolded into a national medium of expression in every walk of life. The indomitable will of Eliezer Ben Yehudah (1857-1922) laid the foundation of Hebrew reborn. His disciples zealously and skillfully advanced the new Hebraic structure, from a holy tongue of prayer and study to a living spiritual bond for all Israel. So deeply rooted has the classical Hebrew language of the Bible become in the land that it no longer fears the competition of any foreign language, including Yiddish. Out of a total of 26 newspapers, 14 are in Hebrew, and only 35 out of 285 magazines are published in languages other than Hebrew. No longer is there any need for the "Defenders of the Hebrew Language." The intensive and cohesive national consciousness has obviated that necessity.

The differences arising both from lands of origin and languages have been more readily solved in the kibbutz. This statement from one of the religious kibbutzim is characteristic of all communes: "Our members derive from Turkey, Rumania, Hungary and Morocco . . . We have one language, one mode of prayer, Hebrew. There is no difference between one man and his fellow. The process of integration is going forward gradually but surely."

Unhappy Memories: Among the most difficult problems in the process of unification is the rebuilding of the lives of the Nazi victims to make them forget yesterday's horrors. In a youth aliyah—young immigrants—institution, one of its wards insisted on sleeping under his bed. He could not become reconciled to the fact that he is no longer in hiding in a Christian home in Poland from Nazi brutal hands. Another youth gathered all the crumbs from his table after each meal and placed them under his pillow. He was still haunted by the bitter memory of hunger while in a German concentration camp. A third refused to part with his sweater on the hottest days. He still "suffered" from the dread of cold which he endured in a Polish forest while in hiding from the inhuman torment to which he had been subjected.

Oriental Immigrants: The Oriental Jews present their own problems of consolidation. Take the case of the young Moroccan Jewish mother who left her infant in the maternity hospital. She would not keep her child because of the care and costs involved but rejected adoption on the ground: "Who will support me when I grow old?" Or consider the problem of the young bride married in her native land at the age of 12. In Israel she refuses to live with her husband twice her age and calls on the law of the land to send her back to school where she belongs, so that she might be released from an intolerable bondage.

The problems presented by the immigrants from the backward countries require understanding, sympathy and patience. They are less educated. Their knowledge of hygienic measures is very limited. Few possess the skill necessary for industry. They have much to learn to become participants in a democratic society. But there is strong determination to help them become first-class citizens. With continued patience the goal is within ready reach.

Housing: Housing appears to be the most painful problem in the process of nation building. One has to see the ma'barot—transitional camps—consisting of one-room tin huts, temporary housing facilities, to appreciate the hardships encountered by the newcomers. When the austerity of their lives is viewed, particularly in cold, damp, rainy weather, all huddled together in cramped quarters, remembering the homes they left behind, their faith in the goodness of man is shattered and things look even bleaker than they are. But this is temporary. As soon as substantial homes are built the new immigrants move into them and are restored to human dignity. By 1956 only 22 ma'barot camps remained, and these too would have been liquidated within a short period if not for the unexpected, large influx of newcomers from Egypt, Hungary and Poland.

The general progressive trend toward durable housing has been in evidence for some time. In 1949, 33,000 new rooms were constructed; in 1950, 50,000; in 1951 the number increased to 85,000; in 1952, 72,000 new rooms were completed; in 1953, 36,000; in 1954, 33,000 and in 1955, 68,000. Thus, gradually, the nationless have found a nation and the homeless have "come home."

New Settlements: Until Israel's assumption of statehood every type of settlement, private initiative, cooperative enterprise or commune was resisted by the native Arab population, at times with the support of the British mandatory government. To overcome such hindrance, the Yishuv had to resort to secret planning and execution. One of these big settlement schemes was unveiled on October 10, 1946 on the close of the Day of Atonement to the complete surprise of the British Intelligence Department and the consternation of the Arabs. The Jewish leadership, deeming the Negev important for future expansion, working in the dead of night, had secretly laid the foundations of 11 new settlements with prefabricated housing and with all the elementary necessities of life in the barren desert. Within eight months water pipes were laid to carry water from far distances to the parched land.

Where experts predicted nothing could grow, sheer Jewish will power planted flourishing gardens. And within less than two years these settlements proved to be of tremendous strategic importance in the War for Independence by helping to win the whole Negev for the Jewish state.

More and ever more new settlements became the answer to the needs of a swiftly growing population, but always with an eye to the greater security of the land. To lighten the defense burdens of the border settlements, the cluster type of colonization was introduced on a larger scale, with the Lachish region as an outstanding example of the new effort and direction in the scheme of concentrated settlement. This area conquered by Joshua about 1230 B.C.E. has always remained a pivotal battlefield throughout Israel's history. It is identified with Samson's exploits, David's defeat of Goliath, Rehoboam's fortresses to guard Jerusalem's southern approach and the Babylonian destruction of those fortresses, making possible the capture of the Holy City.

This modern "Operation Lachish" was completed almost overnight with 21 new settlements and with Kiryat Gat of the famous "tell it not in Gat" as the center for all intercommunity activities, such as common defense, marketing, health, education and culture.

A similar type of cluster colonization, beneficial to the individual settlers and indispensable for the defense of the country, was set up in the Jerusalem corridor. Before the War for Independence this area in the Judean Hills contained six Jewish settlements. Now 40 of them dot this region with a population of 10,000, ever ready to defend the ancient city of David.

Growing up for a nation as for an individual is always both a painful and rewarding process.

Security: The gravest concern to the Israelis since the founding of the state has undoubtedly been the question of security. The urgent needs for defense have often outstripped economic considerations. Settlements had to be established along the borders for strategic purposes, even though economically they were not very productive. Since 1948, 315 such border settlements were established of which 230 were made up of more recent immigrants, with nothing between them and the enemy. Eighty-five of these settlements were recruited from sons and daughters of kibbutzim and idealist youth from the cities. These included some of the fighting groups of Nahal who combine as part of their two and one half years of military training preparation for agricultural life. On discharge from service, they settle as civilian farmers.

Together with the armed forces these border settlements, new and old, constitute Israel's network of defense. The heavy pressure on these exposed settlements is well illustrated by the following two eye-witness accounts: "Right from the start we faced not only economic difficulties but we were confronted with immediate security needs. In the first year Arab infiltrators robbed the harvest from 25 per cent of our land. After a number of clashes, we managed to reduce infiltration in our area and to make our property more secure. . . . We are proud of the settlement we have developed. But, although we cheerfully accepted these assignments, we feel that the heavy load of maintaining our security should not fall on us alone." The second observation is equally significant: "We were frightfully few, 57 in number, and were still almost children who had left behind the warmth and comforts of our homes. Our tents were scorched by the pitiless Negev sun. There was not a tree in sight to cast its shadow. We felt as though we had been exiled to a land where the bullets of murderers flying in ambush might reach us from any side." This situation has been somewhat relieved. These settlements are no longer left to their own resources. In time of emergency, help can come more swiftly and with greater power. Approach roads were built for 308 frontier settlements. Telephones were installed in 208. In 138 settlements electricity was connected and in others, generators provided. The burden of guard duty was also somewhat eased by special recruiting for the Frontier Military Service.

Herzl, the dreamer of Zion, envisioned a peaceful state, but the Arabs made of the dream a nightmare. Jewish physical insecurity preceded and hastened Zionist fulfillment, but self-defense became a primary characteristic of the Yishuv and of Israel, while hopeless, defenseless exposure was the condition of Jewry in the lands of oppression. In the words of one refugee fleeing for life from his native country only to be faced with Arab armed hostility in Israel: "Here, at least, I have the right and the weapons of self-defense, no longer a hunted animal in the wilderness of civilization." Or, as an older pioneer put it: "Here we pay with raids against us and with insecurity, but we do not run."

National Defense: It became clearly evident at the very beginning of Jewish colonization in the Holy Land that Jewish life and effort needed self-protection. Since the bakshish (bribe) loving Turkish police could not be relied on, the Shomer—Jewish Watchman—was born of necessity to defend the Jewish community and its possessions. This organized Jewish police force, the Shomrim, was dissolved by the Turkish government in World War I to be reborn as the Haganah—Self-Defense—consisting of those who were trained in the Turkish Officers' School at Istanbul and those who received their military experience in the British Jewish Battalion First Mule Corps, captained by Vladimir Jabotinsky.

The Haganah grew into a well-disciplined body of guardians of Jewish life and property against Arab attack, employing retaliation if need be and havlaga—self-restraint—when the Yishuv's welfare required it. As the British policy against Israel tightened its harshness, the dissenters from the Haganah tactics of patience and nonprovocation formed the underground Aizel, made up of the initial letters of the Hebrew name, Irgun Zvai Leumi—the National Military Organization—with Menahem Beigin, successor to Jabotinsky, assuming leadership in 1943. Because of Beigin's apparent (though unreal) cooperation with the British mandatory government, a dissident group broke away from the Irgun under the leadership of Abraham Stern, a university student bent on a policy of forthright action and violence if necessary, to compel the British government to recognize Jewish claims to statehood.

Outgoing High Commissioner MacMichael outlawed the Haganah and thus gave the Sternist group added provocation to further embarrass the British government. In 1944 two of Stern's followers, young lads, went to Cairo where they assassinated Lord Moyne, British resident minister of the Middle East.

This act was aimed at the mandatory power for oppression of the Yishuv. It was instigated primarily in retaliation for the inhumane order to turn away from the gates of Palestine the refugee-loaded, unseaworthy *Patria,* back to the open sea where it went down to its doom with all its human freight aboard. The assassination was regarded by many as a political crime. Churchill threatened to reverse his stand on Zionism. Responsible Jewish leadership did not approve of the Sternist acts of terror. But Jewry was united in hostile public opinion against the British government for the acts of its mandatory power resulting in the tragic incidents of the *Salvador,* the *Atlantic,* the *Patria* and the *Struma.*

In fulfillment of the Zionist program, the problem of defense proved to be a formidable and very painful one. When the War for Independence was successfully concluded, the government's major task was the organization of a united armed force responsible to the civil administration. This has become an accomplished fact. The Haganah disbanded, the Irgunist and the Sternist forces and their members were fused into the Zahal, made up of the initial Hebrew letters of Zva Haganah L'Israel—Israel's National Army. Thus beginning with the Shomrim to the completion of the first decade of independence, the Jewish people who for nearly 2,000 years were perforce defenseless have learned the art of self-defense and have become the strongest single military power in the whole of the Middle East.

Learning and Culture: Since the loss of Jewish independence under Rome, the one and only true aristocracy among Jews has been that of learning. Elsewhere in this volume there is a fuller discussion of the educational and cultural growing up of the new Israel. It is sufficient here to state the simple fact that despite the many problems of immigration, defense and land settlement, the People of the Book have not forgotten their love of learning.

The early Zionist settlers came to Palestine because of Torah; its study in the Holy Land gave greater assurance of personal salvation.

The young Zionist was concerned not only with saving the Jewish people from persecution but to create a favorable climate for Jewish culture. Even in the countryside, where the opportunities for learning are not as great as in the urban settlements, Jewish illiteracy was unknown. The worker on the land never sank to the intellectually inferior level of peasantry. He became an intelligent farmer, deeply involved in the building of a nation and always concerned with the progress of mankind.

Return to the Soil: For centuries the Jew was divorced from the soil. Prohibited from owning or working the land and excluded from the various guilds, he made a virtue of necessity. Not permitted to engage in manual labor, he assumed the role of the middleman as his only means of livelihood. Therefore, his first attempt at colonization was through Arab labor, but Jewish self-fulfillment through labor had become an essential principle of the Zionist enterprise.

Morally, if not legally, the land belongs to those who work it. The Zionist pioneers, mindful of territorial limitations, the stubbornness of the soil and the inadequacy of water, literally moved mountains to restore a land neglected by the Arabs for centuries into fertile fields. But despite the intractability of the soil, its absorptive capacity increased even beyond the phenomenal growth of the urban community. While the Jewish population of Israel since 1948 mounted by nearly 150 per cent, the urban population was only approximately 55 per cent; that is, the major increase was on the farm and in the small settlement. Of more than 900 settlements inhabited by the present Israeli population of 2,000,000, 50 are cities and towns with 1,400,000 souls and 850 are rural settlements with 600,000, a very high percentage of land settlers judged by standards of modern civilized countries everywhere.

Whatever the future of the kibbutzim, for the present at least the youth remaining in the settlements of their birth or joining similar rural ventures is estimated to be between 80 and 90 per cent. Governmental propaganda is slanted toward the encouragement of youth settlement on the soil. When a few years ago Ben Gurion left the political arena for a quiet life in the Negev, the cynical interpreted this move as a token of "indispensability" with the thought that he might be called back to even greater power in time of emergency; others ascribed it to a need for physical rest, but those in the know maintained that he was motivated to set an example to influence the younger generation to devote their lives to the soil in the South.

Israel's strength has risen in proportion to its agricultural progress. To work the land and to possess it was no easy task for Jews who for so many centuries were strangers to agricultural pursuits, but Zionism did succeed in reuniting the Jew with the soil of the Holy Land. This is its greatest triumph.

As Zionist achievements advanced, it became more difficult for Jews individually and collectively to increase their land acquisitions. The constant restrictions imposed first by the Turkish government and later by the mandatory power against Jewish purchase of land were a major obstacle. In addition, the economic laws of supply and demand skyrocketed the purchase price of Arab-owned land with every increase of Jewish population. Private purchases were the source of many defects in a large-scale settlement project. Stymied by inflated prices caused by competitive buying, it could not cope with the program of national land acquisition nor deal adequately with strategic planning for statehood.

The Rothschild colonization project, though not under Zionist auspices, became an important step in the right direction toward the Zionist goal. In 1957 the Rothschild land assets of 180,000 dunams were relinquished to the State of Israel. But even this great philanthropic gesture was not commensurate with the needs of a rapidly growing nation.

The second World Zionist Congress in 1898 grappled with the land question and finally approved Dr. Schapira's proposal of the Jewish National Fund for the purchase of land in Palestine as the everlasting possession of the Jewish people. The land thus acquired was to be leased for 49-year terms, on the principle of the Biblical jubilee, to Jewish settlers willing and qualified to work it.

The Jewish National Fund was set up as the official agency to solicit the pennies of the Jewish masses by means of the pushkes—boxes—placed in homes, offices and business establishments everywhere. It also received substantial gifts and bequests, and, later, it became a constituent of the United Jewish Appeal. It devotedly carried on its function of land purchase and tree planting up to the time of the establishment of Israel, having acquired 1,800,000 dunams of land and planted 53,000 dunams of trees.

With the rise of the state, the Jewish National Fund also became the custodian of all government-owned land inherited from the mandatory power as well as the lands abandoned by the Arabs when they fled from Palestine during the War for Independence. Compensation for the property they left behind has been tentatively offered, subject to the hoped-for general peace settlement between Israel and Arab states.

Because of the new functions assigned to the Jewish National Fund and its allocation from the United Jewish Appeal, since the birth of the state this organization has been able to increase its land holdings to 9,000,000 dunams, not including its acquisitions in the southern Negev. Also, it has approximately quadrupled its afforestation area, from 13,250 to 48,750 acres.

To the problem of land acquisition and afforestation must be added the primary need of clearing the land and providing the necessary water, without which no soil cultivation is feasible.

To make two blades of grass grow where only one grew before represents the practical application of scientific approach and method, but Operation Israel went even beyond that wizardry.

No one questioned Jewish brain power, but many doubted Jewish brawn. Even the agricultural top authorities wondered whether the Zionist pioneers were capable of the backbreaking job of clearing and preparing a fallow, long-forsaken land for cultivation. They blasted rocks, they picked up stone by stone, they cleared the ground inch by inch, they produced water where there was none to be had, they plowed, they seeded and when they harvested, they exclaimed with the Psalmist, "They who sow in tears shall reap in joy."

Financial Aid: According to the Biblical story of Israel's exodus from Egypt some 3,500 years ago, the slaves of Pharoah left "with great wealth." In the modern Jewish exodus of the 20th century, the large proportion of those who settled in the Promised Land had been stripped by their tormentors of all their worldly possessions. They required financial help both for transportation and to start life anew in their ancestral homeland.

The cost of settlement per family proved very heavy, approximating $15,000 for elementary necessities: housing $4,000; other necessary construction $2,000; water $3,300; livestock $1,300; tools $700; working capital $700; planning and direction $1,200; miscellaneous and emergency needs $1,800. In the urban communities, the average cost is estimated to be $10,000. From where did the huge sums come? Few immigrants arrived with sufficient capital to be established agriculturally or to engage in some profitable enterprise in the urban community. Private and group investors, motivated by Zionist ideals, created economic opportunities for additional settlers. But the major financial burden for large-scale settlement fell upon the World Zionist Organization through its various agencies and upon Israel's citizens who frequently tightened their belts to make their contributions toward the settlement of new immigrants.

There was disagreement in the Zionist leadership, particularly between Brandeis and Weizmann, concerning the efficacy of voluntary gifts of funds as the economic basis for the building of a nation. The struggle was eventually resolved by giving priority to large-scale philanthropy for nonprofit national undertakings with private investments to follow.

The floodgates of Jewish generosity were thrown wide open at the end of World War II, with each crisis in Israel's life stirring greater willingness on the part of world Jewry to offer ever-increasing financial aid. The United Jewish Appeal, a combination of the Jewish Joint Distribution Committee and the United Palestine Appeal (consisting of the Keren Hayesod—Foundation Fund and Keren Kayemet L'Yisrael—Jewish National Fund) have been indispensable for the task of large-scale Jewish settlement in Israel.

In more recent years three other financial sources came to Israel's aid: 1) the United States through money grants and loans, surplus food and Point Four aid; 2) substantial sums derived from the sale of bonds of Israel and 3) German reparations income.

Eventually Israel will have to rely upon her own financial resources for an independent and secure national existence.

"If life you desire, you must be willing to struggle and sacrifice for it." This ancient Jewish adage is applicable to the stupendous Zionist uphill endeavor for a resurgent Jewish state: Arab resistance, British collusion and intrigue, refugeeism, War for Independence, Fedayeens, boycotts, unresponsive, waterless land, afforestation, integration, financial stringency and United Nations threats have been the growing pains of the new nation.

History bears eloquent testimony to Israel's Herculean efforts to grow up to become a nation among the nations.

IV. Israel Among the Nations

Abraham, the first Jew, was called "The Hebrew," interpreted by Israel's sages to signify his hazardous position as the trail-blazer of a new faith and people. He stood alone, the rest of the world opposing him and his aspirations.

Abraham's descendants suffered the fate of aloneness during the two millennia of their exile, praying and hoping for a cooperative world in which Jewish nationhood reborn would be welcomed into the family of nations.

Will rejuvenated Israel be forced to continue to stand alone or will the enlightened nations extend to her the hand of friendship?

Israel is the legitimate child of the United Nations. It was a Caesarian birth demanding the expert skill of world statesmen. The labor pains were hard and prolonged.

On April 28, 1947, the critical first special session of the General Assembly of the United Nations to consider the Palestine question began. It brought forth its final decision November 29, 1947, 33 members voting in favor of the Jewish state, 10 abstaining and 13 opposing, the negative votes consisting of six Arab states, four other Moslem countries plus Cuba, Greece and India. The resolution was clear and concise: "Having met in special session at the request of the mandatory power . . . having constituted a Special Committee and instructed it to investigate all questions and issues relevant to the problem of Palestine and to prepare proposals for the solving of the problem; having received and examined the report of the Special Committee including a number of unanimous recommendations and a plan of partition with economic union approved by the majority of the Special Committee . . . [the

General Assembly] recommends to the United Kingdom . . . calls upon the inhabitants of Palestine to take such steps as may be necessary to put this plan into effect . . ."

Perhaps, if the final vote had been completed on the previous day, the necessary two-thirds majority might not have been obtained. This is one instance when the "if" in history is not a mere theory in retrospect. The alertness, diplomacy and talented dedication of Zionist leadership had finally succeeded in turning the tide in favor of the creation of a Jewish state in Palestine.

Were the Arabs equally wise, the Middle East would not long remain an explosive area in a turbulent world. Zionists pleaded for more than the United Nations was willing to grant. The territory assigned was too limited for a viable state and the borders resembled a jigsaw puzzle, consisting of seven sections—three for Arabs, three for Jews and Jerusalem as a separate enclave.

Internationalization of Jerusalem was not to Zionist liking. The economic union, which was proposed by the United Nations with a second state to be created in Palestine for the native Arabs, seemed to have merit; but the Zionists were justifiably skeptical of wholehearted Arab cooperation, which was a prerequisite for implementation. If the Arabs had acceded to the U.N. resolutions, there might never have been the Arab refugee problem, which has remained to plague the Middle East and trouble the civilized world.

The Arabs, however, were determined to concede nothing. They set out to nullify the General Assembly resolution by violence if not by votes. They invoked every instrument of propaganda to make the great powers withdraw their favorable action at the General Assembly. The U.S. State Department, never too friendly to Jewish aspirations for national rebirth, in the face of virulent Arab opposition began to reconsider the wisdom of its leadership in the United Nations in favor of a Jewish homeland in Palestine. There were other American pressures upon the State Department urging it not to "alienate Arab friendship for America."

So effective did Arab propaganda become, aided and abetted by oil interests, that the United States withdrew its original support for a Jewish state on March 30, 1948. Into the lap of the Security Council of the United Nations fell this extremely controversial issue.

If left to public debate and behind the scenes maneuvering, the Jewish state in Israel might have been stillborn. But events more potent than world parliamentary discussions and unsavory international deals changed the situation within six weeks after the U.S. withdrew its sponsorship of Israel's reborn nationhood in Palestine.

Arab-Jewish tensions, claims and counterclaims are detailed and examined in the last chapter of this book. In the immediate context, Arab hostility toward Israel is interjected only in explanation of the varying and often contradictory attitudes within the United Nations toward the reconstituted Jewish commonwealth.

The British were tired of the mandate. They forfeited Zionist confidence when they closed Palestine's doors to Jewish immigration and prohibited transfer of land from Arab to Jew, the two basic planks upon which the Jewish future of Palestine precariously rested.

Likewise, they never gained the trust of the Arabs. Britain to them was always an evil colonial power. Their relationships were further strained by the issuance of the Balfour Declaration and the small favors granted Zionism in the honeymoon days of Anglo-Jewish friendship. Ernest Bevin, in charge of British foreign affairs in the crucial period following World War II, was an angry, bitter and frustrated man. He was hostile to the Zionists who made demands. He was enraged at the United Nations for its resolution favoring the creation of a Jewish state in Palestine. Hence Bevin's unbending policy of "a curse on both houses," the Zionists and the United Nations.

He carried out his threat to terminate the mandate and not to implement the U.N. resolution but to let Jew and Arab in Palestine fight it out, confident that the Arabs would drive the (damn) Jews into the sea. So the British mandatory government and 100,000 men of its armed forces packed up what they could, leaving considerable armament strategically behind where it would fall into hostile Arab hands.

The date of the British departure was set for the early hours of May 15. Palestinian Jewry, faced with the problem of the Sabbath, by tradition too sacred for official proclamations, issued its Declaration of Independence on the eve of the Sabbath, May 14, 1948. Within hours Harry S. Truman, then president of the United States, gave the embryonic Jewish state de facto recognition, followed by Guatemala on the 15th, Soviet Russia on the 18th and other nations subsequently.

Temporarily this ended further equivocation within the U.N., but seven Arab states took the law into their own hands to defy, betray and annul that which the United Nations created by its resolution on Palestine. Egypt, Syria, Iraq, Lebanon, Jordan, Saudi Arabia and Yemen, united by one common hate, waged war against the new infant State of Israel. In less than a month, from May 15 to June 11, 1948, Israel, with incredible courage and supreme sacrifice, achieved an armistice which resulted in territorial enlargement, thus proving to the world not only its military prowess but also its ability to survive as a nation under conditions of war, stress and travail.

Zionism as a Jewish philosophy of revival and survival envisioned the future Jewish state in a dual role: one, the ultimate solution of the problem of Jewish homelessness and two, the natural development of a distinctive Jewish national culture. Inherent in the idea of Jewish culture was the contribution to the welfare of mankind which Israel could offer. In support of such a vision it was pointed out: ancient Israel gave to the world the Bible, the ten commandments and the great prophets. From Judaism were derived two great world religions,

Christianity and Mohammedanism. Is it not logical to believe that under normal conditions Israel would again give birth to new ideas and ideals for the betterment of mankind?

In this spirit of cooperation as well as in the pursuit of greater world recognition of its nationhood, the new State of Israel sought the right and privilege to become a member of the United Nations. On May 11, 1949, a year and six days after the proclamation of its independence and 11 months after the signing of the armistice agreement with the belligerent Arab states, Israel gained admission to the United Nations on the passage of this resolution by the General Assembly: "Having received the report of the Security Council; noting in the judgment of the Security Council that Israel is a peace loving state; noting furthermore the declaration of the State of Israel that it unreservedly accepts the obligations of the U.N. Charter and undertakes to honor them from the day it becomes a member of the U.N.... the State of Israel is elected into membership of U.N."

There was high jubilation in the Jewish world. Israel acquired a status of equality among the nations. It could now present its case to the court of world opinion as a matter of right and no longer by sufferance. Henceforth it would be a legally recognized partner in the official deliberations of mankind to secure peace and stability for the peoples of the earth. But from the very moment Israel's aspirations to become a member of the United Nations were realized, it was forced into the perilous role of standing alone. Though in theory the United Nations is constituted of individual members with freedom to act independently for self-interest, in practice this does not apply.

Most U.N. deliberations and conclusions are based on alignment with groups or voting combinations. Israel was placed in the peculiar position described in the Bible, "And it shall not be reckoned among the nations." She would not be the willing tool of the East even if favored behind the Iron Curtain. The

Western Powers would not accept Israel within their bloc for fear of the threat of the Communists who seek Arab favor.

Israel is indeed a "peculiar people." Geographically it belongs to Asia; yet in political ideology it belongs to the Western World.

Jewry, upon whom Israel depends for major help, is world-wide; yet in the United Nations the new state finds no support, only occasional sympathy. Great Britain could not be relied upon. It was (and is) still hoping to recement relations with the Arabs. The United States, torn between justice and expediency, vacillated to fill the vacuum created by the loss of Anglo-French influence in the Middle East. Russia, to gain a foothold in the Arab world, would readily sell the Jewish state down the river. Only France, disillusioned by Arab antagonism, has recently become Israel's ally. But in the main, the Republic of Israel, creature of the United Nations, stands alone between the two opposing camps.

Why has the climate toward that new republic so radically changed in the U.N. since it was admitted into membership on June 11, 1949? Has Israel really changed from a peace-loving people to one of aggression deserving world condemnation and the threat of sanctions? An understanding of world forces which contribute to the instability of the Middle East is important for a true evaluation of the new nation among the nations.

First it must be recognized that while Zionist efforts of a half century resulting in the birth of the state were contributing factors toward tensions in the Middle East, most of the current conflicts would still plague the world even if Zionist aims and fulfillment had never seen the light of day.

Abba Eban, Israel's eloquent spokesman at the United Nations made this crystal clear at the 1958 General Assembly Special Session. "The disorders in Lebanon and the peril of Jordan had arisen in the context of relations between Arab States. The representatives of Lebanon and Jordan have told the United Nations where they believe the causes of these disputes to lie." Similarly, the Iraqi upheaval, the Sudanese disagreement with Egypt and the challenge to Nasser's leadership in Africa have no direct relation to Israel's rise to statehood.

Arab nationalism was born almost simultaneously with the issuance of the Balfour Declaration, but not because of it. At the termination of World War I, Great Britain and France carved out from the defeated Turkish Ottoman Empire a number of Arab states, dividing their spheres of influence—Lebanon and Syria under French tutelage and the rest under British authority. Heretofore, the new Arab states had no marked borders among them nor separate economies. A common religion, language and common laws cohered them in an otherwise mutual lack of interest. Arab nationalism was fed by the growing number of younger intellectuals and the blunders of the two colonial powers.

Three factors were responsible for the favorable attitude toward Arab nationalism by the civilized world. The romantic portrayal of the Arabs by Lawrence of Arabia set the groundwork. The missionaries contributed their share. They came to the Moslem world to scoff, to convince the Arabs of the superiority of Christianity but remained to pray, openly expressing their admiration for their sister religion. British and French governmental staffs, beginning with the rise of Arab nationalism in 1919 up to World War II, found the Arabs acceptable. In contrast to the demanding spirit of the Jews in Palestine the average Arab was submissive, even servile. The Arab's picturesque dress and manner of living made an appeal to the European officials, "something exotic to write home about." In addition, Jerusalem was a dull place; Beirut was the playground of the Middle East.

Neither Great Britain nor France, however, took sufficient cognizance of the growing Arab nationalist mood. They continued their outworn policy of status quo. In every struggle for the improvement of the lot of the masses—to remove poverty, disease and illiteracy—they aligned themselves with the feudal interests. Their jockeying for position led first to the decline of French prestige and power, even to the dislodging of English hegemony, including its suzerainty over Egypt.

In the awakened world of the 20th century, Arab nationalism is authentic. It is the normal aspiration of every people to gain independence, to be master of its own destiny. But pan-Arabism is artificially stimulated, negatively motivated, by hate for Israel and imperialistic ambitions.

While the Arab nations have much in common—ethnic affinity, geographic contiguity, language, religion and culture—their divisive elements are very potent. They may temporarily cover up their differences, but they cannot obliterate them. Conflicting national temperaments, personal ambitions, envy resulting from economic disparity between the "have" and "have not" oil states make it impossible to cement them into a federated union that can long endure.

The current gravitation toward Nasser is not motivated by ethnic reasons since Egypt is not really Arab. Nor has Nasser's stature grown in the Arab world because of any improvement in the daily life of the average Egyptians, for very little has been done under his dictatorship to lighten the burden of the impoverished masses. His popularity is primarily due to the expulsion of the British, his nationalization of the Suez Canal and his advantageous arms deal with Russia. The bandwagon of success is the magnet of attraction; imperialism has become the grand Arab delusion.

Israel is a convenient scapegoat in the Middle East struggle for power between East and West. Hatred of the new state is the tool with which the Arab nations are wielding their bargaining power in a divided world.

Israel's position within the United Nations changed radically from an attitude of sympathy toward her to condemnation since November 29, 1947. The Arab members are understandably prejudiced. But why the change of heart on the part of those whose favor previously had made possible the rebirth of Jewish nationhood in Palestine?

Among the five permanent members of the U.N. Council, Russia has drawn more closely to the Arabs. Therefore, this survey of Israel's worsening situation among the nations will deal first with the Soviets.

1. Russia voted for a reconstituted Jewish state on November 29, 1947. Ironically, it is very doubtful whether the U.N. Palestine Resolution would have materialized without Russian support. Future historians with Kremlin records at their disposal may be able to disclose the exact motives for Russia's strange, favorable action in behalf of Israel reborn. Two factors seemed to argue against the possible cooperation of the Soviets with the Palestine Resolution: one, the intensification of the cold war with the former allies of the Western Powers and two, the traditional Bolshevik antagonism toward Zionism.

Russia and her satellites consistently opposed every major issue favored by the Western bloc. Established precedent of opposition within the United Nations to Jewish nationhood argued against Russian collaboration in favor of a Jewish state. The Russian Revolution of 1917 made both anti-Semitism and Zionism illegal, the former on moral grounds (subsequently repudiated) and the latter for political reasons.

Jews were among the most persecuted people under the czars. It was therefore natural for the leaders of the Revolution, prompted by antipathy against the imperial regime they overthrew and by the alleged principle of equality for all citizens, to make racial prejudice illegal. Zionism, however, was branded as reactionary and antirevolutionary, due in the main to yevsetzke—renegade Jews—influence. These revolutionists of Jewish ancestry were given control of the Jewish minority in Russia. They were historic enemies of Zionism, now bent upon its complete obliteration together with the uprooting of every vestige of Jewish religious life and Hebrew culture.

Another reason for the repression of Zionism in the Soviet

Union is the supposed conflict of interests. Zionism aims at emigration, while Russia opposes the loss of any of its creative forces. An effort to create a Bolshevik substitute for Zionism, Jewish colonization in Biro-Bidjan, soon proved abortive with no further attempt to encourage Jewish minority survival.

In view of Russia's antagonism toward Zionism and its formidable opposition to the West, why did the Soviets endorse the Palestine Resolution? Was it an altruistic act motivated by a sincere desire to help solve the problem of Jewish homelessness?

Russian foreign policy never concerns itself with the plight of the downtrodden unless it serves Communist interests. Clearly, it was not sympathy for the Jewish people but a malignant political action to displace Great Britain's sphere of influence in the Middle East that prompted Russia to join the United States in voting for the U.N. Palestine Resolution on November 29, 1947.

Later events bear out this conclusion. Russia reversed her pretended friendly attitude toward Israel in support of the Arab intransigence in order to gain a foothold in the Middle East after Great Britain lost her prestige and the United States began to fill the vacuum thus created.

To throttle Western influence in the Middle East, Russia turned its propaganda machine against the U.S., condemning it as a more vicious type of colonialism than that of England and France combined. As to Israel, Russia, now openly anti-Semitic, branded it as reactionary and as a tool of the Western Powers to enslave the Arab world, thus fanning the flames of mounting Arab hatred and at the same time gaining a foothold for the Soviets in the Middle East.

Russia stood ever-ready to align herself with every Arab complaint against Israel in the U.N. Even before hearing the defense, the Kremlin was quick to condemn Israel as an aggressor. Nikita S. Khrushchev's wholesale condemnation of the new state bears this out: "The activities of the State of Israel are deserving of censure. From the outset of her existence Israel began threatening her neighbors and conducted an unfriendly policy toward them. Clearly such a policy fails to answer the needs of the State of Israel, since behind the back of those who implement it, stand imperialist powers known to all. They are seeking to make use of Israel as a weapon against the Arab peoples in their shameless desire to exploit the natural resources of the area."

Russia's appetite for Middle East supremacy predated the rise of Bolshevism and became avaricious when the Bear in a new guise was displaying its claws. To counteract the Baghdad Pact, created by the Western Powers to impede Communist infiltration in the Middle East, Russia, through propaganda and contributions of arms, succeeded in persuading most of the Arab states to adopt a policy of so-called "positive neutralism." With Egypt as a willing partner, Russia succeeded in dividing the Arabs on the Baghdad Pact, the destruction of Israel remaining the only issue on which all Arab states would be presumed to unite.

Russia, better known as an exporter of revolution rather than rubles, even went beyond the shipping of arms and the encouragement of hate against Israel. In competition with the United States, she offered Egypt financial aid for the construction of the Aswan Dam. In an effort to wean the Arabs from the attractive U.S. dollar, the Soviets frequently warned and condemned Israel, through the organs of the United Nations and through the medium of Russia's special brand of propaganda, for acts which would have been easily justified or simply overlooked if committed by another nation under similar circumstances.

Peace in the Middle East is less the concern of Russia than her control of that area. Russia would denounce an Arab state for negotiating peace with Israel. In a recent Jordanian crisis, prior to the puppet Arab state's joining the Iraqi Federation, the Russian radio condemned King Hussein for allegedly planning peace with the Jewish state. On this chessboard of world politics involving Middle East hegemony, with Russia and the U.S. the chief contestants, each Russian move is calculated to sacrifice the little pawn, Israel.

2. The British position vis-à-vis Israel in the United Nations, though often veiled, is nevertheless discernible. The motivating factors influencing British behavior toward Israel stem from the circumstances that brought the English into the Middle East and their unhappy sojourn and exit from that seething cauldron of unrest. Not even the indomitable Sir Winston Churchill could reverse the tidal wave of history. British colonialism was doomed despite its comparatively enlightened rule.

The age of nationalism was hastened by two world wars which had weakened the stout Britishers. This resulted in greater dependence of Britain upon the United States, already linked by ties of common language, law and culture. America, with its economic and military resources, had become a dependable ally in the two world conflicts and in the rebuilding of war-ravaged civilization. Conversely, England has become the first line of defense for the United States, more so than the expanse of the Atlantic, making the two countries interdependent. Despite seniority in the art of diplomacy, Great Britain yielded to the persuasive influence of America, granting the right of self-determination to large segments of its world-wide empire.

The British career in the Middle East was, in the general pattern of a reawakened world of nationalism, short-lived. Allenby's army in World War I broke up the Turkish Empire, freeing vast Arab lands and populations, which became independent states in the Middle East: Egypt with an area of 386,198 square miles and a population of 23,410,000; Saudi Arabia 870,000 square miles and 6,500,000 population; Yemen 75,000 square miles and 4,500,000 population; Iraq 171,800 square miles and 4,842,000 population; Jordan 37,500 square miles and 1,500,000 population; Lebanon 4,000 square miles and 1,450,000 population; and Syria 171,800 square miles and 3,856,000 population, while Israel at the time of the Armistice numbered less than a million inhabitants in an area of only approximately 8,000 square miles, constituting about 2 per cent of the Middle East population and less than ½ of 1 per cent of its territory.

Contrary to the excessive romanticizing of the pro-Arab Lawrence as to the alleged Arab revolt, the new states gained their freedom without making any real contribution to the war effort. In World War II, when Nazism threatened to engulf every vestige of democratic life, Egypt assumed a doubtful neutrality; Iraq was convulsed by a pro-Hitler revolution and the rest of the Arab states rendered more lip service than military aid to the Allied cause. Egypt and Syria did not declare war on Germany and Japan until February 26, 1945, followed by Lebanon on the next day, on the very eve of Nazi defeat, not in support of free world war efforts, but to be enabled to attend the San Francisco conference for the founding of the United Nations on March 1, 1945. British influence dominated the area, though for a while France controlled the destiny of both Syria and Lebanon.

Palestine soon loomed as one of the major obstacles in England's design to become master of the Middle East. The Balfour Declaration, which was issued on November 2, 1917, turned out to be a serious stumbling block. It pledged to facilitate the creation of a Jewish homeland in Palestine, subject to two conditions: one, not to prejudice the civil and religious rights of existing non-Jewish communities in Palestine; two, not to prejudice the rights and political status enjoyed by Jews in any other country. The second condition proved to be only a pious wish.

As to the pledge to facilitate a Jewish homeland in Palestine, the Balfour Declaration was artfully translated and distorted to make it seem more of a pledge to the Arabs than to the Jewish people. Gradually it was whittled down by "white papers," commissions and investigation reports to vitiate the clear intent of the Balfour Declaration. By a variety of subsequent tortured interpretations, in order to appease the Arab world, Great

Britain twisted the meaning of the subordinate clause of the Balfour Declaration, "the protection of the civil and religious rights of the existing non-Jewish communities," to become primary in importance, and "a Jewish homeland in Palestine" secondary in effect. The British Foreign and Colonial offices, in their anxiety to foster Arab friendship (at the expense of the Jewish homeland), were not too meticulous in their construction of even the subordinate clause which specified civil and religious rights but made no reference to political rights.

There was never any danger to Arab civil and religious rights that would result from the establishment of a Jewish homeland in Palestine. The Moslem religion enjoyed complete freedom. Civilly, the Arabs enjoyed equality under law, with full participation in the Civil Service, with Arab language and culture secure throughout the land. There was no pledge of Arab sovereignty in the Balfour Declaration. But British rule was determined to undermine its original commitment to the Jewish people for the sake of what it considered of greater importance, Arab good will, which proved to be very dubious.

This British policy of Arab appeasement and only occasional small favors to the Jews might have resulted in a Jewish ghetto-like community in Palestine if not for world events preceding and following World War II. As Palestine neared its first half million Jewish settlers, British statesmen declared Zionist aims as fulfilled, since this number made a viable Jewish cultural center in Palestine feasible.

Nazi rise to power brought imminent danger to German Jewry. Despite threats of Arab rebellion, the doors of Palestine were kept partially open a while longer. During World War II, however, when the need for sanctuary was most acute, the doors of Palestine were shut in the faces of Jews fleeing from brutal Nazi slaughter.

With Rommel at the gates of Egypt, conquest of the Middle East as a strategic Nazi goal seemed close at hand. In general, the Arabs remained safely aloof from the conflagration and some even gave support to the Nazi army. Palestine Jewry pleaded for the privilege to organize a Jewish brigade to aid the Allies. After undue procrastination the petition was finally granted, but only in a limited way. Why? Because Great Britain feared to arouse Arab antagonism now being voiced through a British-sponsored Arab League.

Britain's immigration policy in Palestine became even more stringent and heartless at the close of World War II, while the few surviving German Jews were wasting away in refugee camps. As a result, the British were harassed by aggressive action in Palestine as well as by Jewish pressures supported by sympathy in the U.S. It therefore resolved to get rid of its headache by tossing the mandate into the lap of the United Nations, and this action led to the eventual recommendation of the U.N. for the creation of the Jewish state in Palestine.

The British government, however, refused to implement the decision of the United Nations. It expected to void the resolution by this means. Failing in this, it hoped that by withdrawing from Palestine, the Arabs themselves would have free reign to put an end to Zionist aims. In this way Britain hoped to regain her lost influence among the Arabs, dissipated through the Balfour Declaration. When results proved otherwise, and other great powers had already given recognition to the Jewish state, Britain reluctantly followed suit.

The record of the British policy of vacillation toward the creation of a Jewish national home in Palestine is rendered more graphic by a consideration of these salient dates and events:

1917. Great Britain issued the Balfour Declaration.

1922. The Churchill White Paper cut off Trans-Jordan from Palestine with the added dictum that Palestine was never intended to be as Jewish as England was English.

1930. The Passfield White Paper based on the Shaw Commission Report and Simpson Investigation reduced the intent of the Balfour Declaration, trumping up a new definition of a Jewish national

home in Palestine and introducing the new principle of "absorptive capacity."
1937. Palestine Royal Commission recommended "partition."
1938. Peel Commission submitted recommendations against "partition."
1939. MacDonald (Malcolm) White Paper, for all practical purposes, annulled the Balfour Declaration, allowing 50,000 new Jewish immigrants to Palestine during the next five-year period, with an extra 25,000 visas for refugees at the discretion of the high commissioner.
1945. Ernest Bevin of the postwar Labor government rejected proposal to admit 100,000 displaced persons into Palestine and vitiated other recommendations of the Anglo-American Inquiry on Palestine.
1946. Morrison-Grady Plan proposed recommending a federated state with Arab and Jewish cantons.
1947. Bevin referred the Palestine question to the United Nations with a pledge to implement its recommendations, but he repudiated his pledge after the Palestine Resolution was passed by the General Assembly on November 29, 1947.
1948. Great Britain withdrew from Israel May 15, 1948.
1949. Great Britain recognized the State of Israel on May 13, 1949.

Except for public declarations during elections, British policy on Palestine in reality was never a party issue. The Conservatives and Laborites only competed for votes; but they exhibited no wholehearted desire to implement the Balfour Declaration. When the promise of a Jewish national home was being dishonored by the Conservative government the Labor Party protested the injustices to the Jewish cause; when Labor came into power, its restrictions on Jewish national aspirations were severely criticized by the Conservatives.

However, Britain's hopes to restore her waning influence in the Arab world were never abandoned. She stood ever-ready to support Arab claims against Israel as a means to this end.

Though not authenticated, this apocryphal story is believable: After the British-French evacuation of the Suez Canal area, the British secretary of foreign affairs favored, in Parliament, Israel's withdrawal from the Gaza Strip and Gulf of Aqaba as well as its return to the 1947 territorial boundaries recommended by the U.N. When asked at a party conclave why he betrayed the interests of Britain's erstwhile ally in the

Suez affair, he is reported to have replied: "We have not lost hope for mending our fences with the Arabs. We must continue our efforts to recement friendship with them."

Within the United Nations, the British attitude on questions dealing with Israel is based on Arab appeasement despite the futility of this policy in the past. Not even Jordan, which has been artificially created by England and had been aided with money and military leadership by her, could be relied upon for support as an ally. Yet England cannot resign herself to her forced exit from the Middle East and would sacrifice Israel if need be to regain her former dominant position in the Arab world. She would cheerfully sell the new state down the river of Arab oil.

3. Israel's history will gratefully record the warm friendship and major aid given her by the United States, making possible the rise of the Jewish republic and its survival against heavy odds in the early years of its existence.

From the very beginning of American history there has been a spiritual affinity of the United States with the Jewish people. The prophetic aspiration of Israel's restoration in Zion was a familiar concept to those who were influenced by the teachings of the Hebrew Bible, the basic source of American moral law. This sentiment was voiced by two great Americans, both of Jewish faith. Mordecai Manuel Noah (1785-1851), American consul in Tunis, declared, "We will return to Zion as we went forth, bringing back the faith we carried away with us." Emma Lazarus (1849-1887), American poetess of note, also spoke for America when she said, "There is great need for a home for the homeless—and a nation for the denationalized."

The Balfour Declaration, the first political achievement of Zionism in the world arena, would not have been issued without the moral support of the U.S. In 1919 Woodrow Wilson publicly declared: "I am persuaded that the Allied Nations, with the fullest concurrence of our own government and people, are agreed that in Palestine shall be laid the foundations of a Jewish commonwealth." He reiterated this statement a year later to strengthen the Jewish claims before world public opinion. Though the U.S. did not join the League of Nations, Congressional approval of a "Jewish homeland in Palestine" and of the mandate to Great Britain by the League of Nations was adopted in 1922 and approved by President Harding.

Franklin D. Roosevelt, less dependable for practical aid, frequently made favorable utterances in behalf of a reconstituted Jewish nation in the Holy Land. Truman's sincere interest in the restoration of the Jewish people in Zion expressed itself in his firm demand to open Palestine to 100,000 homeless Jewish refugees and later, on November 29, 1947, he gave U.S. approval to the Palestine Resolution of the United Nations. The disappointment caused by the reversal of that support on April 16, 1948, allegedly in order to avoid threatened bloodshed, was more than made up by granting the new State of Israel de facto recognition on the day of its Proclamation of Independence, May 14, 1948.

The United States' favorable attitude toward Zionist aims has been officially expressed on numerous occasions by both the executive and the legislative branches of the government. They are worthy of record:

1917. President Woodrow Wilson was consulted on and approved the text of the Balfour Declaration.
1918. President Wilson gave formal approval of Zionist aims.
1919. President Wilson publicly endorsed the proposal of a Jewish national homeland in Palestine in aid of the cause when he personally appeared at the League of Nations in the making.
1921,
1922. President Warren G. Harding on various occasions expressed his approval of Zionism.
1922. Joint resolution of Congress endorsing the establishment of a Jewish national home in Palestine was adopted and signed by President Harding.
1925 American-British Mandate Convention was ratified by the United States Senate.
1928, 1929, 1930,

1932. President Herbert Hoover repeatedly confirmed U.S. policy favoring Zionist aims.
1935, 1936, 1937, 1938, 1939, 1941, 1942, 1943,
1944. President Franklin Delano Roosevelt frequently expressed his favorable attitude toward a national Jewish home in Palestine.
1945. President Harry S. Truman made request of British Prime Minister Atlee to grant 100,000 visas to Jewish displaced persons.
1945. Joint Congress resolution was adopted, calling on the president to use his best influence to open the gates of Palestine to a larger Jewish immigration.
1947. United States took the lead in the United Nations in favor of the Palestine Resolution which was adopted on November 29, 1947.
1948. On March 30, United States withdrew her affirmation of Palestine Resolution substituting a trusteeship proposal.
1948. On May 14, immediately following the proclamation of the State of Israel, President Truman granted to it de facto recognition.

It is clear that without the political support of the U.S., Israel could not have come into being. Without material help from America, the new state could not have survived. In the words of Ben Gurion, Israel's prime minister: "All through the years we have received financial assistance, the value of which cannot be exaggerated." But while America remained generous in rendering financial aid, it did not continue to give Israel the necessary political support.

Why did American policy toward Israel change? On the surface it might be attributed to a change of party leadership in the U.S. government. Without minimizing the influence or questioning the sincerity of any important individual in the State Department or the party in power it is fair, however, to conclude that the U.S. policy toward the Middle East, including Israel, has been motivated primarily by self-interest rather than by an anti-Jewish attitude. But though the intent is pro-America, this self-interest may prove to be misplaced, unjust and shortsighted, as well as damaging to the cause of America.

The implied interest of the U.S. in the Middle East is based on the following considerations: a) Avoidance of serious conflict that may lead to a third world war. b) Exclusion of Communism from the area. c) Maintenance of air bases, particularly in Saudi Arabia. d) Guarantee of oil resources for the West.

The accomplishment of these objectives is linked to stability in the Arab countries. But how is this stability to be attained? Temporary expediency will not suffice. International justice, the basis of permanent stability, cannot be realized through appeasement. Just and wise decisions must be founded on facts without prejudice.

The State Department of the U.S. has seldom reconciled its Middle East diplomacy with the realities of the situation. The Arabs are more zealous with their threats than in their ability or readiness to execute them. For example, they threatened many European firms with Arab boycott if they continued to transact business with Israel. Most Europeans rejected the blackmail without suffering any consequence. The Arabs warned West Germany against paying reparations to Israel at the risk of severed relations, but the threat did not materialize. Some large American corporations, however, did take the Arab pressure seriously and ceased to do business with Israel. Furthermore, in keeping with well-known Oriental tactics, the Arabs make exaggerated demands in their negotiations in order to allow for bargaining.

In appraising the Middle East political situation, the U.S. State Department is wont to look through rose-colored glasses. Consider the attitude of the U.S. toward Egypt, the largest of the Arab nations. The U.S. favored King Farouk, despite his personal and official corruption, on the ground that his throne was a stabilizing influence in the land. When the revolution brought Naguib to the head of the Egyptian government, he, in turn, became the State Department's idol, the new Messiah of the Middle East. Nasser's unceremonious removal of Naguib promptly brought him American official acclaim as a paragon of idealism and nobility, heralded as the economic, political and social savior of Egypt.

The State Department has not benefited from historic experience which has proven Arab friendship to be illusive and undependable. The Arabs gained their independence through Allied efforts in World War I, but in World War II they failed to remember their indebtedness to Great Britain and France. Promises and written agreements made by Arab leaders proved worthless. They "played ball" with the Nazis.

The Arab accepts concessions as a sign of weakness rather than of generosity or good will. U.S. dollars, arms and political support failed to produce the expected appreciation in loyalty and friendship. Should expediency necessitate desertion of America to gain Russia's favor, the Arabs would shabbily disregard all that America has so generously contributed to them.

America's policy of appeasement would not prevent conflict between the Arab states and Israel; neither would an unfavorable attitude of America toward Israel keep Russia out of the Middle East. Such moral weakness would serve as a poor strategic weapon for the prevention of a world conflagration.

The underdeveloped Middle East is oil rich, capable of producing between one-half and two-thirds of the world's needs. This alluring black gold could not escape the attention of American enterprise, the major concern being profit, not a just peace. Were oil to be less essential for the Western World, the American flag would be less apt to signify dollars in the Middle East. American policy has favored the Arab states not with the intent to undermine Israel but because of the mistaken notion that the Arabs must be appeased for the good of the Western World.

Oil has influenced America in placing expediency above moral considerations. Without denying the importance of Arab oil in peace and war to Western industrial power, two important elements have been overlooked in the relation of oil to America's Arab appeasement policy. In the first place, Russia is self-sufficient in oil. It is more interested in providing the Arab world with the sinews of revolution than with rubles. In case of war, how long would it take for an enemy to destroy

Arab oil fields? Rumanian oil sources were easily bombed and cut off in World War II. More recently, the Syrian sabotage of oil pipe lines during the Sinai Campaign bears out this premise. U.S. policy of isolating Israel to guarantee the flow of Arab oil to the West is as unrealistic as it is immoral.

The second factor too readily overlooked, in addition to the Russian aspect, is the Arab need for selling oil to America and Europe in order to acquire dollars and other needed foreign exchange. Furthermore, the present American policy of appeasement would not in itself deter the Arabs from swerving politically, if not ideologically, toward Russian Communism. Even if Israel were destroyed, there could be no assurance that the Arabs would align themselves with the West. They have repeatedly and arbitrarily broken alliances in the past.

The formation of the Asia-Africa bloc has again evidenced the tendency of America to befriend the Arabs at the expense of Israel. This balance of voting power could prove disastrous to Israel. Russia's prompt support of this bloc hastened American support.

At times, the American alignment came in conflict with Western powers when their colonial interests were challenged. By professing friendship for the Arab world, influencing South American delegations and cooperating with the Asia-Africa bloc, the U.S. in effect has often isolated Israel in the U.N. Was it a Freudian slip or an intentional attempt to justify the American imbalanced judgment and action in the Middle East tension that the U.S. secretary of state, John Foster Dulles, explained before a Congressional committee the long-standing enmity between Arab and Jew on the ground that the Jews are alleged to have killed Mohammed?

American policy in the Middle East is not of its own making. Because of the State Department's blundering tactics and lack of moral courage to take the initiative, Russia has been dictating American policy. The United States reacted out of fear of what Russia might do but did not pursue an affirmative policy of its own.

On the numerous occasions when Israel registered complaints against the Arabs for acts of attrition, plunder and murder, the United States as well as the U.N. refrained from any expression of moral indignation. Israel's plea for the right to purchase ammunition for purposes of self-defense in the face of the Russian-Egyptian armament deal was denied for the alleged purpose of discouraging an arms race in the Middle East. The State Department moralists further argued that there should be no parity between Israel and her enemies in ammunition since the Arabs are more numerous, the specious logic being, the bigger the nation the greater its moral right to possess force with which to destroy its smaller opponent. The State Department moralists fortified their position by piously quoting the prophetic verse, "not by might nor by strength" does a nation survive. Therefore, they argued, Israel should not rely on munitions for self-defense but, by implication, it was all right for the Arabs to rely on munitions.

While United States arms were denied to Israel for self-defense, the Arabs, seeking aid from Russia, obtained through their bargaining power armaments far beyond their needs. The Arabs boastfully asserted that they would employ American arms against Israel only. In the words of the Syrian prime minister: "We shall take the weapons [American] and use them against the Jews." After the State Department muddled the "off again, on again" shipment of arms to Saudi Arabia, that state's minister of defense made known in no uncertain terms: "The intention is an attack on Israel." Jordan, too, made the solemn promise: "We shall not use these [American] weapons against our brother Arabs. They are reserved for the Israelis."

The refusal of arms to Israel was another graphic illustration of present-day abysmal standards of international morality. It was based on the false assumption that it was necessary to appease the Arabs in order to avert Russia's sinister designs.

Furthermore, Israel presented no blackmail threat to join the Communist fold if she was unsupported by America.

American policy, or the lack of it, has wavered between half-hearted support for Israel and professed friendship for the Arab states, a policy based on no moral considerations. The Arabs outnumbering Israel twenty to one offer larger markets. They and their Moslem friends control many votes in the U.N., while Israel has only one. Israel symbolizes the spade and sapling; the Arabs, the barrel of oil, source of power in peace and war.

Israel's expedition into Sinai in 1956 brought down the wrath of the United Nations, with the U.S. and Russia in the lead. This is the second instance when these two great powers were on the same side of the fence on a major issue affecting Israel, her creation and condemnation. Britain and France, with or without previous knowledge of Israeli plans, joined the successful expeditionary forces in the direction of the Suez Canal, to reclaim their rights violated by Nasser months previously. Not to be outdone by Russia, the United States, joining hands with her venomous foe, promptly denounced her proven allies, including Israel, as aggressors, demanding their immediate withdrawal from Egyptian territory.

Israel regarded the expedition as an act of defense to avert an imminent armed Egyptian invasion of the Jewish state, the fixed date of which had been learned by Israeli intelligence. The war plan in the making was precipitated by Fedayeen attacks, organized by Egypt, while Russia was adding to the vast store of armaments in the Sinai desert. The Arab nations considered themselves in a continuing state of belligerency despite the signed armistice between them and Israel.

By Egypt's own admission the Fedayeen were organized and directed from Cairo: "Egypt continues to pride itself on the deeds of the Fedayeen which are only symptomatic of the strength that will wipe Israel out in the future." Egypt also loudly proclaimed: "We exercise our rights of war with Israel. An armistice does not put an end to the state of war. It will not prohibit Egypt from exercising certain rights of war." On another occasion Egypt categorically declared: "There will be no peace on Israel's borders because we demand vengeance, and vengeance is Israel's death."

Other Arab nations fully shared Egypt's aims and intentions. Ibn Saud vehemently declaimed: "The Zionist threat is like an incurable cancer; the only treatment is surgical." An ex-premier of Iraq predicted: "The Arabs have now an opportunity to turn the Baghdad Pact into a strong rope with which to strangle Israel." And an Arab government newspaper editorialized: "There is no place for Israel, except in the sea." Concisely phrased by Israel's official spokesman: "Thus we were placed between two alternatives: either to be destroyed and thereafter to serve as a subject of funeral orations and expressions of grief, or to destroy the bases of aggression mobilized in Sinai by our largest and most formidable enemy."

The loud avowal of America's moral indignation was not in line with its own action under similar circumstances. When the Mexican government did not halt its raids into U.S. territory, President Wilson ordered General Pershing's expeditionary force to pursue the Mexican bandits into their own country across the Mexican border. But Mr. Eisenhower blandly ignored this clear precedent.

In the case of the Suez incident, had the U.S. not interfered, England and France might have solved the Suez problem for all time, bringing the international waterway under the control of the U.N. Nasser, suffering defeat, could not have long survived. Suicide or assassination might have been his fate. Perhaps this would have prevented all the subsequent evil events, including the Iraqi revolution, the murder of Feisal II and pro-Western Nuri as-Said. Sobered, a new Egyptian government might have been ready to discuss peace with Israel.

Instead, the Middle East remains at the boiling point, with Nasser restored to his position of power, all due to the ill-advised pressure by the U.S. on Britain, France and Israel out of fear of the Russian bluff of intervention. And it was obviously only a poker game bluff, because at the time Russia had her hands full with the Hungarian Revolution and a struggle for power at home.

While an inflexible policy may not be feasible in a changing world, neither are blatant contradictions or straddling on both sides of an issue effective. The U.S. is pledged to joint action with Great Britain and France on matters pertaining to the Middle East, yet frequently acts unilaterally. She recognizes Israel's right to exist but does not guarantee her borders. She advocates a free democratic world but courts the friendship of Arab autocracy. She fathers a Baghdad Pact but will not join it. She proposes to solve the problems of the Middle East through the U.N. but projects plans and methods of her own outside of the world organization. To keep Russia out, she confers the blessings of an Eisenhower Doctrine on the Middle East but does not include Israel in the benefits of that doctrine. The only consistency is a fear of the possible effects of Russia's actions.

4. After Holland, France was the first nation to kindle a spark of freedom and a measure of equality for the Jew. However, even the revolution of 1789 did not completely cleanse the country of anti-Semitism. A century later the Dreyfus case convulsed the liberal world, eventuating in Herzl's Political Zionism. Little concerned with the problem of Jewish homelessness, France nevertheless endorsed the Balfour Declaration in 1918 as a necessary by-product of World War I. But Paris balked at the acceptance of the mandate out of fear of potential British domination in the Middle East and because of the absence of a definite border between Palestine and Syria, the latter belonging to her sphere of influence.

Throughout the period of the League of Nations, French support of a Jewish national home in Palestine wavered between negation and lukewarmness. In the United Nations, France voted for the birth of Israel but thereafter, in the hope of regaining her influence in the Middle East and to retain her colonial position in Africa undisturbed, she gave comfort to the Arabs, to the hurt of Israel. The Suez Canal incident and the rebellions in her colonies, aided and abetted by Nasser and company, resulted in a bond of friendship between France and Israel within and outside of the United Nations.

5. China, the Security Council's fifth permanent member, distant from the troubled spot and uninvolved in Middle Eastern interests, in the main followed the leadership of the United States, but with eye and ear attuned to the whispers of the Asia-Africa bloc.

But what of the rest of the nations of the world organization? It would be logical to ask: Can a whole world be wrong? The United Nations General Assembly voted 70 to 2 against Israel in the dispute over the Sinai incident. The answer is, world or no world, this was a melancholy surrender to power politics.

Many nations in the General Assembly expressed their sympathy for Israel's plight, but when the votes were counted, Israel stood alone with France her only supporter. True, Canada, Australia, New Zealand, some of the North European countries as well as a few Latin American nations frequently indicated their sympathetic understanding of Israel's position, but the "follow the leader" policy has almost invariably deterred them from independent action.

In the main, four factors are responsible for this anomalous situation. One, the founders of the United Nations envisioned a world body consisting of individual members, each sovereign in judgment and vote. This sovereignty is nonexistent. Actually, the world organization today does not function through the free and independent action of its member nations. Many of the votes are cast as a result of influence or "deals" or pressures of nations to whom voters are indebted for past or future favors. Two, while the founding fathers of the U.N. foresaw the need for regional organizations to promote specific and similar interests in a given area, it did not envisage the formation of blocs of nations whose alignment would be based on world power and exchange of favors rather than on the merits of the case in hand. The increasing tendency to vote in blocs is tantamount to a denial of national sovereignty. Three, the General Assembly was created as a legislative organ without the judicial power which would have enabled it to act as prosecutor as well as judge. A majority vote reached through the method of the geographic or ideologic bloc does not represent a fair and unprejudiced decision, especially when equities of the issue are bypassed, retaliation condemned and provocation condoned. Both the Security Council and General Assembly of the U.N. may order a cease fire decree to prevent the spread of conflict between opposing nations, but the world organization as it is presently constituted is too politically involved to sit in judgment on what is right and wrong when the decision may indirectly affect the voters themselves. Four, Israel is peculiarly situated in a politically divided world. It stands alone, isolated by blocs and regional groupings for obvious reasons. The Arab states are solidly massed against her. Russia and her satellites consistently vote with the Arabs to win their favor. The Western nations, in an effort to maintain Arab good will, are quick to condemn Israel, though sympathetic toward Israel's plight.

The South American countries were among the most friendly in voting for the U.N. Resolution in favoring the establishment of the Jewish state. They did not support the U.S. proposal, made in the face of Arab threats, to create a trusteeship for Palestine in lieu of statehood. But in the final analysis, most of the Americas, though friendly to Israel, as a rule follow the U.S. in casting their votes in the U.N.

The Asia-Africa bloc, with which the Jewish state is geographically identified, barred Israel from its councils and endeavored to exclude her from the U.N. in support of the Arab position at the initial organization of the bloc. Composed as it is of peoples from Arab states and of the Islamic faith, the nations of the bloc, having themselves tasted the bitter cup of foreign oppression, normally, should have favored Israel as a new state. Why then was there such a lack of sympathy with and hostility against Israel?

The following conditions are responsible for the prevailing situation: The Jewish communities in the Afro-Asian countries have been too small to impress those countries with Judaism and the national aspirations of the Jew. Nor did Zionism penetrate those countries. The movement was too concerned with education and propaganda among the Western nations to spread itself thin among the peoples of Asia and Africa who themselves were not yet politically independent. Conversely, they who were formerly powerless to help consummate the Zionist aim and program are now in a position to antagonize Israel's statehood.

On religious grounds, too, East and West have not met. Unlike the Christian world which shares with the Jewish people the Holy Writ, the peoples of the Asia-Africa bloc do not possess this common bond. In addition, the white race symbolizes to them the spirit of "colonialism." Therefore, they frequently identify Israel with the oppression of their masses. Ben Gurion, sensing this misunderstanding, commented: "Little do they know that we have suffered at the hands of white people even more than they." Fortunately, time is on Israel's side. Some of the newly created Afro-Asian states, particularly Ghana and Burma, have entered into friendly and cooperative relations with Israel to their mutual advantages. Others may follow suit despite, or perhaps because of, Nasser's will to dominate the Arab world.

Israel's admission to membership in the U.N. was predicated on the principle that it was peace-loving and would live up to the Charter of the world organization. The new Jewish state upholds that view but protests the unequal treatment accorded her as a nation among nations.

The Arabs organized Fedayeen suicide squads to attack Israeli life and property. The Fedayeen who managed to return unscathed became heroes, honored and rewarded for executing sneak attacks on innocent, unarmed civilians. Israel's punitive measures in retaliation invariably evoked Arab complaint before the U.N., accusing Israel of ruthlessness. Lex talionis, or the law of retaliation, a recognized medium employed in the past by many a nation to repel repeated acts of violence against its borders, was stigmatized as illegal and immoral when utilized by Israel to secure the life of her citizenry. When a "day of reckoning," such as the Kybia incident, resulted in the loss of innocent lives, including children, Israel regretted it no less than any other members of the United Nations. Unfortunately, this is the natural consequence of all warfare on a large or small scale. "Once the power of evil is released, the innocent suffers together with the guilty."

World powers, wooing the Arab nations for control of the Middle East, arrived at a new rationalization: It is reprehensible to fight fire with fire, but if compelled to do so, the response must be commensurate with the attack. It must never be more effective in its results. In the first eight years of Israel's existence the Arabs committed thousands of inimical acts of aggression resulting in 434 Jews killed and 942 wounded. The U.N., ready to condone murder in retail, will denounce deeds in kind exceeding one at a time. In the words of an Israel editorial: "The U.N. has allowed itself to be maneuvered into this curious doctrine, that sub-war, Fedayeen attacks, boycott, open belligerency, sabotage, hit and run murder are legitimate political weapons, and only military retaliation in the field is forbidden, even if a campaign is planned to root out the warlike bases of attack."

Threats and condemnation were issued by the great powers without fair hearings. To avoid possible repercussions against the Western World by Arab states, muddled disputes were referred to the Secretary General more recently.

The augmented authority from administrator to investigator and conciliator conferred upon the Secretary General's office may yet come to plague those very nations that encouraged such unprecedented procedure. There is strong feeling in Israel that she has been singled out as the whipping boy in the U.N., treating every complaint against her as if it were a major issue. Justice is not meted out equally to the strong and the weak.

The facts bear out this conviction. Neither the Cyprus situation nor the Algerian conflict brought down the wrath of the nations on England or France. Similarly, India's disregard of the U.N. decision on Kashmir did not result in condemnation proceedings. As a matter of fact, Nehru openly defied the U.N. in his well publicized statement: "We are not bound by resolutions which are against our country and interest." Glaring, indeed, was the spotlight of Russia's brutality in the Hungarian revolt, which did not even call for the imposition of economic sanctions. Moreover, when the Arab states flagrantly and defiantly challenged the U.N. Palestine Resolution by engaging in a war of extermination against Israel in her infancy, what threats or condemnations did the U.N. voice against the guilty Arabs?

Such inequities are the result of a system whereby blocs of nations can maneuver the vote to gain political advantages. It is the old question of whose cow gets gored. Consider the case of Israel. Organized Arab Fedayeen attacks marked by plunder and murder brought no protest from the U.N. But when Israel in self-defense struck against this evil, the U.N. threat of sanctions and condemnation resulted. If it was considered equitable to reprimand Israel for retaliation, it would follow that those who had been guilty of creating the provocation should be held equally responsible for their part in the crisis. One without the other is a travesty on international law and justice.

Arab stubborn resistance to peace negotiations with Israel could gradually soften were not the United Nations so lamentably divided between East and West, each seeking partisan advantage rather than a just and workable peace.

With no intent to counsel the Western Powers in their effort to hold onto the Middle East with the essential oil for European economy, the assumptions held by some keen observers unburdened by outworn policies of the Western chancelleries are worth noting. In their opinion, unless the feud between East and West is amicably settled, the Arab states are bound to move closer to Russia not out of sympathy for Communism but because of the stigma of colonialism they continue to associate with the Western World. Under these circumstances Israel and Turkey alone remain the true allies of the Western Powers in the Middle East.

Since the Sinai incident, Israel's situation in the U.N. has been somewhat eased as other Middle Eastern problems have begun to occupy the world's stage. Nasser's fraternization with Khrushchev, Syria's absorption by Egypt's United Arab Republic, the Iraq-Jordan Federation, the flare-up in Lebanon with the U.S. armed forces within her borders, the Iraqi revolution and British forces in Jordan have made the U.N. more aware that the Middle East tensions are not of Israel's making. But Israel's continued dangerous position in a sea of Arab enmity demands international guarantees of her borders. Israel in effect says: We appeal to you, the free nations, to safeguard our peaceful existence. But if you fail us, we claim the natural right to defend our lives and property against those who would destroy us.

Unattached to any bloc of nations, Israel from her infancy has been compelled to rely on her own resources.

With faith in the Lord of Hosts, with confidence in her own will, integrity and courage and with hope in the triumph of international justice, Israel, having weathered the storms of her troubled years, begins the second decade of her national rebirth.

V. The Staff of Life

Through the ages of Jewish yearning for the restoration of Zion, spiritual rebirth was the major consideration. God would provide the bread, housing and raiment, life's essentials. Until the last decades of the 16th century, Jewish longing to live in the ancestral Holy Land was not spurred by the need for a physical haven of refuge from persecution in the lands of exile. The all consuming interest was the full religious life which Zion signified to the pious.

As the physical need for a Jewish national home became intensified in contradistinction to the urge for spiritual fulfillment of individual Jews, there came the recognition of the ancient Jewish principle that a heavenly Jerusalem, the spiritual edifice, can be built only on the earthly Jerusalem, the material foundation of the Jewish homeland.

The establishment of a Palestine office in 1908 under the leadership of Dr. Arthur Rupin (1876-1943), German-Jewish economist and sociologist, was among the first significant Zionist steps toward a planned Jewish colonization effort in the Holy Land.

The modern architects of the Jewish state have not lost sight of the problem of material self-sustenance. So far, however, this goal is still in the process of fulfillment. Without subsidies from world Jewry and other sources Israel as a national entity would suffer heavy, if not fatal reverses.

What then are the prospects for the realization of a self-sustaining economy in Israel? At present the cost of the military establishment and the settlement of new immigrants are severely straining Israel's progress. The crucial question is: If and when peace is established and the "ingathering" completed, will Israel then be capable of self-containment or will she indefinitely have to depend on the generosity of world Jewry for her existence?

To assess the problem with any degree of accuracy we must familiarize ourselves with a number of factors. What are Israel's national assets, human and material? What progress has been made so far in the various economic areas? What are the state's essential needs?

The present situation is both widely criticized and defended. A nonpartisan, objective presentation of the opposing views, less heat and more light, may offer a fair evaluation of Israel's current economic condition and future prospects.

The new Zion's natural resources are limited, but willing, even eager constructive hands have conquered a stubborn soil neglected by Arab sloth and incompetence to the point of utter ruin for many centuries. These human assets in essence represent the real wealth of the country. Out of a general Jewish population of about 1,750,000 in 1957-58, 650,000 were gainfully employed. Various occupations served the country's needs. Workers on the land in agriculture, afforestation and fishing constituted 18 per cent of the gainfully employed. Industry and crafts embraced 21.6 per cent of the workers. The largest percentage, 29.4 per cent, were engaged in health, education, public and personal services. Trade, banking and insurance absorbed 13.9 per cent of the employable population. Public works and building construction employed 9 per cent of the laboring class; transportation and storage, 6.6 per cent; public utilities 1.2 per cent and mines and quarries 0.3 per cent.

It is noteworthy that Israel's population is predominantly of a youthful, vigorous age which is indispensable for the successful development of a new, pioneering land. Persons from one to 14 years constitute 33.5 per cent of the population, between 15 and 29, 23 per cent; between 30 and 44, 21 per cent; between 45 and 64, 18 per cent while those from 65 and upward constitute only 4½ per cent of the Jews in Israel. Combining these categories we find that the productive persons between 15 and

64, the most active years in a worker's life, constitute 62 per cent of the working population. This is a fortunate circumstance. It is a very high average for any country.

To this reservoir of manpower should be added another important factor, high intelligence plus idealism. While Israel's workers, as in most countries, are concerned with improved labor conditions, their spontaneous devotion to the security and advancement of people and land supersedes their class interests. Their patriotic allegiance transcends all material considerations. Without reluctance they readily forfeit benefits to class and party for the good of the state.

Labor in Israel is exceptionally intelligent and intensely interested in cultural activities. Many of those who are now in the labor group cheerfully abandoned their previously chosen intellectual pursuits to help build a firm foundation for Israel. With brain harnessed to brawn and with unparalleled concentration on the fascinating task of building a nation, the workers in the Holy Land have elevated and sanctified labor. Thus labor is the very heart of the program of the rebuilding of Israel.

Agriculture is the basic economy of every country. It has taken on added significance in Israel because the Zionist ideal from the beginning called for a return to the soil. Conditions imposed upon the Jews in many lands during the long, dark night of their exile divorced them from the land, forcing them to become almost completely an urban people. Zionism set forth to correct this abnormal phase of Jewish life.

The State of Israel, consisting of 8,000 square miles, has now under cultivation approximately 4,000,000 dunams (approximately 1,000,000 acres) with additional tracts being readied. Considering its topography, hills and mountains difficult of cultivation, lack of water particularly in the Negev, marsh and swamp lands, and washed down, denuded, treeless soil, in view of all this, the agricultural progress today by far exceeds the arithmetic proportion of 1,000,000 acres of cultivated land to 8,000 square miles of Israel's territory.

The land is indeed poor in water resources. The proportion of water to land is one of the lowest in the world, 177 square miles of water area to 7,815 square miles of land. This is the crying need of the country, to give life to the soil through irrigation and to generate power for industrial development.

The meager water resources have been utilized to the fullest but the needs are far from satisfied. Through various devices, water has been transported to distant parts of the land in order to cause the dead desert to awake and flourish again.

The primary need of every nation is food. Only the richest countries are completely self-sufficient in the supply of life's necessities. Most countries are to some extent dependent on other nations. But no nation can long survive if it has to depend extensively and permanently on the outside world to keep body and soul together.

Food production is the foremost factor in the program of the new Israel's life and thus has made the return of Jews to agriculture imperative.

For a better understanding of the problem of bread in Israel, it is important to consider the variety of methods employed on the land as well as in labor, production and marketing. Several factors are responsible for the various agricultural projects which in 1955 produced 230,000,000 IL ($126,500,000) in revenue.

The individualism of the Jew did not permit him to adhere to one exclusive pattern of farming. The settlers originating from different parts of the world brought with them their respective ideas and methods. Thus various categories of social philosophy influenced and often determined the direction of agriculture in Israel.

(1) First came the *Moshava* (plural, Moshavot)—the village of private land ownership. Many of these settlements developed into towns, but the principle of private ownership and management has not altered.

(2) Second, and perhaps the most striking in its impact not only on the economic but on the political and social develop-

ment as well, has been the *Kibbutz* or *Kvutza* (plural, Kibbutzim or Kvuzot)—the collective commune. It differs radically from the Russian collective farm. It is a voluntary grouping together of likeminded people. No outer force unites them; their cohesiveness is not dependent on any outside authority. There is no compulsory quota of production, nor ceiling price on produce. A member of a kibbutz is free to leave at any time without fear of retaliation, and he may seek aid and affiliations elsewhere. Each member contributes his labor in accordance with his ability and the need of the group. In return he receives the benefits of housing, food, education, culture and social service.

The kibbutz maintains children's quarters, releasing the parents from home cares to give their undivided attention to their respective labor assignments. While there is room accommodation with privacy for each member, the dining and social facilities are common to all. Here democracy is not a theory or an ideal to be fulfilled in the distant future, but a present, working reality. The kibbutz is managed democratically with all the members constituting the general assembly, arriving at policies and decisions through majority rule.

(3) Mutual aid is the essential element of the *Moshav Ovdim* (plural, Moshvei Ovdim)—workers' settlement. As in the kibbutz, the moshav ovdim is governed by a general assembly consisting of all the members, but it is not concerned with the personal lives of the settlers. Its authority is limited to the advancement of the settlement by cooperative efforts, decisions on transfers of farms and property to outside parties and approval of new members. The moshav ovdim is based on self-labor of the farmer and his family on land leased from the Jewish National Fund in the same manner as that of the kibbutz. The farms are worked as private enterprises but with a high degree of cooperative and mutual aid. The settlement cooperatively owns agricultural equipment; sells its produce cooperatively and makes its purchases cooperatively. The

moshav ovdim is the predominant settlement in Israel today. It has absorbed since 1949 more immigrants than all other types of villages together.

(4) *The Moshav* (plural, Moshavim) is a small holder's settlement with no rigid rules against hired labor, nor do the farmers jointly own heavy agricultural equipment. While the moshav ovdim, through the central organization, is a Histadrut affiliate, the moshav is independently federated.

(5) *The Moshav Shitufi.* The cooperative or partnership settlement is close in its economic ideology to the kibbutz. Ownership and management are collective in character but unlike the kibbutz, each family owns its own house, cares for its own children, with dining and social life centering in its own individual premises. The labor to be rendered is decided by the cooperative management which also determines the needs of each family.

(6) Less independent and more transitory in character are the *Work Villages* of the newer immigrants employed in public works, afforestation or farm labor in the nearby agricultural settlements. Most of the work villages formed since 1947 have become moshav ovdim, passing from wage labor on land cleared for settlement by the Jewish National Fund and government, to working the land as their own farms. As they develop in their agricultural efforts, they also establish community institutions along the lines of the moshav ovdim.

(7) *The Ma'bara* shelters the most recent immigrants for whom no permanent housing is available at the moment and who live in temporary huts as wards of the state. The state plans to transfer the newest ma'bara immigrants (numbering 18,000 families in 1958-59) as soon as feasible to permanent housing and equip them with the skills necessary for gainful occupation just as they did with previous contingents of ma'bara dwellers.

The newest type of settlement, the regional, came into being since the rise of the state, made possible by the larger land reserves under national control. The three regional settlements

—Lachish of Biblical fame, Ta'anach in the Afulah vicinity and Adulam in the Jerusalem corridor—number 90 villages with a population of nearly 30,000. Kiryat Gat, the central urban hub of the Lachish area with its phenomenal growth in numbers, commerce and cultural facilities, is indicative of the great possibilities in regional settlement, initiated not alone for a faster pace in agricultural development but for purposes of common defense, better marketing, educational and cultural advantages as well. Instead of isolated, self-contained, individual settlements of pre-state days the Jewish Agency and government have initiated the cluster idea, on a regional basis—a number of settlements in close proximity to each other working together for the common good.

The collective and cooperative settlements have their counterpart in the *Kibbutz Hadati,* the religious communal villages. In addition to the theories which they share with the various kinds of settlements, they emphasize as their highest aspirations their reverence for and observance of Jewish religious law.

The kibbutzim and other types of settlements approximating their program were founded on two principles: one, self-labor and the other, work on the land. In recent years, these principles were modified by new developments resulting from Israel's rapid growth and because of the changes that time has wrought in the lives of the original settlers.

From the moment the state was launched, the number of new immigrants increased rapidly. Many of them were assigned to industry and commerce, but the state vigorously persuaded large numbers to settle on the land. Some were provided with opportunities in new settlements; others became day laborers on nearby farms. To supply the new immigrants with employment in an emergency, the kibbutzim, though committed to the principle of self-labor, were induced by the new conditions to employ nonmembers. This inconsistency between ideology and practice brought confusion into the kibbutzim, particularly in the minds of the younger generation raised on the principle of the sacredness of self-labor.

Time has also modified the other principle, subsistence from the land only. The kibbutz has grown in numbers through natural increment and through the acquisition of new members. To maintain the ever-enlarging kibbutz, it became necessary in a number of instances to organize industrial enterprises to supplement the farm income. These and other new problems now trouble the cooperative commune. Their solutions lie in the unpredictable future.

The cooperative movement in Israel represents a most important asset. At the end of 1955 there were over 2,500 cooperatives embracing every form of productive endeavor. The largest proportion is to be found in the agricultural field, 862. In the category of production, supply, factories and transportation there were 329, with motor transport almost exclusively in the cooperative sphere.

Two hundred and seventy-five stores servicing 425,000 persons and 489 housing developments also carry on as cooperatives. One hundred and seven financial institutions serve the credit needs of 261,000 persons on a cooperative basis. The provident and pension funds are also cooperatively conducted numbering 425, and miscellaneous categories make up the balance. This movement has found its best champion among the Jewish citizenry. The non-Jewish population numbering 200,000 citizens maintain only 67 cooperatives of all types. Three-quarters of the members in the various cooperatives come from the laboring class, affiliated with the Histadrut—General Federation of Labor. They are derived primarily from the kibbutzim and moshavim.

The attainment of self-sufficiency has been a driving force in Israel's life with the most effective direction as yet undetermined. The aim is to produce everything possible, even if unprofitable. The propaganda for tozeret-ha-aretz—domestic production and consumption of goods made in Israel—blankets the land. Some deny themselves certain necessities to avoid the use of imported items. The Israelis are aware of their limitations of production and even of the higher costs involved, but they take pride in their own handiwork and are confident they will eventually reach competitive capacity of production in every area. The zealots in behalf of Israel-made merchandise even decline gifts of items made in foreign lands if substitutes are available in their own country.

To balance imports with exports is the crux of the problem in Israel. The answer to that problem will determine whether the economy of the land will reach the point when it is sound or Israel's existence will indefinitely have to continue to look for outside help.

It is axiomatic that increased export depends on increased production. So far the rate of progress has been phenomenal not only in population but in agricultural and industrial expansion as well. Since the birth of the state in 1948 when the total cultivated area was 1,650,000 dunams (400,000 acres) and the irrigated land 300,000 dunams (75,000 acres) close to 4,000,000 (1,000,000 acres) were put under cultivation and 1,000,000 dunams (over 250,000 acres) irrigated.

Much land now in the process of drainage and clearance will considerably increase the volume of crops. The Hulah region, which took six years to drain and make ready for production in the face of Syrian military attacks and a temporary halt of labor at the behest of the United Nations, has an estimated capacity to support 60,000 new settlers. If and when the U.S.-proposed Jordan Authority to be shared by Arabs and Jews is implemented, 250,000 dunams of additional cultivated land will become available to Israel.

In afforestation, before the establishment of the state, the Jewish National Fund, the land and tree agency of the Zionist movement, could boast of only 5,000,000 trees, but since then the numbers actually planted or in the process of planting have increased to 20,000,000.

The phenomenal agricultural achievement is evidenced by these facts: almost everything is now grown in Israel for home consumption with some products in sufficient quantities for export as well. Israel now produces 70 per cent of the country's food needs. In such staples as milk, eggs, poultry, vegetables and potatoes the country is now self-sufficient; in the development of other essential items, rapid strides are being registered in the race between production and consumption.

In 1954-55 Israel exported $37,000,000 worth of agricultural products. Its largest volume of exports are citrus fruits and table wines, as much as 70 per cent beyond the needs of home consumption. In the first decade of Israel's statehood, citrus fruit production doubled, from six to twelve million cases, of which eight million were exported.

The Biblical picture of a "land flowing with milk and honey" is true of Israel today. One hundred seventy-five million liters of milk were produced in 1956. Dairy products, despite a reduced number of cows, showed encouraging figures. In 1952-53 there were 3,869 liters of milk per cow; in 1953-54 it rose to 4,197 liters; in 1954-55 to 4,636 and in 1955-56 to 4,800 liters, an increment of 1,000 liters per cow in four years.

The laying hens, too, have "cooperated" with Israel's economy. Three million of them accounted for close to 500,000,000 eggs in 1956. While meat is chiefly imported, fish is plentiful on the home market. Eleven thousand tons of fish, 7,000 of which came from breeding ponds, were added to the table of the Israelis in the past year.

When the Jews returned from Babylonian captivity in 536 B.C.E., they brought with them 736 horses, 245 mules, 435 camels, 6,720 asses. The Bible enumerated these domestic animals in detail because of their importance to the practical needs of resettlement. Likewise, today, the livestock in Israel is an index of the land's economy. The machine has taken the place of the beast of burden as the instrument of agricultural production. But livestock for food, with its by-products, remains an important factor in the life of the country. Israel possesses today 110,000 thoroughbred local cattle, 250,000 sheep and goats, 50,000 draft animals, 3,500,000 laying hens and 250,000 ducks, geese and turkeys.

In agricultural yield there is a substantial and consistent increase. 567,000 dunams of wheat were sown in 1956-57 as against 473,000 in the previous year. Vegetables and potatoes have also shown a marked increase from year to year, 284,000 tons in 1953-54 to 291,000 tons in 1954-55, now supplying all the needs of the home market.

An upward swing seems to be evident in every field of farm and garden enterprise. In 1955-56, despite various pest attacks on wheat and cotton crops, the increase over the previous year was substantial. New crops such as apples, melons, bananas are now produced in sufficient quantities to satisfy the demands of home consumption. The value in overall agricultural production rose from 377,000,000 IL in 1954-55 to 454,000,000 IL in 1955-56, made up of the following categories: field crops 37 per cent increase, fruit 58 per cent, meat 27 per cent, citrus 10 per cent, milk 9 per cent, vegetables and potatoes 8 per cent.

The essential requirements have been adequately met. Electricity for home, farm and industry has kept pace with the general progress of the country which in 1957 produced 370,000,000 kws. of electricity.

Unlike most of the Arab nations in the Middle East, Israel is oil poor. Extensive and persistent search is being made for the "black gold" in commercial quantities. The recent discoveries yield 10 per cent of the nation's needs. Israel imports 1,000,000 tons of crude oil to meet its minimum requirements.

Other natural resources are estimated to reach 10 per cent of revenues from exportable items consisting of products from the Dead Sea such as potash, bromine, ethylene dibromide; from the Negev, phosphates, copper, manganese, etc.; from Oron, phosphate rock and from the Haifa region, a variety of fertilizers and chemicals.

Economic growth is much in evidence in other areas as well. Industry and mining in 1954 yielded a national income of 339,000,000 IL and in 1955, 417,000,000 IL. Electricity, building, public works and communications showed an income of 225,000,000 IL in 1954 and 250,000,000 IL in 1955. Banking, finance, real estate and various services produced an income of 407,000,000 IL in 1955.

Of very high value are the roads which were built under the British mandate and extended since the beginning of the state. When the British quit Palestine the new state fell heir to 2,000 miles of roads of every type and description. By 1958 Israel added 500 miles of good new roads, 400 miles of feeder roads and has improved 1,000 miles of old roads for communication and transportation purposes, and maintained for defense needs as well. In case of an invasion, if one artery is blocked the army now has alternative routes for military use and for food supply delivery to the civilian population.

The country's railroads, including the link with Beersheba, almost doubled since 1950 when it consisted of 268 miles of track of standard gauge and 101 lengths of side lines. By 1957 it increased to a total of 650 miles of tracks of which 450 are of the standard broad gauge and the balance of 200 miles are sidings. Though the trend is toward other forms of transportation, there has been a marked increase both in number of passengers and tonnage of freight carried. In 1953 the state-owned railroad carried 2,416,000 passengers and 98,542,000 tons of freight; in 1954, 2,934,000 passengers and 124,223,000 tons of freight and in 1955, 3,254,000 passengers and 131,485,000 tons of freight.

The motor transport system is extensive, consisting of 25,000 trucks and over 2,000 buses. Israel counts 16,500 private cars, and in 1956 there were only six Cadillacs registered in the Vehicles Bureau. When compared to the number of Cadillacs in Saudi Arabia, Israel's frugal and austere life becomes conspicuous. Twenty nine thousand taxis serve the country's needs.

Most of them are imported used cars requiring continuous repair and consuming excessive quantities of gas and oil. In 1955-56 close to 2,000,000 passengers used taxi service averaging a little more than one taxi ride per resident.

Air transportation, too, has made strides. In 1955, 1,373 planes from abroad landed at Lydda airport with 36,613 passengers and nearly 2,000,000 pounds of freight and mail. During the same year 43,191 passengers departed by planes which also carried 1,300,000 pounds of freight and mail. In 1957, in spite of the aftereffects of the Sinai Campaign, there was an increase in air transport. Incoming flights delivered 52,936 passengers, 824,077 kilograms of freight and 199,880 kilograms of mail, and in the same year departures carried 48,473 passengers, 639,879 kilograms of freight and 141,177 kilograms of mail. In 1958, the year of Israel's tenth anniversary celebration, there was continued marked improvement.

Of greater economic dimensions is the volume of shipping in Israel. Israel began with 6,000 tons shipping capacity. In less than a decade it rose to 100,000 with expectations of an additional 136,000 tons as part of the German reparation fund. In 1955, 1,212 ships of all kinds touched Israel's shores, 267 of them Israeli-owned. In 1956, 92,000 passengers entered and left Israeli ports. The number of seamen grew from 100 in 1948 to 1,550 eight years later, of whom 1,419 were Israeli and only 114 foreign citizens. In view of the fact that until recently there were very few Jewish sailors anywhere in the world and almost none in Israel, the shipping industry has scored a major achievement. For the further development of sea manpower, the government has founded a nautical school with a present attendance of 400 students preparing for the navy and merchant marine. Cargo shows an equally impressive record: in 1956 loading amounted to 639,591 tons of which 175,275 tons were from Israeli ships; unloading, 2,983,047 of which 618,311 tons were on Israeli ships.

In the field of communications, the telegraph and the telephone play their significant roles. The telephone in particular is showing a notable advance in Israel. Its use is a barometer of economic progress. In 1954 there were in all 57,000 private, party and extension lines, only 33 telephones per every 1,000 population. In the following year the number increased to 66,000 or 37 per 1,000 population. Nearly 90,000 telephones, private, party and extension lines are now in use in the Holy Land, that is, one telephone for every 18 inhabitants, which compares favorably with the U.S.; whereas in all the Arab states with a population of 40,000,000, there is only one telephone for every 10,000 inhabitants.

Tourism is an important economic asset. In 1955, 48,000 persons toured the country spending $6,500,000, excluding cost of fares. Of this total of visitors 68 per cent were Jews and 32 per cent non-Jews. Of the 48,000 tourists about 18,000 came from America.

To accommodate the visitors Israel now has 125 hotels with 3,500 rooms and 11 youth hostels. Several of the hotels are palatial and some of them are air-conditioned, ocean-front edifices.

Between 1948 and 1957 close to 250,000 additional rooms were built to house the new immigrants. The gains to the building industry and allied trades from this remarkable expansion of living accommodations are self-evident.

The Israelis not only welcome visitors but are tourists themselves. In 1955-56 about 40,000 Israelis traveled abroad. Among them 25,000 left the country temporarily for family and social reasons and 5,000 for commercial purposes. Other categories of travelers abroad included 2,500 students and 2,000 emissaries representing the Jewish Agency, the government and private institutions of learning, culture and philanthropy.

The growth of life insurance is an added indication of Israel's advancement. In 1950 there were 68,000 persons insured in 56 domestic and 12 foreign companies. In 1951 the number mounted to 75,000 with 64 Israeli companies and 11 foreign.

This advance continued. In 1952, 83,000 were insured in 72 home companies and 11 foreign. In 1953 the numbers rose to 91,000 in 78 domestic companies and 13 foreign.

The average individual income based on the total national income rose from 865 IL per capita in 1954 to 978 IL in 1955. Even if consideration is given to the disparity in prices between 1954 and 1955, *i.e.,* according to 1954 value of the IL (the 1955 978 IL was only worth 918), the per capita increase, though less, is still significant for Israel's economic standards, a net increase of 53 IL per capita. The rapid improvement of housing standards in the kibbutzim and moshavim is additional evidence of the more abundant life. A quarter of a century ago life in these settlements was almost primitive. Today, particularly the older settlements enjoy modern facilities and comforts unknown in the earlier pioneering days.

There is no gainsaying the progress made in all fields by Israel in her first decade. But some of her best friends, unprejudiced students of her national economy, are apprehensive of the future. Even established and larger nations, with abundant natural resources and free from fears of military intervention, look to one or another great power for aid to set up a sound national economy. For obvious reasons, the government budget does not spell out in detail the requirements for military purposes, but it is estimated that the costs exceed an annual outlay of $100,000,000, or an aggregate sum of over a billion dollars in the first decade of Israel's existence. Because of her peculiar circumstances she certainly needs outside aid. But for how long? This is a serious question. The day must come when the Jewish state will have to stand on its own feet if it is to continue to function in a competitive world.

Further material development is imperative in order to keep pace with the progress already made and reach the goal of economic independence.

Among the crying needs is more cultivated land to reduce the expenditure of almost $75,000,000 for the import of food to maintain the Israeli population on a none too plentiful diet.

There is no longer any hunger for additional land or need for territorial expansion. The present area, though limited, is enough to satisfy the bread needs even of an expanding population. Within Israel's borders three sources of additional land are available. Many Arabs now living in Israel might, either for a monetary consideration or to satisfy their desire to live in Arab countries, be willing to sell their lands to Jews. This type of land acquisition will have to await the establishment of peace with the Arab nations, affording individuals free movement from one country to another. Extensive land that is good but still in an unproductive condition is in the hands of religious organizations. Negotiations for voluntary sales have been proceeding for some time with some measure of success. Such organizational possessions and those of individual Arabs have large potentialities for increasing Israel's breadbasket.

The other sources are in the northern and central sections and in the Negev which for the present lie fallow because of the neglect of centuries and the lack of water. In the statement issued by the Jewish National Fund: "Israel is still an undeveloped country. Four-fifths of its territory are wild desert and dunes, rock-strewn hills and swamps." To balance its economy and strengthen its security the soil must be able to support its people. With ingenuity, sweat and tears much of these lands can be reclaimed to make Israel eventually self-sufficient, at least as to food supplies.

Ambitious plans to cultivate the still unproductive areas face two major hurdles. The stony, rocky land, which through Arab neglect has been denuded with the topsoil washed away, needs backbreaking toil, as a labor of love, for the purpose of clearance, reafforestation and replenishing the soil to make the land fruitful again. This is now consistently being done and will undoubtedly revitalize many dunams now barren. The northern and central land potential, however, is insignificant compared to the vast stretches of the Negev.

Ben Gurion, conscious of the need and believing in the possibility of making the Negev flourish, has been urging Israelis to settle in the southern wasteland. His retirement to S'dai Boker during a temporary period of relief from the duties of the prime minister's office, whatever the political motive, was prompted by his desire to set an example for the younger generation, to move them to pioneer in the Negev in behalf of Israel's expansion and development. Ben Gurion does not recognize the inherent impediments as insuperable. In his own words: "We are under no obligation to accept the heritage of desolation from the past. It is within our power to afforest the wastes, fertilize the sand dunes and revive the dust of the earth. Indeed this is the true conquest of the desert."

To accomplish that Herculean assignment, however, requires more than will, brain and brawn. Water is the unconditional prerequisite to awaken the Negev desert. The digging of wells will not suffice. Either the piping of fresh water from far distances or the use of desalted seawater is required. The latter has passed from the dream stage to that of a long deferred hope trestled on science. In Israel and elsewhere such a process has already been discovered, but it is too costly for practical application. A less expensive method has been found in America. Time will tell if it can meet Israel's needs. Ben Gurion has faith that the hope will become a reality. To quote him: "But the great problem of supplying water to the expanses of the South and the Negev is that of extracting the salts from the seawater. The great task which Jewish science must achieve is the discovery of a cheap and practical method of purifying salt water with which it will be possible to slake the thirst of the Negev."

Those who know Ben Gurion are aware of his boundless confidence in the know-how of Israel's scientists. His predictions go beyond the project of water desalting. He envisions atomic power for peaceful uses and the sun as energy to be captured and stored to provide all the necessary light and power for the country. "The Negev today derives less benefit than any other region from the absorption of the sun's rays by plants, but this energy can be transformed into an active, dynamic and electrifying force." Faith is capable not only of moving mountains; it can harness the sun and lay the foundation for the economic security, prosperity and welfare of all Israel.

Admitting that remarkable progress was made in the first decade of Israel's sovereignty and that Jewish scientific ingenuity will renew the life of the dry, barren soil, the road to self-sufficiency must be cleared of various obstructions, according to critics, some politically motivated and others staunch adherents to the principle of private initiative as the major prerequisite for the upbuilding of the land. In their opinion, of the $6,000,000,000 poured into Israel since her national rebirth from all sources, United Jewish Appeal, Bonds for Israel, American aid through gifts, loans and a variety of private funds, only half was soundly invested, the balance, while perhaps usefully spent, made no substantial contribution toward economic self-sustenance.

Those who disapprove of the present industrial trends point to the dangerous imbalance between exports and imports. While it is true that there has been a definite improvement in the total of exports, an increase in imports vitiated the benefits from the seeming gains. In 1949 imports exceeded exports by $253,000,000; in 1950 by $261,000,000; in 1951 by $333,000,000; in 1952 by $276,000,000. In 1953 and 1954 the situation improved, $222,000,000 and $198,000,0000 respectively. In the past three successive years the climb of exports over imports continued.

There are, however, competent students of the national economy who present a more favorable interpretation of the alleged alarming situation of exports over imports. They maintain that the gap between exports over imports is gradually closing as indicated by these telling illustrations: Not withstanding the threefold increase in population by immigration in the last decade, imports per capita declined from $243 in 1949 to

$212 in 1957, while exports per capita more than doubled, from $28 to 1949 to $73 in 1957. Another favorable factor is the substantial reduction in imported consumer goods—32 per cent in 1948 and 15 per cent in the first nine months of 1957. The larger imports of capital goods spells out two benefits: one, their long-term use and two, their capacity to produce added consumer goods, both for the home market as well as for export. The road to national financial stability is beset by many stumbling blocks but with purpose and zeal, claim the defenders of the present policy, the goal can be achieved.

The critics of the current economic status in the land ascribe the unfavorable conditions to a number of factors. They assert that Jews in the Diaspora are good business people but poor soldiers, while in Israel they make excellent soldiers and poor business people. The reason they give for this inverted order is that military service is in the hands of the younger generation whose minds and hearts are unshackled by half-baked philosophies, while in the economic sphere the early pioneers grew old in their position of leadership and remained indoctrinated by preconceived theories of economic development.

The severest criticism of the government's policies, which to a major extent reflect Histadrut action, is that they stifle private initiative. The General Federation of Labor has fashioned an industrial empire permitting little room for free enterprise. The government, according to its critics, has its tentacles everywhere, discouraging individual initiative, frowning upon incentive and permitting political partisan interests to penetrate every industrial sphere in the land. Critics of the present policies claim that privately owned and managed enterprises suffer from direct competition by government or Histadrut or both. The government has the power and exercises it to eliminate competition and to destroy private business through credit control and currency exchanges. Private business also suffers from another disadvantage, the red tape which snarls the Bureau of Licenses for export and import of raw materials.

Party patronage is another stumbling block. It is very strong in Israel, with minor parties which form the government coalition often abandoning their differences with the party in power in order to receive a proportionate share of jobs for their adherents. Jobs are the cement of party structure. The Labor Party is most conscious of the "principle" of reward for political activity. Its workers may be shifted from government to Histadrut or Jewish Agency as necessity requires but protectzia—political preferment—is assured for the "faithful."

Another serious barrier on the road to fulfillment as viewed by the critics of the present leadership is the inefficiency if not hypocrisy of work methods, padding, feather-bedding and obstructing the discharge of disloyal or inefficient workers, all tending to reduce and hinder production. The complaint that a spirit of indolent bureaucracy prevails in the land is illustrated by the oft-repeated jibe: One afternoon a frontier villager came to the Jewish Agency on an important matter. He found all offices open with no occupant, except one in the process of being cleaned by a charwoman. Upon inquiry, "Don't they work here in the afternoon?" the spontaneous reply was: "Oh, no! It is in the morning that they don't work here; they just sit around. In the afternoon they don't come." According to some critics, the Israeli worker produces only half as much as his British counterpart but his wages are 10 per cent higher and while his fringe benefits are one-third of his pay, those of the British worker are only 10 per cent.

Economic students discountenance the national pride which leads Israelis to believe that everything must be produced in the land even if commercially unsound. Israelis cherish the chauvinistic idea that, "everything that can be done elsewhere, we can do better here." Such an attitude may be good for the national ego, but leads to ill-advised ventures that have no chance of competition in the open market. And not the least of the criticism is against the mounting taxes which set up another impediment on the road to expansion. The new Treasury Building is popularly named the "Wailing Wall."

The financial problems of the kibbutzim and moshavim also loom large. Many of them are overexpanded, financed by short-term loans on capital investment projects with heavy rates of interest. These projects in the main were intended to improve the adverse living conditions which the pioneers endured until recently. No fair-minded person can deny them the right to try to ease their hardships. Their private living quarters have undergone a metamorphosis: more than one room per settler, private showers and commodious common dining hall with attractive social accommodations. But when the improvements cause financial strain, can the policy of sound economy be ignored?

The moshavim in particular present a severe problem: the difficulty of eking out a decent living. The moshav is frequently too small in size and the cooperative equipment is too unwieldy to move about freely. The older settlers can no longer labor with the vigor of their youthful days. They now demand greater living comfort and fewer working days. Economists estimate that 275 work days a year are required to provide a minimum subsistence for a family. Many farms, however, reach only a total of 200 to 250 work days per annum. Therefore, unless farm work is supplemented by other productive employment, some form of state or Jewish Agency subsidy must be provided. It is true that since the state began to function very many of the agricultural settlements were founded on the promise of public aid until they could attain self-support. But it is alarming to note, the students of economics maintain, that out of more than 700 agricultural settlements in 1956, 400 were still under the paternal care of the Jewish Agency.

Youth in the agricultural settlements presents another problem. No exact figures are as yet available to determine the number of young adults who are willing to remain in their agricultural settlements. Youth everywhere gravitates toward the city, where opportunities for personal advancement are better.

In Israel, while the pioneer parents endured privation they raised their children in the lap of security and comfort. Protected from the hardships suffered by their parents, the youngsters do not always develop the stamina needed to meet the challenge of agricultural pioneering problems. Besides, in view of the attractions of the city and unpreparedness for a life of austerity, youth is ideologically confused. The kibbutzim, founded on the principles of self-labor with no profit from the work of nonmembers, let down the bars, affording employment to day laborers to meet a national emergency in order to provide work for new immigrants. The reluctance of the kibbutzim to accept larger numbers of the newcomers as equals in their social structure also resulted in confusing the youth. Parental teachings did not square with the unexpected developments arising from the nation's rapid expansion. Thus the younger generation faced a reversal they could not understand and suffered a loss of faith.

What the future holds in store for the kibbutzim and moshavim, their apparent new trends and the children's place in the scheme of things set up by their parents, time alone will tell. But those who frown on socialist experiments in the land do not predict a healthy development for the kibbutzim and are pessimistic regarding the younger generation's future in the communes. For the present, however, studies indicate that 85 per cent of the youth remains in the kibbutz to work side by side with the older generation.

Another complaint is the failure to invite and encourage investments by foreign capital. This is regarded as a shortsighted policy of the government in power. The telephone is only one example of this provincial policy. As soon as the state came into being, bids were made by foreign investors with experience and ability to take over and develop the telephone system with guaranteed royalties to the government. Their meritorious proposal was rejected because of the government's policy of national ownership. The results are self-evident: inadequacy of new installations plus charges of 200 IL per new private phone with the threat of an increase to 500 IL as an advance payment on future calls.

The nationalization of the Dead Sea project has also produced unsatisfactory results. Many an undertaking which might have been successfully developed through free enterprise is either partially or fully owned and operated by the government or Histadrut, closely allied to the party in power.

The question already posed is the most pressing economic problem: can Israel become self-sustaining unaided by the outside world? Israel cannot and does not wish forever to rely on the income from the United Jewish Appeal, bonds, or financial help from the United States. Unless increased production results in greater economic wealth what substitute will there be for the German reparations income, which was a windfall in the first place, when the fixed amount is exhausted within a few years?

Israel's realists are also fully aware of the gradual diminution of American generosity toward the development of the land and that it cannot go on indefinitely. Even large-scale contributions of world Jewry will depend on crises in Israel, real or fancied. The most substantial sums were naturally raised in time of danger. As life in Israel is normalized, the sizeable voluntary gifts from Jewry of the free world will shrink to mere philanthropic handouts.

The critics of the economic planners of the state view the situation with alarm. Unless the blocks on the road to success are removed, Israel, they claim, is doomed to dependence on the generosity of world Jewry and friendly governments of the free world. Israel's independence, not only economic but also political, can be achieved only by greater production resulting from free and unhampered individual initiative and private enterprise.

The national policy, while severely criticized in some quarters, does not lack defenders even among those unaffiliated with the Socialist Party. Firstly, they hold that the major Socialist Party in the government's coalition is not irrevocably wedded to an inflexible Marxian doctrine. Judged by past performances, as the government learns of failing experiments in Socialism, it will bow to the demands for better opportunities for free enterprise. Histadrut's position, too, is becoming less rigid in its quest for national ownership or monopolistic, cooperative enterprises. As a matter of fact, the defenders of the present economic program disclaim the existence of a government nationalization policy. Free enterprise, they maintain, instead of being stifled is considerably encouraged through government loans, tax rebates and conversion of pounds into foreign currency. The government enters only into such business where pioneering is essential and where private enterprise would be reluctant to invest because of the small prospects for immediate returns.

Secondly, the defenders of the present policy present a more favorable picture of what they consider to be the realities of the current situation. They focus their attention on a balanced budget. The money derived from sources outside of Israel, they claim, is devoted to the large-scale immigration program. When the "ingathering" is completed and amalgamation of the newcomers into the life of Israel is achieved, outside aid will not be required. Surely, they maintain, when peace is established and the heavy burden of financing the armed forces has been drastically reduced, the national budget will be met from the normal resources of the land. The defenders of the Government's position also look to increased production by immigrant workers who, given time, will develop better skills and more efficient methods of labor.

While the kibbutzim have been successfully wrestling with their problems, the cooperative moshavim have made genuine economic contributions. The conscientious labors of the cooperative farmers have been well rewarded. Many of them started out with one cow and now count ten or fifteen. Friends of the government view the kibbutzim, too, as a most valuable asset despite some of their present shortcomings. The subsidies they receive are more than compensated by the fact that they constitute the first line of defense since so many of them are colonies bordering on the Arab states.

Furthermore, friends of the kibbutz movement deny that the communal villages discourage the acceptance of new members. On the contrary, they claim the new immigrants are reluctant to join the austere pioneer life of the kibbutz. But where they do, they become equal partners with the veteran member who have given a lifetime of service, except in housing, where the principle of "last in, last served," prevails. Even in this area there is gradual adjustment through government regulations. As to the improved housing conditions in the kibbutz, causing an economic strain, the answer is that the communal villages produce much more than the proportionate number to the national economy. The kibbutz has indeed grown economically, not only in producing for the nation, but in its own accumulated possessions as well, as indicated by the increased inventory of stock and equipment. The standard of living has improved considerably for the entire population. Surely the kibbutzim are entitled to a little greater comfort after their many years of self-sacrificing labors.

As to the high taxes, the government's defenders, while admitting that they are among the highest in the civilized world, deny that they are burdensome. They claim the laborer's taxes are relatively moderate while a maximum of 50 per cent tax is levied on the profits of the wealthy, which is a lower scale of taxation than in many other countries.

Regarding the imbalance between imports and exports, it is held that there has been definite improvement except during the year preceding the Sinai incident, when extra imports were necessary to be stored for the emergency.

Thirdly and above all, they point out, there is the intangible asset which cannot be scientifically appraised or evaluated. Dr. Weizmann, first president of the new Jewish commonwealth, related this story to illustrate this greatest of all assets, the people of Israel. Soon after the issuance of the Balfour Declaration, the distinguished leader invited a prominent French agricultural authority to examine the wisdom of a project to purchase land in Palestine. A decade later he again met the land expert, who jestingly advised him of his "conversion to anti-Zionism" because of his Palestinian experience. "My opinion disfavored the purchase. By all economic laws, the projected venture should have failed. Your Zionists have proven me wrong. But I shall forgive them. The pioneers made the desert blossom despite my reputedly expert economic theories."

The truth is that the ordinary laws of economics do not operate with a people dedicated to an ideal. Such a people accomplishes the impossible. With the indomitable will to build their nation against all odds, the Israelis will find the way that leads to a secure foundation for the fulfillment of their national aspirations.

VI. Not By Bread Alone

Even the nonreligious in Israel are not immune from the impact of the deeply controversial question of religion. The state's attitude is clearly enunciated in the government's Basic Principles: "The period of the ingathering of the exiles has brought together in their homeland Jewish groups which had been living for centuries under the influence of cultures and environments remote one from the other, divided in their views and outlooks and differing in their customs and manners. The unification of the nation and the establishment of a normal national life make it necessary to foster freedom of conscience and religion; to prevent any religious or antireligious coercion from whatever source it may come; to insure that public religious needs be met through the resources of the state; and also to ensure freedom of religion and conscience to non-Jewish communities and the satisfaction of their religious needs by the state."

Through the help of the ministry in cooperation with local religious committees, services of prayer and worship are maintained in 340 settlements. Aid is given in support of rabbis, religious teachers and ritual slaughterers. Edifices for public worship are provided and kept in repair. Prayer books and ceremonial objects are also supplied. Institutions of learning of Jewish law and lore are subsidized. The state officially recognizes the rabbinate and rabbinical courts to which it gives aid and authority to function properly. The Department of Marriage and Divorce is within the province of the respective authorized religious denominations.

Through the Ministry of Religions, the state's cooperation and aid are freely extended to all denominations, Jewish, Christian and Moslem alike. This ministry numbering close to 300 employees in 1955 with a budget of 3,500,000 IL encourages, subsidizes and initiates many religious activities. It takes charge of all historic holy places and participates in celebrations of special public religious events.

In proportion to their numbers and religious requirements, the Moslem, Christian, Druze and Bahai religious administrations are accorded equal authority. Even the Karaites and Samaritans, though few in number, are granted assistance to carry on their religious affairs.

The Ministry of Religions, though predominantly Jewish in personnel and interests since almost 90 per cent of the population is Jewish, does not favor one religion over the other. Religious freedom for all is axiomatic in Israel. The various Christian denominations even conduct missionary activities to convert Jews with no interference on the part of the ministry. Jewish children attend Christian missionary schools to which they are enticed by the promise of economic aid or by educational advantages not found elsewhere.

Even conversions are permitted. The individual has the right to profess a new religion. In 1955 there were these changes of faith: 20 Christians and four Moslems embraced Judaism. Nine Jews and three Christians adopted the Moslem religion. Four Jews were converted to Christianity. Changes from one Christian denomination to another totaled 46. Tolerance and respect for other religions is the general attitude of government and people.

The holy places of all religions receive scrupulous attention. Official cognizance is given to religious festivals of Christians and Mohammedans, even to the extent of providing Christmas trees, an important item in the economy of a land where all trees are precious and vital.

On the various festivals of the minority religions, the government radio provides special programs with the president's message of good wishes widely broadcast. In this atmosphere of religious freedom an incipient movement to proselytize non-Jews to Judaism is now in evidence. An organization has been formed in Tel Aviv under the name of the Movement for the Dissemination of Judaism, with the subtitle, the Organization for Sincere Converts in Israel and the World.

The state has not faltered in adherence to these Basic Principles: freedom of conscience and religion to all; financial aid from state funds for public religious needs and no religious or antireligious coercion from any source whatever. But within the Jewish community these principles are often ignored by groups and parties of conflicting views and interests. The struggle by one element or another for the enforcement of religion or for its elimination is vigorously fought in Israel. The next generation will in a large measure determine the outcome.

Extremes govern the religious issues in Israel with few moderating voices heard above the raucous protests, name calling, crimination and recrimination.

In the main, three groups or parties officially claim religion to be their major concern. The ultra-Orthodox Neturai Karta —the Guardians of the City—secluded in the older Meah Sh'arim sector of Jerusalem, display a fanatical zeal accompanied by exhibitionism and arouse attention not warranted by their insignificant numbers. They refuse to give even de facto recognition to the existence of the state and if permitted the choice, would prefer to make their residence in the Jordanian sector of Jerusalem in the vicinity of the Wailing Wall. Their rejection of the state's authority is based on the conviction that Zion restored without previous Messianic leadership is godless. Since the Neturai Karta arrogate to themselves the guardianship of the most strictly interpreted Jewish traditions, Israel's major religious parties often remain silent or even support the demands of the extremists to avoid accusations of timidity or weakness in "the battle of the Lord."

The Guardians of the City also gather strength from their sympathizers in the Diaspora. The occasional tactless acts of retaliation on the part of their opponents rekindle their fiery protests not only through harsh words but sticks and stones as well. They are an unmitigated nuisance alike to the religiously observant and nonobservant Jews.

To maintain law and order, the government's police power is at times brought into action. Every fine for the disturbance of the peace affords the Neturai Karta a claim of martyrdom with a corresponding expression of sympathy from their real or politically motivated allies.

The Orthodox Agudat Israel was non-Zionist and some of its leadership was anti-Zionist prior to the establishment of the state. Strict and unyielding adherence to Jewish religious tenets and practices has been its platform since its founding in 1912, with no Zionist plank to further the development of a Jewish national homeland in Palestine through human efforts.

Since the birth of the state, Agudat Israel has entered the political arena, utilizing its organized strength for the advancement of Orthodoxy in the land.

The Mizrachi, an integral part of the World Zionist Organization since 1900, with the platform of "the land of Israel for the people of Israel, in conformity with the Torah of Israel," is also dedicated to Orthodox Judaism but with greater flexibility in the application of Jewish religious law to life's new demands in Israel.

The major portion of the Jewish population in Israel consists of those who are personally religious-minded and do not look to the state for the enforcement of Jewish religious law and life, or those who are neutrally indifferent toward any form of religious expression, or still others who favor a secular state with the individual Jew divested of religious traditions, which they consider a burdensome hangover from the long Jewish exile.

Judaism as a religion, broadly defined, signifies the binding together of man with God, man with his fellow man and man with his people. The last, man's duties as a citizen toward land

and people, is unquestioned in Israel, except by the Neturai Karta.

The Jew's obligations to the land which for him has never ceased to be holy, are explicitly expressed in Jewish law and lore. Even after Israel's sovereignty ceased between 70 C.E. and 1948, the Jew in prayer and hope remained loyal to the principle of Jewish nationhood, even when it was only an ideal, and fulfilled all feasible obligations to that principle during those centuries.

Since Israel's resurgence, a patriotic spirit equal to religious fervor has taken hold of the entire population. Therefore this phase of the threefold unity constituting Judaism has become a vigorous force for solidarity in Israel's life. Among the religious, nonreligious and irreligious there are no essential differences as to the duties of man toward his fellow man. Even without the benefit of reliable statistical data concerning the moral and ethical relations within one group or another, it is safe to conclude that the standards of human behavior are no lower among those who are not identified with the official religious camp in Israel than those who are.

The kibbutz movement, though dissociated from religious belief and practice, has made good relations between man and his fellow man the basis for a more perfect social order. Therefore religious divisiveness in Israel is not motivated by major differences as to the ethical precepts of Judaism. There may be a variety of opinions regarding the economic implications arising from the aspiration for a better society, but they pose no impediment to a unified and cohesive Jewish nation.

The essential religious controversies lie in the area of worship, ritual, ceremony and the dominance of religious laws pertaining to the family, such as marriage and divorce.

There can be no compulsion in the realm of faith. Persuasion and voluntary conviction are always in order, but one's private beliefs cannot be legislated. Yet, in this very area, there is considerable explosiveness.

When the first temporary constitutional assembly was convened to draw up the Declaration of Independence, there were strenuous objections to the invocation of God's blessing in the document. The problem was resolved by substituting the expression, Tzur Israel—Rock of Israel—freely translated in English as God of Israel. The religious representatives who signed the document in behalf of their constituents inscribed next to their names the Hebrew phrase, B'ezrat Hashem, meaning, With the Help of God.

The Israeli Parliament does not open or close with prayer, an indication of the predominant attitude of the nonreligious in the law-making body.

Nationalism has acquired the character of a religious cult in Israel, as evidenced by songs the people sing and the heroes they praise. Some have altered the battle cry of Mattathias the Hasmonean by substituting: "Let him who is courageous join me" instead of "He who is for the Lord, let him join me." Others have shortened the chant based on the threefold unity of God, Israel and Torah by eliminating the God element. Frequently, the irreligious are charged with alleged dejudaization of the religious immigrants from the Oriental countries. The accused in turn inveigh against all efforts to keep the newcomers "imprisoned" in the beliefs and practices of the "dark ages."

The clashes between the religious and the irreligious might have endangered the founding of the new state at its very outset if wiser counsels had not prevailed. To avoid a national crisis, the enactment of a permanent constitution was adjourned sine die to allow time and precedent to become the decisive factor in the religious issues facing the country. As a stopgap, the state continued the British mandatory law pertaining to religious authority, subject to specific modifications by the Knesset, the Israeli Parliament.

However, despite all conflicts of religious issues it is true that the state and Church are not completely divorced from each other in Israel. The extreme left feared that the state might become a theocracy while the extreme right predicted that Israel would be godless. Neither was right. The broad policy of the state has continued to allow for freedom of religious expression, which, as a corollary includes the right of the nonreligious to live their lives as their conscience dictates.

To achieve this balance is no simple task. It is very much like walking a tightrope. A few illustrations will suffice. The present Sabbath laws in Jerusalem and Tel Aviv prohibit transportation in public vehicles. Those who have no private cars or cannot afford taxi service are thus deprived of what the nonreligious consider their personal right to observe the Sabbath or not observe it as they see fit. Thus the law which was intended to prevent offending the sensibilities of the religious, simultaneously though unintentionally curbs the way of life of the nonreligious. The religiously observant object to athletic events on the Sabbath while others approve such activities as innocent and healthful forms of relaxation. The nonreligious favor swimming pools for both sexes while the ultrareligious consider mixed bathing, particularly in Jerusalem, as a desecration.

In the economic area, too, there are conflicts of interest. The spokesmen for the religious elements would prohibit every form of labor on the Sabbath except those activities unquestionably essential for the preservation of life and the state. Others, while accepting the Sabbath as the official day of rest, would permit labor in order to satisfy economic necessities. They would even permit the raising of pigs, though that is an abomination to the religious groups. They would go so far as to sanction the sale of pig meat on the principle that diet is a personal matter and therefore of no concern to the state.

Israel maintains a Ministry of Religions—supported by the taxes of the entire population, a principle unpopular among the nonreligious. However, despite all differences on matters of religion, the varying degrees af acrimony have been confined to the sphere of discussion, except for the Neturai Karta, without resulting in strife calculated to wreck the national unity.

The Chief Rabbinate in Israel consists of two heads, one representing the Ashkenazi, of East European Jewish origin, and the other Sephardic, of Spanish Jewish origin. Officially the Chief Rabbinate is the final arbiter on all religious disputes. The two heads act as one and work cooperatively enough to give the appearance of complete unity. Both chief rabbis have the same goals. But in practice the two are as different in temperament as they are in personal ambitions. The present Ashkenazi head, if given the choice, would prefer scholarly pursuits over administrative duties, which the office requires. He has no taste for temporal power. His age and failing health preclude him from assuming dynamic leadership. The Sephardic chief rabbi is the more vigorous of the two, ever ready to assume greater responsibilities and leadership. Even those at variance with his views recognize his independence of thought, freedom from party influence and sincerity of conviction.

As men of erudition and dedicated lovers of country and people, both Ashkenazi and Sephardic heads enjoy high regard and affection in the Yishuv, but their united official voice is in a minor key because of the gradual usurpation of authority by the Ministry of Religions. The ministry really "runs the religious show" in the land, including the Chief Rabbinate, which is not strong enough to protest against the inroads made into the areas of its legitimate authority.

As an indication of the comparative strength of influence of the Ministry of Religions and the Chief Rabbinate, the following figures are significant. Out of a total budget of 3,477,-500 IL, the head office of the ministry controls 2,451,800 IL while the Chief Rabbinate is granted only 124,000 IL, approximately 4 per cent of the budget. While it is true that the religious courts operated at a cost of 900,000 IL are under the Chief Rabbinate's auspices and the budgetary allowance appears much larger, it is equally true that the Ministry of

Religions wields a major influence in the appointments of the judges and administrative staff of the rabbinical courts. A Chief Rabbinate more zealous of its position may some day find itself in serious conflict with the Ministry of Religions in a struggle for the exercise of more power and influence.

Family and marital relations are the chief concern of the religious courts. For them, nothing is more important. The observance or nonobservance of a ritual concerns primarily the individual. The matter of marriage and divorce, however, involves the community of Israel, due to the ensuing problems of legitimacy and the legal definition of the term, Jew. Since no civil marriages are consummated in Israel, persons of different faiths cannot intermarry, unless one of the parties accepts conversion.

Recently, a crisis developed in the Cabinet in connection with the issuance of identification cards to all the residents of the state. The religious members objected to the majority's definition of what constitutes a Jew. The Ministry of the Interior, supported by a Cabinet majority, proposed that any one claiming himself to be a Jew should be so recognized. Accordingly, the child of a mixed marriage, though the mother be non-Jewish, should also be accepted if both parents give their consent.

The prime minister, who is in sympathy with this proposal which is contrary to the accepted religious legal definition of a Jew, argued that there should be greater stress on the Psalmist's identification of Jewishness over and above the legalistic requirements: "Lord, who shall sojourn in Thy tabernacle? Who shall dwell in Thy Holy Mountain? He that walketh uprightly, and worketh righteousness..." Those who insist on the legal requirements equally aspire to the highest moral life as proclaimed by the Psalmist, but find no contradiction between the legal and moral aspects of the matter. They maintain, however, that he who legally does not possess the status of a Jew cannot without formal admission to Judaism be recognized as such. Furthermore, the Jew who transgresses the moral law directly affects only his individual life, but the acceptance of one as a Jew merely on his own assertion disregards the inevitable problems of marriage and descent, which involve the worldwide community of Israel.

Legal authority in matters of the family is vested within the various religious groups, despite the leftist tendencies of the government. This is due primarily to expediency and not to the recognition of a principle. The hasty organization of the new state prevented a consideration of the basic constitutional laws of the land including the complicated area of family relations. As pointed out above, temporarily, and for the indefinite future, the British mandatory laws covering the marital status, remain in force. The various recognized religious denominations continue to have sole authority in the realm of marriage and divorce laws.

This situation has not been modified to any considerable extent during Israel's first decade of sovereign power out of fear of precipitating a major religious crisis in the land. This concession to organized religion served the government as a device for bargaining with the religious parties in areas of political and economic importance.

Occasionally, the country is aroused by specific hardship cases resulting from official strict Orthodox interpretation of the religious marital laws, but the resentment peters out. To illustrate: a marriage was prohibited on the ground that the prospective bride's mother was a convert to Judaism but the conversion was effected in Germany by a liberal rabbi not in conformity with Orthodox practice. Another case involving public dissension was caused by rabbinic refusal to remarry a divorced couple, though they remained single in the interim, on the ground that the husband was a Kohen (of priestly descent) and therefore prohibited from marrying a divorcee.

The organized religious parties in Israel cannot hope to gain an electoral political victory in the foreseeable future. Although a majority in Israel are in sympathy or identified with some form of religious thought and practice, the combined religious parties cannot gain a majority vote because the greatest number of those who cast their ballots are motivated by many considerations other than religion, such as economics, foreign affairs, the relative merits of candidates and the like. But despite their minority status in Parliament and government the religious parties maneuver advantageously to gain their ends. Because the combined labor organizations do not command a working majority in Parliament, they often rely on the support of the religious parties to form a coalition government. In addition religious representation in the Cabinet is deemed essential for favorable relations with free world Jewry where religion is the major Jewish raison d'être.

Thus the bargaining power of the religious groups is greatly enhanced through political deals. They have succeeded in making public kashrut—dietary laws—the law of the land. No public institution or governmental agency may serve food which is not in accordance with Jewish traditional practices under the supervision of the rabbinate. This law applies as well to the armed services, which are also provided with chaplains to care for religious needs.

While public utilities and other essentials for the health, welfare and security of the land are not subject to strict Sabbath laws, all other activities are at a standstill on the Sabbath except in times of emergency because of the political influence of the religious parties. The government's proposed unified public educational system was considerably modified to placate the opposition of the religious elements resulting in a grant to Agudat Israel, the rightist religious party, for an independent educational system. The religious parties were also considerably successful in modifying the proposed law requiring girls to participate in military service by permitting the religious elements among them to choose civil instead of military service.

Party system and party loyalty are very strong in Israel. In a democracy like that of the United States no religious political parties exist. Direct political intervention by religious organizations would conflict with democracy in action. In some other countries in the free world, religious political parties also function with national programs of their own. But everywhere it is recognized that true religion cannot be legislated. It can be taught by precept and example but cannot be coerced.

In Israel, the religious political parties concentrate more on political pressures rather than on persuasive tactics to gain their ends. This often leads to greater concern for party power than for moral influence, keener interest in political spoils than in spiritual endeavor. As a result, proceedings in Parliament have frequently been motivated by expediency rather than principle.

As the religionists are not united in thought and action, a duplicated if not competitive drive for laws to advance piety and stricter religious observance is inevitable. Under such conditions the more liberal will not act in accord with the dictates of their conscience lest they be charged with timidity and half-hearted allegiance to their religious convictions.

Does all this mean that Church and state are united in Israel? By no means. While all religions are recognized and supported by the state, citizenship privileges and responsibilities are in no wise dependent on any religious affiliation or the lack of it. Neither civil service nor political office require religious adherence. Parliament consists of members who belong to various denominations and of those who disclaim any religious ties.

In a recent judicial decision, yet to be confirmed by the Supreme Court of Israel, a Jewish teacher in the public school system who was dismissed for conversion to Christianity gained reinstatement on the ground that a man's religion is his personal affair.

In theory at least, a Moslem or Christian citizen of Israel may aspire to the highest office in the land. In the United States, where political democracy is intrenched, thus far only a Protestant has found it possible to occupy the White House. Great

Britain, mother of modern democracy, limits the crown to hereditary royalty belonging to the Church of England. Lebanon too has a constitutional provision which reserves the presidency for the Christian majority while the prime minister must be of the Moslem faith. A similar unwritten law, namely, that the president, who is the titular head of Israel, should be of the Jewish faith, would naturally make a strong appeal to many who are mindful of the Biblical injunction that only one of Israel's lineage may be the nation's head.

In other countries outside of Communist domination, heads of governments and important public officials maintain warm and cordial relations with the Church. In Israel, except for the current president, the relationship is distant. The government leadership seldom makes an appearance at public worship or at important religious functions, lest its presence be construed as a sympathetic attitude toward Jewish tradition. A spirit of aloofness characterizes the official relationship between political heads and the Synagogue in Israel. This is not apocryphal. The harsh reaction by the religious elements against the apparent callousness toward religious interests displayed by public officials is certainly not conducive to a cohesive Jewish life in Israel. And yet with all this, there is no separatism or isolationism in the land. The majority of the people have learned to live with one another regardless of their differences. Frequently they even display good humor in their intergroup criticism. Not only in official circles, such as Parliament, but even in nongovernmental activities, the religious forces and their opponents often plan and work together, forgetting their differences.

Conflicting and confused opinions prevail concerning the state of religion in Israel. The irreligious fear that there is a theocracy in the making, threatening individual freedom of conscience. The deeply religious see the threat of an atheistic society. Neither extreme view holds in Israel. Religion in Israel is much in evidence in the areas of both faith and practice.

Faith in the God of history is almost universally approved; belief in a personal God is found to a lesser degree.

The three major cities symbolize the degrees of religiosity in Israel. Jerusalem, called the "City of the Past," is the religious fortress; Tel Aviv, known as the "City of the Present," represents the moderate or lukewarm religious tendencies; and Haifa, the "City of the Future," inclines towards the nonconformists.

Unlike other countries, where religious roots grow strongest in the rural areas and weaker in the more sophisticated urban communities, in Israel the reverse is true. The reason is historically discernible. Most of the halutzim—the pioneers who settled on the land—came to Israel convinced of the merits of the Marxian or kindred philosophy of life, due to their bitter experiences in the Exile. Therefore they strove to build a society unburdened by religious traditions. The city or town settlers, consisting mainly of middle-class immigrants, did not bring with them the rebellious spirit characteristic of the believers in "Socialism in our day."

No reliable statistics are available to reveal the thinking of Israeli Jewry about religion, but tendencies in religious practices are gradually becoming clearer. In public worship Jerusalem takes first place, with the vast majority of its population in attendance at the synagogues on the high holy days. In Tel Aviv the proportion of observant Jews is smaller, in Haifa there are still fewer and in the nonreligious rural communities the percentage of worshipers is insignificant.

The dietary laws are more universally observed, due in the main to national or local legal enactments rather than to religious conviction. In the field of religious education there has been considerable progress, both because of the state's interest and a more popular realization of the void that has to be filled in the life of the younger generation.

Generally speaking, the synagogues in Israel do not attract the youth of the country. The houses of public worship do not reflect the sacred poet's "beauty of holiness" either in physical appearance or in the conduct of the service. Since Israel is primarily the land of the "ingathering of the exiles," the variety of forms of worship serves only to stir a curiosity satisfied by a single visit to the synagogues as if they were museums featuring the antiquities of the generations that have passed.

The day has not as yet arrived for a synagogue type of structure and service sufficiently meaningful and inspiring to attract the younger generation. The architecture and appurtenances of an edifice in a large measure symbolize the ideal which the structure represents and the devotion paid to that ideal. Israel has many imposing public buildings for educational, cultural, dramatic and political activities of the various communities, but one searches in vain for distinguished synagogue edifices. The one religious structure of impressive dimensions and architectural distinction constructed for the Chief Rabbinate recently dedicated in Jerusalem aroused criticism for its costliness in time of sharp economic stress by those very people who did not hesitate to build elaborate labor temples, concert halls and the like. The major difficulty, however, lies not in the paucity of adequate structures but in the lack of understanding of the importance of public worship for the unsynagogued.

The living word of God through the sermon is almost completely unknown at public worship in Israel. This is in line with the past practices of the Eastern European synagogue where, if a sermon was delivered at all, it was no part of the regular service of prayer. Only the large Jewish communities maintained their own professional preachers, who dealt primarily with abstract theological and ritualistic deviations, not with problems of man's relation with his fellow man and seldom with questions of current national or international interest.

The prestige and influence of the synagogue in Israel would be considerably enhanced by the inclusion of sermons dealing with important topics of personal, communal and national concern. The occasional sermon that is heard in Israel is an exhibition of casuistry, planned to display the Talmudical erudition of the preacher rather than to present a living message of current interest. The vital problems of life are dealt with on the platform of the public lecture forum or political arena but the synagogue's voice on the issues of the day remains muted.

The lack of decorum and esthetic appreciation in the synagogue is encountered in other religious spheres as well. The usual marriage ceremony is a mechanical, legalistic function devoid of spiritual meaning and beauty. When conducted in the marriage bureau it becomes only a ritualistic formula of mumble and jumble. Other ceremonies, too, lack the amenities. There is urgent need for leadership to restore inherent dignity, warmth and significance to the ceremonial phase of Israel's religious life.

The inflexible status quo attitude of the clerical hegemony of Israel is a major stumbling block on the road to religious awakening. A few brief illustrations will tell the story. At the founding of the state, one of the truly great spiritual savants in the land proposed the convocation of a Sanhedrin—a replica of the ancient ecclesiastical and judicial tribunal—to consider religious problems in the light of the transformed national status. The Chief Rabbinate, pressured by the extreme rightist bloc, tabooed the proposal. At the dedication of the Chief Rabbinate Building, the proponent of the renewal of the Sanhedrin was invited to be a guest speaker with the proviso, however, that he make no reference to his original proposal. He declined the invitation.

The more recent suggestion to convene world-renowned Talmudic scholars in Jerusalem, merely to exchange views informally, was also rejected, lest the assembly give the appearance of a Sanhedrin authorized to make permissible customs and practices traditionally prohibited.

The same unrelenting attitude brought reproach to a young scholarly rabbi for arguing in favor of excluding electricity from the Biblical prohibition: "Ye shall not kindle a fire on the Sabbath."

In one synagogue, at the insistence of the Hebraically-minded, the dominant Sephardic pronunciation was introduced into the service. The Chief Rabbinate supported the opposition to this innovation on the ground that custom is even more sacred than law!

Another community, while constructing a new synagogue, became embroiled in a contentious question of decorum and the introduction of a prayer for the welfare of the state and the highest officers of the land. Again there was victory for the die-hards. This myopic rigidity of the present religious authorities will not attract the unaffiliated to Jewish faith and practice despite Parliament's approval of sectarian laws obtained through political maneuvering by the ecclesiastical parties.

The mode of prayer and ritual, though important even if unadjusted to changing conditions, is not considered essential by the Israeli people. Life goes on just the same. The irreligious will remain irreligious and those deeply devout in thought and practice will continue as such. But when religious leadership takes no cognizance of the need for reinterpretation of Jewish law and practice in the area of individual economic subsistence and national well-being, the consequences may be serious. The religious elements, for example, are plagued by the problem of Sabbath laws such as animal care, milking cows or the observance of the Sabbatical year and the like.

The religious workers on the land need a more liberal interpretation of the law if they are not to be subjected to the choice between pangs of conscience and severe economic losses. On questions of self-defense or preparations against enemy intrusion, the Israeli Chief Rabbinate has gone on record permitting such activities on all religious red-letter days. And they have not forbidden work in indispensable national industries such as electricity, telegraph and telephone.

But what shall the religiously observant worker do? Should he desecrate the Sabbath for the national welfare or should he permit the nonobservant Jew to carry the load?

How about the laws of the Biblical Sabbatical year? Should the earth lie fallow for an entire year or should the land through a legal fiction be titled to a non-Jew for the Sabbatical year, allowing the produce to be used by Jews? The Chief Rabbinate closely allied with Mizrachi favors the latter; the Agudat Israel Rabbinate insists on the former.

A similar problem arises in the practice of grafting fruit and vegetables. Numerous other legal problems face the Chief Rabbinate. To deal adequately with them requires maximal courage and wisdom. Perhaps some day a vigorous rabbinic leadership will be able to cope with the involved religious problems of the day arising from the new national status of Israel.

The Jewish woman in Israel enjoys equality except in the area of religion, where she is still a second-class citizen. Segregation of sexes at public worship is not a crucial issue. The unsynagogued are unconcerned with this problem; the religiously observant are satisfied with the status quo. Only occasionally is the modern woman's absence from public worship explained as due to the segregation of sexes. The reason is deeper. In civil life the Jewish woman is permitted the fullest expression of her talents, while in the religious sphere she is limited by law and practice. Her spiritual training is inferior to that of the average male and her responsibility for religious leadership is at zero. In sacred law and lore she is not on a par with the male; in ritual and ceremonial activities of a public nature, her position is insignificant. The results are self-evident. Many a Jewish home, traditionally the spiritual fortress of Jewish life, is far from that in Israel. The Hebrew tongue, matters of state and secular culture are the interests, to the exclusion of religion, that dominate the home presided over by a mother unconcerned with the Jewish religious heritage. A revival of the Jewish woman's participation in the religious life of Israel will depend largely on bridging the gulf between her status in the civil order and in the religious area of her life.

The initial rebellion against formal religion has spent itself.

The danger to spiritual life lies now in apathy and indifference. The early reaction against the synagogue is not indigenous to the Jew in Israel. It was imported from abroad, fomented by Marxian philosophy which the early pioneers acquired under alien strains and stresses.

There were also the "enlightened," known as the maskilim, who abandoned their religious fervor in the lands of their birth for a reawakened Jewish nationalism. The leftist kibbutzim established themselves with goals for a new social order, divesting themselves of ritual and ceremonial as outmoded vestiges of a bygone age. The Bible was the major significant Jewish heritage which they retained. But the post-Biblical literature, Talmudical law and lore, the spiritual life of the Jew of the Exile had no further interest for them. They regarded the long period between the dispersion under Rome and modern Zionism as a blank page in Jewish history. Their greatest interest in the Bible was in the prophetic portion. While the devout and pious Jew turns more frequently to the Psalms as the medium of prayer, praise or thanksgiving, the Israeli nationalist is more imbued with the prophetic teachings because they deal with the problems of social justice and national rebirth rather than with the yearning of the individual soul.

The Socialists and the "enlightened" Jews denied the need for religious guidance and regulations. The Sabbath was observed as a day of physical rest minus the rigorous prohibitions and admonitions of Scriptural and Talmudical law. The festivals were reinvested with their original agricultural meaning or national significance but were stripped of traditional religious content. Even the high holy days were divorced from the synagogue and shorn of their ritual and ceremonial phases in the home. Yom Kippur—the Day of Atonement—became another day of rest from labor, devoid of its central doctrine of at-oneness with the Supreme Being.

The number of those who fast on Yom Kippur in the kibbutzim has increased in recent years, but officially such observance is still looked upon as a throwback to the Middle Ages of clerical fanaticism. Edifices for public worship in most of the leftist kibbutzim are nonexistent, with no Holy Scrolls in many of the communes. Little ghettos are provided for aged parents in nonreligious kibbutzim where they may practice their religious rites, including the observance of the Jewish dietary laws, wherever feasible. But the two generations have no common denominator in religious thought and practice.

In the leftist circles the third generation, the children of the pioneers, is raised in ignorance of religious life. While circumcision is universally practiced, training in prayer and observance of ritual and ceremonial is completely ignored. Some of the younger elements may not see anything of religious practices until they reach adolescence, when they unexpectedly come in contact with observant Jewish families. Others discover Judaism for the first time when they join the army where, under chaplaincy guidance, Kashrut and the Sabbath ceremonies are officially observed.

The bar mitzvah ceremony which marks religious maturity at the age of 13 bears no ritual content in the leftist kibbutzim. There is no public worship, no Torah honors, only a social reception at one of the commune's meetings at which time the bar mitzvah is presented either with a Bible to symbolize his coming of age or in some instances a small weapon to signify that henceforth he is to be a defender of Jewish life and property against enemy invaders.

Since the launching of the state, liturgical ceremonies sanctifying marriage ties have been universally observed even among the leftists, but thus far not out of conviction but rather in compliance with the law of the land. Occasionally marriage sacraments are conducted on a wholesale scale. The officiating rabbi is invited to solemnize the union of a number of couples at the same time, thus saving the commune the expense involved in arranging individual receptions and celebrations.

The irreligious are no longer dogmatic in their skepticism.

Second thoughts have begun to penetrate the inner sanctum of those who not long ago actively rejected Judaism as a living faith.

The leaders of the kibbutz movement have set as their goal the creation of an ideal society unencumbered by the claims of Jewish tradition. After many years of personal sacrifice for their ideal of a reborn Jewish nation in a reconstructed Marxian world, they have become disillusioned. The international situation has not improved, nor has the individual become a better human being. The new world of their dreams has not been realized. Many of the intelligent elements feel the void in their lives. Some are now beginning to question the wisdom of having tossed religion into the discard.

Both the older and younger generation are actively groping for spiritual verities beyond economic needs and even beyond a planned social order. The failure of Socialist experiments in Russia and her satellites has sharply disappointed many of them. However, they have not officially abandoned Marxian philosophy nor have they appreciably returned to religion. It is not easy to repudiate oneself or deny a lifetime philosophy. But they are no longer certain that the Marxian program is the panacea of all human ills. Many of them in their hunger for spiritual values are now not so sure that the ways of their forebears were all wrong. They are in search of God but have not gone so far as to articulate it. It is still in the embryonic stage waiting for dynamic and inspired leadership to point the way.

This inner struggle, gradually becoming more vocal, could be resolved much sooner if only there were a more sympathetic understanding on the part of the nation's religious leadership as to the nature of the spiritual difficulties now disturbing the doubters and the apikorsim.

The attempts at rapprochement are meager and faltering. There is vast Jewish scholarship in the land capable of interpreting the Jewish law on any question. But Israel lacks the unique type of spiritual and resourceful capacity "at the top" needed in order to confront the challenge of the day.

When a year ago the Sephardic chief rabbi arranged for an official visit at the leftist kibbutzim, the reception accorded him was cordial enough, but the results were drab. Instead of utilizing the visit as a symbolic binding up of the wounds inflicted by both on each other, the effort was vitiated by the inadequate approach to the real problem facing the kibbutzim and by the inept publicity that followed. The public was misinformed that the kibbutzim acceded to the chief rabbi's request to have mezuzot—parchment scrolls containing the Biblical verses of Deuteronomy VI:4-9, XI:13-21, and Numbers XV:37-41—attached on the doorposts of their dining and social halls. First, the request was premature, and second, the diplomatic reply was that consideration would be given in due time to the matter.

Perhaps some day the skeptics will find the road to a revival of Jewish religious practices and observances, but for the present at least, it does not appear that such awakening will result from the efforts of the religionists who are now exercising their power. And when the day does come that the leftist groups are drawn closer to Jewish ritual and ceremonial life, it is doubtful whether they will go the whole way as demanded by inflexible orthodoxy, which dominates Israel's religious sphere with the tacit approval of the state.

What can be done to attract the intellectual and dogmatic Socialist to the synagogue and all that it symbolizes? The adjective "dogmatic" is used advisedly. For those who accept the Marxian philosophy literally, including the closed mind belief that religion is the opiate of the people, are certainly no prospects for an alliance with any religious program.

As to the large numbers of the more open-minded unsynagogued in Israel, various opinions prevail. Some claim that increased production on the land warranting a five-day work week will be conducive to wider participation in religious activities. As leisure is increased, more time will be available for spiritual interests.

Others claim that the synagogue, in all its ramifications, is not as important for life in Israel as it is in the Diaspora. As one Israeli put it: "When I studied medicine in an American university in the non-Jewish environment of a midwestern city, I attended Sabbath services diligently. I hungered for Jewish association which was readily found in the synagogue. Here, at home, I meet my people everywhere. I therefore am in no need of the house of worship for Jewish association here. Here the very streets are Jewish. They bear the names of Jewish heroes, martyrs, saints and scholars. Hebrew sounds fill the air. All conversation leads to Israel's achievements and needs. The synagogue in Israel is not essential to make us conscious of our Jewishness. The whole environment is Jewish. Furthermore the synagogue or temple in America is esthetically inviting, the services beautiful and the sermons meaningful. Here, the religious structure is shabby, the service undecorous and there is no significant message from the pulpit. On the last high holy days, observed in the midst of a national crisis, when I did attend the services to seek communion with God and my people, the rabbi's sermon dealt with the innocuous question of a new ritual bath instead of the vital issues of the day. Under these circumstances the synagogue and I can enjoy no intimate relationships. Here we are Jewish automatically, like breathing. Here I have all the association with my people I could possibly crave."

To make the Israeli synagogue attractive and influential, the religious leadership in Israel has neither the will nor the know-how to deal with this problem. It is, therefore, urged that this task be undertaken by a new type of rabbi of high intellectual attainment, erudite in both traditional Jewish learning and general world culture and deeply concerned with the every-day individual and national problems of the Jew in Israel and in the Diaspora. Those who can meet this challenge, who have attained a fluent command of Hebrew and are motivated by idealism and who are willing to make the necessary economic sacrifices, are rare. But assuming that there are rabbis who are thus qualified, how could they be elected or assigned to rabbinic posts without the consent of the Chief Rabbinate and the Ministry of Religions, constituting a clerical authority which monopolizes official religion in Israel? Should they exercise any independence of thought or action they would promptly be blocked by those who insist on a monolithic religion in Israel allowing for no deviations even of a trivial character.

To counter this difficulty it has been suggested that a beginning be made with children's congregations under the right kind of rabbinical tutelage. When they reach adulthood they will find a way to make the synagogue function as it should. This remedy, even if countless difficulties be overlooked, presents many obstacles which appear to be impenetrable. The irreligious parents would not encourage their children to engage in such a program. The religious committed to their party affiliations will not allow their youth to deviate from the established ways of worship and practice under a spiritual guidance on which the elders would frown.

Religious leadership recruited from abroad is not the solution either. The Israelis feel self-sufficient. Outsiders, unless invited by them, would be snubbed.

Furthermore, while some of the proven successful methods of the Diaspora Synagogue Center could be adopted for Jewish spiritual life in the holy land, all new developments in religious thought and practice, if any, must be home-grown.

Anyone who theorizes that the Reform or Conservative synagogue evolved in America could be duplicated with any success in Israel is greatly mistaken. The intellectual, cultural and spiritual leadership of Israel must in the main come from Israel itself. The old type rabbi steeped in Jewish law and lore alone, without worldly knowledge, philosophical understanding and practical wisdom, is acceptable to the static powers that be. The modern rabbi whose secular higher learning and cultural attainments exceed his Hebraic training and traditional background will be considered an am ha-aretz—a Jewish illiterate—and will not be approved even by the nonreligious liberals in Israel.

If organized religion were more concerned with the future of Judaism in the Holy Land than with maintaining a status quo, it would attend to the need of training a new spiritual leadership combining rabbinic studies with a university education. This proposed new type of rabbi would have to be made aware of the pressing problems of the nation and be able to meet the challenges which constantly arise.

Israel's rabbinate of tomorrow must comprise effective public speakers in order to win the hearts and minds of their congregations. They must possess the will and organizing ability to fill the House of God with religious and educational activities every day in the year. The new rabbinate if it ever develops must be dynamic in the role it plays, commanding an active participation in all community enterprises, not satisfied with a limited function confined to answering questions on ritual and ceremony.

Life in the community of Israel, progressing at a rapid pace, is maturing from day to day. The religious leadership must not fall behind. There are definite spiritual stirrings in Israel among elements who only yesterday were indifferent and even hostile to Judaism. From many indications it is becoming clear that religion in the Holy Land inherently possesses vast potentials of accomplishment. With an intelligent, courageous and consecrated rabbinate, willing and able to cut through the thick underbrush that until now has obstructed progress, there could be a farreaching revitalization of inspirational religious thought and practice in the Holy Land.

VII. Above All, Learning

There is no illiteracy in Israel. Even the Oriental immigrant women who have not had the advantage of learning in their native lands are gradually acquiring at least the ability to speak and read Hebrew.

In September, 1949, shortly following the War for Independence, an educational law was adopted to make school attendance compulsory for all children between the ages of five and 14. Those who fail to complete an elementary school education at the age of 14 are required by law to attend continuation classes up to the age of 18.

In the first decade of its national existence Israel created the necessary opportunities and instruments for the advancement of education and culture, projected on the foundations of the early Zionist pioneering days.

Achad Ha'am (Asher Ginsburg, 1856-1927), philosopher of Jewish life and distinguished man of Hebrew letters, advanced the cause of a regenerated Hebrew culture in the Holy Land prior to Herzl's call for a Jewish state. Cultural and political Zionism, however, were not mutually exclusive. They were two phases of the same movement, differing only in emphasis and method. Herzl never lived to see the fulfillment of his dream of an international charter recognizing Jewish rights to Palestine. But Achad Ha'am, who settled in the Holy Land in 1921, saw with his own eyes the foundation of the Hebrew culture reborn.

Ever since the beginning of Jewish immigration to Palestine, the school edifice has been given priority over housing facilities. More than anywhere else in the world Jewry in Israel has become worthy of the appellation: "People of the Book." Israel can boast of more schools, more books, more authors, scholars, musicians and artists in proportion to her population than any other country in the civilized world. When as a result of the Sinai Campaign in 1956 the gift shops in Israel suffered financially because of the lack of tourists, those shops which also handled books did not feel the financial pinch because the Israelis continued to purchase and read books. The hunger for knowledge and the love of the esthetic in art, drama and music are constantly on the increase.

Out of a population of approximately 2,000,000, close to 450,000 attend schools of one type or another instructed by a teaching staff of over 25,000. The state budget for schooling, in the neighborhood of 50,000,000 Israeli pounds, is supplemented by an equal sum derived primarily from world Jewry for university level training and yeshivot (Talmudic academies) studies.

To begin with, the kindergarten department has close to 65,000 youngsters who participate in supervised play in preparation for the elementary school system, which embraces 310,000 pupils. The secondary schools teach about 25,000 students; agricultural and vocational schools number 11,000 pupils; teachers' seminaries train 3,000; schools for working youth number 11,000 students; yeshivot account for approximately 5,000 students. Miscellaneous, such as business, nursing, postal telegraph and nautical schools, number 10,000 students. Colleges and the university have a student enrollment of over 8,000.

The state's responsibility covers a primary education for all between the ages of five and 14. The Government Program issued the following pronouncement dealing with the goals of a universal elementary education: "The values of Israel and the achievement of science; love of the homeland and loyalty to the state and the Jewish people; training in agricultural works and in handicrafts; the realization of the pioneering ideal; the aspiration toward a society based on freedom, equality and tolerance; mutual assistance and love of humanity."

These broad basic principles laid down as the government's policy for Israel's entire population are entrusted to the Ministry of Education for implementation. The government, however, recognizing that the Jewish citizens of the land have additional relations and obligations beyond the borders of Israel, assumes these further responsibilities. "In elementary, secondary and higher education the government will do its best to deepen Jewish consciousness among Israel's youth, to strengthen their bond with the Jewish people's past and its historic heritage, to reinforce their moral affinity with world Jewry through inculcation of the knowledge of the common fate and history which unite the Jews all over the world in all generations and in all countries."

To accomplish both aims, the training of loyal and capable citizens devoted to one another, to country and humanity and to develop a closer affinity between them and world Jewry is an arduous task beset by many difficulties. While learning has always been a major goal in Jewish life, the past half century has witnessed an acute divisiveness in the aims and methods of Jewish education. The traditionalists, those on the right, continued to insist on religious instruction as the sum total of Jewish learning; the more liberal elements on the left tended toward a secularization of Jewish education.

Under the mandatory rule and for a time following the establishment of the state there was no unified system of Jewish education. Each party and faction sought to perpetuate its partisan ideals and interests through its educational facilities. The youth was trained to be dedicated to party before country, frequently resulting in children of tender age being unwilling to be associated with those raised under different ideologies. This evil of partisanship among the young has not as yet been completely eliminated, but the Unified System of Education adopted in 1954 is rapidly moving in that direction.

The goal of the present school system is to train citizens who think, live and act above party affiliations. The Ministry of

Education is charged with the duty to direct and supervise education for all with the aim of character building, development of talents and skills and to promote loyalty to the country and its people. Present-day figures indicate that in the elementary school system, 70 per cent of the children are within the state's general school category, 23 per cent attend state religious schools and 7 per cent are in the independent religious schools. The vast majority therefore, 93 per cent, are under the Unified System of Education. Only the schools of Agudat Israel, the right-wing orthodox, maintain an independent existence, and even they are subject to governmental control in the areas of secular subjects of instruction.

The success of a school or system must largely depend on the quality of the teacher. In Israel, as in most countries, there is a shortage of teachers, some of whom lack pedagogic training but only a few of whom fall short of professional dedication. The teaching staff has been caught in the feverish tempo of nation building and in a measure helped to stimulate this mood. Teaching in Israel has become more of a calling or vocation than a profession. In the decade of Israel's existence, with the large influx of new pupils, the teachers' problem has grown considerably. The teachers' training schools were not sufficiently prepared to graduate adequate numbers of teachers or afford them the best preparation for their careers. Israel has now 27 schools for the training of instructors with an enrollment of 4,000, of whom approximately 90 per cent are girls. The deficiencies of the past decade will be gradually corrected through the new and more comprehensive teacher training programs.

The teaching staff is a well-organized body affiliated with the National Labor Union, both for the promotion of their security as well as for the advancement of their professional standards. Salaries for teachers though not the highest in the land are nevertheless proportionate to the better standards of the whole community. Compensation consists of basic salary plus additional cost of living increments. A teacher holding a B.A. degree with about 10 years of experience has an earning capacity of close to 300 IL per month. This income is higher than that of the average Israeli worker, who earns approximately 200 IL per month.

The working hours of the school day decrease after the teacher has reached the age of 50, with less periods of instruction per week as the age of the teacher advances. Women teachers are accorded the privilege of reduction of hours during pregnancy and for the care of children during their infancy. A less tangible but very important aspect of the teaching profession is the esteem which it enjoys in the community. Since the entire country pays homage to intellectual and cultural proficiency, there is high regard for the teacher who by training and calling belongs to the intelligentsia.

Like teacher, like pupil. While it is true that Israel has a proportionate number of problem children, on the whole the pupils are devoted to their studies. This is due to two factors: the traditional high regard of the Jew for learning transmitted at an early age to the youth by the elder generation and the sincere interest of the teachers who with missionary zeal build the intellectual life of the future citizens of the land. The Israeli pupil is a conscious patriot at a very tender age and recognizes his responsibility to participate in the building of the nation through the development of his skills and talents. He soon becomes aware of the meager resources of his own country but would not exchange his allegiance for any other place no matter how enticing it may be.

Since the existing population represents the "ingathering of the exiles," almost every type and color of world civilization is to be found in Israel. Some have come from rich cultural backgrounds, others from primitive countries with no educational facilities. The large influx from Oriental lands has posed two problems. The possible capacity of the Orientals to keep up with the "white" school population and their acceptance as equals despite their color and difference of origin. The government, mindful of the problem of integration, recognizes the successful accomplishments to date but remains conscious that "the social and cultural differences between a great part of the immigrants and the Western settlers have not yet been obliterated." Thus far the school system, through its earnest, intelligent efforts, has allayed the dual fear: the Oriental pupil has proven himself capable of learning equal to that of the "white" and his acceptance by the general school population has been rapid and wholehearted.

The phenomenal increase of population has created the additional problem of insufficient classroom and auxiliary facilities for the proper instruction of the ever-growing school membership. In the older settlements and in the larger cities, the school edifices compare most favorably with the best structures of the community. There has been no economizing at the expense of the school. Investment in the future generation is in response to popular demand. Nothing is too good for the children in Israel. In some areas overcrowding is the natural consequence of the rapid increase in school enrollment. Some schools are hastily constructed and are of a temporary nature to meet new emergencies. But by and large neither people nor government are inclined to neglect the physical facilities of the educational system.

As to the curriculum, to borrow an American term, the three R's are basic in Israel, too. In the primary schools greater attention is given to five other subjects: Bible, elementary science, agriculture, handicrafts and a foreign language. English for the present is in great demand, but French is on the ascendant because of the numerous Oriental immigrants whose native tongue is French.

The first four grades of the eight-year school program require a class attendance of 23 hours per week on a six-day week schedule. The fifth school year calls for an attendance of 28 hours per week and the last three grades, 29 hours per week. In addition, pupils between the fourth and eighth grades receive two to four hours of instruction per week in agriculture and one to five hours in handicraft. The state religious schools also include in the last three grades instruction in Talmud as well as in religious beliefs and practices.

Special attention is given to retarded pupils. There is no accelerated program, however, for the gifted. Physical education is of considerable importance in the curriculum but its realization is short of the goal because of lack of adequate facilities. In the not too distant past the education of Jewish youth was channeled toward mental improvement and piety, frequently at the expense of physical development. This no longer prevails in Israel's educational system which emphasizes "mens sana in corpore sano," intellectual attainment in healthy, vigorous bodies. The great interest in physical education is evidenced by the fact that the Wingate Physical Culture Institute contest of 1956 attracted 42,000 participants from 400 primary schools and 50 secondary schools with 2,500 pupils receiving certificates of distinction for their success and perseverance in a variety of tests. The curriculum deals also with the artistic and esthetic interests of the youth. Music and art are given special attention.

No particular course of study is devoted to the teaching of moral principles. The instruction in ethics and human relations is part and parcel of the subjects generally taught, such as Bible, literature, history, etc. Civics, citizen's rights and duties to one's people, land and government is a required subject effectively presented but, as in all countries, the politicians and public leaders demand an even greater emphasis on the inculcation of patriotism in the hearts and minds of the younger generation.

Almost 7,000 children in the various categories of handicapped and chronically ill receive special training under the auspices of the Ministry of Education.

The educational system is comparatively new and is unburdened by inflexible standards. Therefore, new ideas in education are not unwelcome and experiments are encouraged. Valuable assets auguring well for the future of education in Israel are the pupil-teacher relation and a healthy parental respect for intellectual advancement. Between pupil and teacher the relations are both reverential and friendly. There is a wholesome regard for authority not characterized by domination. The aim is to develop citizens with ability to think as individuals and the will to act in unison for the good of the country as a whole.

Parents are deeply concerned and show an active interest in the school progress of their children. They take pride in their successes and are disappointed in their scholastic deficiencies. This attitude stimulates pupil and teacher alike to maximum effort and accomplishment. The general community keenly desires the best in education for all, irrespective of budgetary limitations. Democratic governments, usually sensitive to popular needs and wishes, respond accordingly. In Israel the government is even ahead of the citizenry in the advocacy of an educational system broad in its base and significant in human values. The government is committed to the ideal of a maximum educational program and initiates steps for its fulfillment.

The place of religion in the school system is both difficult and confusing. The parent has the right to send his child to one of the three types of schools: the *General School* of his own immediate community, the *Mizrachi School* with its definite religious program under the direct supervision of the Ministry of Education or the *Agudah School,* independent of government control except for requirements of general education. Some of the nonreligious send their children to mizrachi schools either because of better teaching staffs or improved standards of education. Others do so in the belief that it is well for Jewish children to acquire a knowledge of their religious heritage to enable them on reaching maturity to decide for themselves what to retain or discard from Jewish belief and practice. The religious elements insist that pupils of different home backgrounds create a confused atmosphere which is religiously and pedagogically unsound. If agudah school students seldom and mizrachi primary school graduates more frequently switch to a general secondary school or become affiliated with a nonreligious kibbutz, their former religious training is quickly all but forgotten. The religious groups recognize this problem and struggle hard to win the minds of their youth so that when they grow to maturity they may be able to resist the secular environment inimical to their early religious training.

The general school is free from any anti-religious bias but has not as yet adopted a positive attitude toward religious beliefs and observances. Recognizing the need for transmitting the essential elements of the Jewish heritage to the up-growing generation, the Ministry of Education recently incorporated in the school curriculum a course of study on "Jewish Consciousness." The goal of the new element in the curriculum is not too clearly defined. If the intent is a greater awareness of the national interdependence of all Jews, why teach the prayer book, religious customs and ceremonies? If, however, religious ties to bind Israeli and Diaspora Jews together are intended, then the innovation will prove ineffective. The success of this new course is largely dependent on the teacher. The devout instructor will teach Bible, prayers, customs and ceremonies as integral features of Jewish life; the nonreligious will present them as antiquities with no application to present-day realities.

During the primary school career of a pupil, he will be influenced by a variety of teachers who profess opposing ideologies, leaving him confused as to the place of religion in his own life. He may acquire the meaning of Sabbath observance, festival and holy day celebrations, dietary laws, prayers and the like but he will not have the interest or the will to make them living forces in his daily conduct.

Nowhere in the world do Jewish children know the Bible as well as they do in Israel, but the emphasis is on the national elements with scarcely any effort made to generate the personal religious fervor which a sympathetic contact with the Bible should engender. The general school adequately prepares the Israeli child for good citizenship, but for spiritual training he must look beyond the confines of the classroom. For bar mitzvah preparation he must have private tuition. The prayer book is used as a text but not as a source of inspiration. The holy days and festivals are historically explained, without encouraging their traditional observance.

Everywhere in Israel the place of religion in the system of education is under discussion. The leaders in education are conscious of the existing shortcomings and problems. As pointed out above, they have introduced as an initial step the study of "Jewish consciousness," a vital factor in the training of the younger Israeli generation. The results and further developments are still unpredictable.

Before we turn our attention to intermediate and higher education in Israel we should briefly consider the kibbutz school, the yeshivah and the ma'barah—transition camps for new immigrants—program of education.

In the kibbutz, the child is the responsibility of the commune from infancy to his 18th year. Through nursery, kindergarten, elementary and intermediate courses, he is prepared for life in the kibbutz. The earliest years are spent in organized play. As the pupil matures, he is taught to assume some measure of work responsibility, eventually dividing his time equally between learning and labor. The religious element in his education is either totally lacking or is frequently presented negatively. The city and town youth minus a formal religious training becomes somewhat aware of traditional Jewish practices through contacts with his general environment. This situation does not prevail in the secular kibbutz. The religious kibbutz, however, represents the most ideal combination of education: effective teaching in the classroom, congenial religious observance at home and a warm atmosphere in the commune, all in harmony with one another for the spiritual way of life.

The yeshiva—Talmudic academy—is both a relic of the Jewish past and a bulwark for the future of Talmudic study in Israel. Jerusalem's older sector leads in the long-established type of yeshivah while in the rest of the Holy City and throughout the country there is ample evidence of a revitalized interest in the study of oral law and lore—Talmud—by the new builders of Zion. In the first category, the old type yeshivah houses both the beginners as well as advanced students, some of whom are married men devoted exclusively to Jewish learning with no thought of personal career or future. These yeshivot retain the methods and atmosphere of past generations and Yiddish is the language of instruction. The physical accommodations are poor; the food served is inadequate. They have neither facilities nor time for play. But their devotion to the study of Torah is so intense that any sacrifice would be readily forthcoming.

Children of elementary school age in these centuries-old yeshivot are required by the state to learn the Hebrew language and also arithmetic. There is some compliance with the law, but only as a concession to the state and not because of any conviction that a pious Jew should "waste" time on secular subjects. Practically all of these children can converse in Hebrew, fluency in which they acquire from their sisters who attend the state religious schools.

The older Talmudic students devote all their time to their studies; the more industrious even devote their evenings as well to Torah. They receive small stipends to keep body and soul together. Some of these Talmudic students, especially the married ones, may be enrolled in two yeshivot, one for the morning session and the other for the afternoon, to benefit from two stipends.

All over Israel new yeshivot have risen to meet the needs of the religious Jews who are deeply concerned with the perpetuation of Torah in the Holy Land. Most of these new yeshivot are housed in modern edifices and employ academic methods of instruction with great zeal not only for learning but for the progress of the land as well.

Some of these Talmudic academies have been transplanted from Eastern Europe in fulfillment of the Jewish pledge that "Torah will never be forgotten in the life of Israel"; others have been founded by scholarly, religious elements in Israel to help unite the two major Jewish forces, Torah and nation, in the service of God. Talmud study in Israel is entering on a new era of expansion.

The new settlers in the ma'barah, both young and old, while waiting for their permanent homes, go through a special process of education to prepare them for the new life. In addition to language, many of them are taught the elements of hygiene, diet, occupation and trade. The task is none too simple. Many of the menfolk bring with them the notion that fathers at the age of 40 are already too old to labor for a living and it is their children's duty to support them. So rooted is this tradition with the Oriental immigrants that, in one instance at least, a whole encampment fled from the assigned ma'barah because "their new Israeli teacher was corrupting the morals of their children" by telling them that their fathers at the age of 40 and over can still be productive and capable of learning new trades to support their families.

One of the truly great accomplishments in Israel's educational system is the refashioning of the lives of the new immigrants. The physically able, young and old, attend classes to acquire the language of the land and learn improved living standards. Those incapable of attending classes are taught at home by private tutors, many of them volunteers. The aim is to adjust the new immigrants as quickly as feasible to the life of Israel, linguistically, economically and culturally.

The secondary school in Israel does not have the democratic base of the primary school. Of the 16,000 graduates of the elementary schools in 1956, a considerable number never entered the high school system. Because of the rapid increase of school population it is estimated that within five years the number of graduates may be doubled, but a corresponding expansion of secondary education is questionable.

Because the secondary schools charge a tuition of between 350 and 600 IL per annum, large numbers of elementary school graduates find the financial obligation an impediment to continued education. For the present at least the government budget dictates a policy of high school education for the more talented students only. The more studious pupils, however, need not be prevented from receiving a secondary school education because of lack of finances. Seven thousand of the elementary school graduates receive through competitive examinations at least a partial free scholarship from the state, the Jewish Agency or other sources. Others with lower qualifications may enter a high school if the parents are willing and able to assume the tuition fee.

Another reason for the comparatively smaller high school registration is geographic. Out of more than 900 Jewish settlements in Israel, only about 100 have a population in excess of 1,000 souls each. The smaller settlements cannot maintain high schools of their own. Boarding plus a tuition fee makes a secondary education for those too distant from a district high school prohibitive. The especially gifted students, however, find their way to a higher education despite all barriers. Under the auspices of the Labor Ministry, in cooperation with the Ministry of Education and Culture, elementary school graduates not attending high school are taught trades and skills and are afforded opportunities for the exercise of their cultural interests as well.

The newer youthful immigrants are enabled to learn and to earn simultaneously. In many instances their parents, incapable of immediate adjustment to the new life, depend on the nominal income of their children to supplement the aid they receive from the Jewish Agency, thus adding slight material benefits in order to help maintain self-respect.

Eight thousand students devote themselves to undergraduate and graduate studies in the higher institutions of learning in Israel: the Hebrew University, the Haifa Technion, the Weizmann Institute, the Bar Ilan University and the Tel Aviv University Institutes. If teacher training schools and agricultural colleges were included in the category of higher education, the number of students would be considerably larger.

The prophecy, "Out of Zion shall go forth the law and the word of the Lord from Jerusalem," has from time immemorial been deeply imbedded in Jewish consciousness. The ideal to make Jerusalem the seat of higher Jewish learning was always present with those who dreamed of a Jewish national home in the Holy Land.

In the 1880's Professor Hermann Schapira conceived the idea of a Hebrew university for the fulfillment of the prophetic vision that Jerusalem was destined to become a light unto the nations. He presented his proposal to the First Zionist Congress in 1897 and it was incorporated in the Zionist program of 1913. Following the conquest of Palestine by General Allenby, Weizmann laid the foundation stone for the Hebrew University on Mount Scopus in 1918, and it was opened by Lord Arthur James Balfour in 1925 in the presence of Jewish and world dignitaries.

As the first president of the Hebrew University, Dr. Judah Leon Magnes, American-born rabbi (1877-1948), and prominent advocate of a bi-national (Arab-Jewish) state in Palestine, helped raise the Hebrew University to international recognition.

The University suffered a temporary setback in the War for Independence when its campus on Mount Scopus fell into Arab hands. A new campus at Givat Ram, one of Jerusalem's suburbs, was established with almost two dozen splendid edifices for instruction, administration and student residence already completed or in the process of erection.

With the Hadassah-Hebrew University Medical Center now under construction, the Jerusalem University will become the most outstanding institution of learning in all of the Middle East. The building costs and the budgetary needs are largely met by Jewry of the free world. The student body, numbering over 4,000 in 1957, comprises mature and serious-minded young people, most of whom showed outstanding ability and talent in their high school careers and passed matriculation examinations demonstrating their fitness for higher studies.

The average student is over 20, due primarily to the fact that the larger number of registrants are required to complete their military training before entering the university. Though class attendance is not compulsory, the students, because of their genuine eagerness for learning, attend lectures regularly, unless the professor or lecturer makes no contribution to their thinking or knowledge. In such cases the teacher will soon become aware of his unpopularity by excessive absences on the part of the students. They are tolerant of a professor's personal idiosyncracies or political views, but they will practically boycott lectures devoid of intellectual stimulus. In addition to intensive study, the students are compelled to seek gainful employment for self-support during their student career.

The teaching staff of nearly 600 includes men of high standing in their respective fields. The university's 4,600 students are distributed among 6 faculties: humanities, science, law, medicine (which includes the school of pharmacy and school of dentistry), social sciences and agriculture. Since its opening up to 1957, the University has graduated 316 Ph.D.'s, 321 M.D.'s, over 2,267 Masters of Arts and Sciences and over 686 Bachelors of Arts. Graduates of the various faculties have already proven their worth through their professional and intellectual contributions to the progress of the people and land of Israel.

The Haifa Technion, founded in 1912, began its formal

courses of teaching in 1924. It has since become the "M.I.T. of the Middle East." Because of its ever-increasing student body, it has outgrown its physical facilities in the heart of the port city and has opened a new campus with six new attractive buildings already completed ideally located on the summit of Mount Carmel. Its staff of more than 450, teaching a student body of over 2,500, is devoted to instruction as well as research. Besides the training of engineers, architects and technicians of various types, the Haifa Technion also serves Israel in the fields of industry and agriculture through advice and guidance. More than half of the engineers now practicing in Israel are graduates of Technion. Like the Hebrew University, its advancement in physical facilities, student body and staff has been made possible and is still being furthered by the generosity of world Jewry.

The largest unit of population in Israel is concentrated in and around Tel Aviv. The Hebrew University is located in Jerusalem. Therefore, persons in the Tel Aviv area who desire college or university training must live away from home with added expenses and fewer opportunities for part-time employment. At present the Tel Aviv University Institutes, founded in 1935, offer opportunities for higher education in limited fields. There is a faculty of 135 and a student body of nearly 1,300 in departments of law, economics, natural sciences, Jewish culture and the humanities. Because of Tel Aviv's large and increasing population, its university institutes are destined to grow and develop either into an independent university or as a branch of the Hebrew University in Jerusalem.

In addition to the higher education facilities within the country, nearly 2,100 Israeli students study abroad in 16 countries, majoring in subjects of special interest to the future well-being of Israel. Practically one-half of this number reside and study in the United States, with the United Kingdom affording educational opportunities to about 400. France and Switzerland train nearly 150 Israeli students each and the rest are to be found in other countries.

The Weizmann Institute at Rehovot is the most fitting living memorial to the great life and career Dr. Weizmann gave to Israel. His distinguished achievements in the political arena for Zionism were completed with the establishment of the State of Israel. The Weizmann Institute's accomplishments are endless. Dr. Weizmann was not only a world-famous Zionist leader but a man of practical vision in the world of science. He recognized the natural limitations of the Holy Land. To rejuvenate its ancient resources and create new ones, the Weizmann Institute was first established in 1934. It was then known as the Sief Institute to further scientific research both pure and applied; it was renamed and expanded as the Weizmann Institute in 1949. A notable scientific staff of 150 is provided with the best facilities obtainable to carry on for a more abundant and significant life in the Holy Land, with a program aspiring to add to the well-being of all mankind.

When the Bar Ilan University, under religious auspices, opened its doors in 1955 at Ramat Gan, there were skeptics who doubted the need for it and the possibility of its success. How differently can mathematics, physics or any other science be taught under religious auspices than under a secular administration, they queried?

Bar Ilan in the brief period of its existence has proven its raison d'être. True, scientific subjects can be taught only as science irrespective of religious attitudes. However, Bar Ilan has demonstrated its worth by making the Bible, Talmud and Jewish philosophy required subjects of instruction instead of electives. Also life in the dormitories and leisure hours are spent in a religious atmosphere with public worship and prayers at meals as part of the student's routine. In addition, it is a new experiment in college education in Israel. The Hebrew University is modeled after its European scholastic counterpart, while Bar Ilan follows the methods employed by the American undergraduate college. With a student body of 300 and a teaching staff of 50, it promises to make a noteworthy contribution to higher education in Israel.

Considering its limited dimensions both in population and geography, Israel, burdened by military and economic problems, has done remarkably well during its first decade in the field of higher education. However, the cultural character of a nation should not be measured by its intellectual aristocracy but by the general level of learning of the majority of its people. In the extension of education Israel has excelled beyond the expectations of the most hopeful. Its cultural activities cover a wide range, some of them under government auspices and others under independent initiative.

Israel today responds sincerely and with alacrity to the monition of the Persian poet: "If thou hast two pennies, spend one for bread and with the other buy hyacinths for thy soul."

There is a hunger in the land, not for bread but for the word, spoken and written. Ulpan, the extension school for adults organized and devoted primarily to the teaching of Hebrew to the new immigrants, has become a remarkable agency for the integration of the newcomer with the new-old land. The number of classes and students varies with varying needs. In 1953 there was a monthly average attendance of 17,500 students in 1,234 classes. The enthusiasm of the students, the single-hearted devotion of the teachers and the most advanced methods of language instruction are largely responsible for the revival of Hebrew as the unifying language of the country. In and out of class, through government aid, private initiative and voluntary home teaching, Hebrew has become the established tongue of the land with no fear of competition from any of the languages which the immigrants bring with them.

In the early Zionist days Yiddish—the vernacular of the Jews from Eastern Europe—was considered a threat to the primacy of Hebrew in Israel. No longer is there any need for the "Guardians of Hebrew" to wage war in defense of the classical language of the Bible. The Hebraic atmosphere is now dominant in the land. Ulpan is no longer an extension school for beginners only. Advanced courses in Hebrew and literature as well as studies of foreign languages have become part of its program.

The number of adult study groups in all phases of Jewish learning, including the humanities and sciences, under private auspices, is difficult to estimate. But they are extremely numerous.

Learning in Israel is more than a routine or pleasant interlude; it has become the essence of living; in fact, a passionate pursuit. It is no exaggeration to state that only few are untouched by the craving for enlightenment in Israel. The familiar dictum: "Talmud Torah k'neged kulom," freely translated, that "learning is coextensive with life," or that learning supersedes all, is applicable to Israel. If this be true in city and town, it is even more so in the isolated, rural kibbutz where the evenings are spent in studies both to promote the efficiency of their agricultural economy and to advance their cultural interests.

The widespread purchase and reading of books is a true barometer of a nation's cultural development. There seems to be no end to book publishing in Israel. In 1955 the Jewish population was a little over 1,500,000. Twelve hundred books were newly published that year with a total sale of close to 3,000,000 copies, averaging therefore two copies per person, including children of all ages. Of the books published, 40 per cent were translations from the literatures of the world, the remainder of the 700 odd titles represented new editions of religious works or new subjects exploring every field of human endeavor.

The libraries, too, indicate the caliber of a people. Besides the National University Library of 800,000 volumes, the country supports 582 public libraries located in every section of the land with a total of 2,000,000 volumes and 135 school libraries estimated to house 250,000 volumes. There are no statistics detailing the vast number of books in private home libraries, but a home in Israel that does not have at least a shelf of books is held in low esteem.

In the field of newspapers, periodicals and magazines in Israel the record would be even more extensive were it not for the high cost of paper and newsprint. The widespread attention that greets the published word of current interest is clear from these figures: the country boasts 28 daily newspapers with an average daily circulation of 340,000 copies and on Fridays the number reaches 416,000. Considering that in many instances a single copy is scanned by all the adult members of a family, it is not incorrect to state that practically everyone in Israel reads a newspaper. Of the 28 daily newspapers, 16 are published in Hebrew, 13 morning and three afternoon editions. The other 12 newspapers, printed in foreign languages, have an average daily circulation of 103,000 and on Fridays slightly higher, 111,000. Because of the high cost of newsprint and frequent shortages, most of the daily papers are limited in size, four sheets to the copy with larger editions on Friday. But despite the size they are newsworthy and of fine quality devoted largely to national and international news with editorials and articles of high character.

The large variety of newspapers is due primarily to the fact that most of them are founded and conducted as party organs. The number of periodicals and magazines published in Israel is equally substantial. Altogether there are 280 periodicals of which 230 are printed in Hebrew and 50 in other languages. With the exception of the most popular weeklies and monthlies which feature pictures and photos as the attraction to win the attention of the reading public, the vast majority of them are serious efforts dealing with literature, religion, economics, politics and all other areas of human interest.

In the world of arts, too, Israel gives a good account of herself. In the year 1954-55, the three largest theater groups presented 31 plays with 1,597 performances drawing an attendance of 1,475,000. The Habimah Theater presented 13 plays with

516 performances attended by 500,000; the Ohel Company presented seven plays with 358 performances attended by 175,000; and the Chamber Theater, 11 plays with 663 performances with an attendance of 800,000. The above figures do not include the small experimental theater, which is also of artistic worth.

In music, there has been a deep interest as well. The Israeli Philharmonic Orchestra alone during 1954-55, presented 146 concerts, with an attendance of over 200,000. Smaller, less prominent concerts helped also to fill the air of the land with harmony. Among the musical bodies are also the Israel Army Defense Orchestra, Air Force Orchestra, Gadna Youth Orchestra, Kol Israel Orchestra, maintained by the State Broadcasting Service, and the Haifa Orchestra.

In the Israel musical sphere must also be included the various chamber music groups and the opera, whose shortcomings primarily are due to lack of facilities rather than to a shortage of talent. Choral groups are to be found everywhere in the land. The Histadrut—National Labor Organization—alone, maintains 200 choirs with 12,000 members.

Because Israel has become the focus of settlement for Jews from every part of the world, folk songs of their respective lands of origin together with the chanting of Biblical passages have found reinterpretation. The study of song and instrumental music and the perfection of the musical arts are given special emphasis in Israel, which now supports a number of institutions devoted to all phases of music with 400 instructors and 2,750 students. Of the 80 members of the Philharmonic Orchestra 12 are sabras—natives—who received their musical inspiration and training in the Holy Land. For much of the progress in the musical arts the contributing members of the American Fund for Israel Institution are deserving of Israel's enduring gratitude.

Some of the other artistic phases of Israeli life such as painting and sculpture have not been neglected in Israel. In the past, due to religious and historic reasons, this expression of the creative arts did not always evoke an affirmative Jewish response. Modern Israel has reversed this trend. Art has become intrenched as a subject of instruction in the general scheme of education. Special institutions are devoted to the advancement of the arts. Almost everywhere in Israel there are museums for the exhibition of artistic masterpieces, native and foreign. Of the three largest museums, the long-established Bezalel in Jerusalem, founded by Boris Schatz in 1906 and which also maintains a school of the arts, drew an attendance of 66,000 in 1954. The Tel Aviv Municipal Museum had an attendance of 70,000 and the Haifa Museum 50,000 in the same year.

Considering the high quality of radio broadcasting in Israel, its programs may be included in the category of culture. In 1955 there were 380,000 radio receivers in Israel, each registered and paying an annual tax.

Surprisingly high is the number of movie-goers in Israel, with American pictures in the greatest demand. Israel now has 160 established movie houses with a seating capacity of 110,000. Tel Aviv counts 20 movie theaters and its bordering city of Jaffa five, Jerusalem has 11 cinemas and Haifa 24. The rest of the country has 95 cinemas distributed from one to five per locality, depending on the population of the locality. The total attendance at these theaters is staggeringly high. In 1955 there were 27,000,000 admissions, of which Tel Aviv's share was over 9,000,000. Haifa had an attendance of 5,000,000 and Jerusalem 2,500,000. Deducting the infants, who are not counted in the admissions, and the very aged and extremely religious, who do not indulge in such forms of entertainment, it appears that in the cities and towns the average attendance per person at the movies is very close to 25 per year, or once every second week.

Israel has an official Board of Review to pass on the fitness of all the motion pictures shown, but only seven of the large number viewed were found objectionable, three for political reasons, three for depicting brutality and crime and one for propaganda reasons. The Board of Review treats the population as adults capable of serving as their own board of censors to discriminate between the good and the trash, and will not substitute its will for the will of the people.

Together with the movies, American jazz makes a fairly popular appeal to the younger generation. Athletic contests are also a powerful drawing card to the youth. The Sabbath being the only day free from regular occupations, most of the sports events take place on the day of rest, with religious elements, of course, absent. While nominal admissions are charged to cover the expenses of the teams, sports are not conducted for profit. The income is used for the maintenance of the fields and for the transportation costs of the players but not for salaries or bonuses of any kind.

The younger generation is well organized in clubs for the spending of leisure in hikes, sports, social and cultural events and for the advancement of their patriotic programs under the auspices of such movements as the Boy and Girl Scouts and the Gadna, student military groups.

Israel is very much alive—a dynamic, pulsating country with a vibrant people. To the Israeli, illiteracy is akin to the misfortune of blindness. Therefore, next to their primary concern for the defense of country, they wage war on ignorance through elementary, secondary and higher education. Learning is limited to neither age nor to class. The acquisition of knowledge is everybody's business.

The people of Israel are indeed the "people of the book." They read, they listen, they attend forums and participate in discussions. They thus become keenly aware of their immediate world and of the world of mankind around them. They recognize that none can live without bread but they are resolved that none shall live by bread alone. The cultural, the intellectual, the spiritual and the esthetic exert a potent, tangible impact on them. Like the sun worshipers of old, they seek the innermost of life. And they are on their way to the attainment of a new kind of existence, the free, creative, joyous life.

VIII. The Heart of a People

Israel is not yet politically or even ideologically a welfare state. But unless the present trend is reversed, it will gradually move toward it. Neither the idea nor the trend makes many Israeli jittery. Even if the conservative elements adhering to the principle of free enterprise were in power, the process might be retarded but not completely halted.

The present coalition government, with the Socialists in the dominant role, does not vigorously strive for "Socialism in our day." Ben Gurion's party is guided more by practical considerations than social theories. The blueprint for the welfare state is held in abeyance until and if theory and practice merge. In the meantime there seems to be general agreement that everything that can be done must be done for the underprivileged and socially maladjusted.

Social welfare in Israel is concerned with all who lack the capacity for self-help and with the rebuilding of the life of the individual as a member of his family, including the child, the young and the adult, the aged and the sick. Deep and spontaneous interest in the well-being and dignity of the individual and of his family, accompanied by practical measures to improve the status of woman, to protect the helpless and support the poor, is a long-cherished ideal rooted in Israel's past.

Jewish tradition has always distinguished between hesed—a casual act of kindness—and zedakah—righteousness or justice—interpreted as an obligation to aid the unfortunate. To serve God in truth is to serve His children in need. Hence the Biblical injunction against harvesting the corners of the field, the law to leave the gleanings for the poor and the apportionment of tithes for social needs.

Maimonides, renowned philosopher and codifier, made zedakah—justice to the poor—the very heart of Judaism. "It is incumbent upon us to be heedful of the commandment of zedakah above all other commandments. The basis for the existence of the Holy Throne and the religion of Israel is zedakah. Furthermore, Israel cannot be redeemed except through justice to the needy. As it is said, 'Zion will be redeemed through law and its returnees through justice.' "

Judaism is not only concerned with the care of the needy but with their dignity as well. Therefore the "hand-out" or the dole, which degrades human personality, is frowned upon by Jewish tradition. For charity in that sense of the term there is no word in the Hebrew language. According to Maimonides the highest form of charity is that which makes charity unnecessary, by the grant of a loan, or the offer of a partnership or by providing the needy with gainful employment so that he need not rely on gifts or favors. This principle of constructive help for the purpose of rebuilding lives has become the established policy of the State of Israel in the conduct of its Welfare Department.

Since the welfare agencies, public and private, regard the family as the unit of society, it is well to consider first the constitution of the family as a legal entity and then the social problems arising when the family is broken up as a result of the dissolution of marriage.

Monogamy is the law of the land. Jewish religious law prohibiting polygamy began with the ban of Rabbi Gershom ben Judah in the 11th century, applicable only to the Ashkenazim of German Jewish origin. The Sephardic Jew, primarily of Oriental origin, did not adhere to the ban. The Israeli state law, however, applies to all the inhabitants of the land, including the Arab minorities who were granted a five-year period in which to adjust themselves to the new legislation. Sephardic Jews who bring with them to Israel more than one wife may continue their marital status except when a wife is still a minor, since the state prohibits child marriages. The minimum marriage age for women is 17 years and consent of parents is of no avail to set aside this age requirement. No minimum age has been set for men. The average age of men marrying in 1954 was 27 years and four months and of women, 22 years and eight months.

Oriental Jews differ from those of European origin in their marital attitudes and relations. Among the former, dowry is the obligation of the groom rather than of the bride, with added material consideration to her parents for the privilege of acquiring a wife. When the marriage, however, is between a younger man and a formerly married woman, it is the wife who brings the dowry to compensate for the difference in age and premarital status.

The Oriental Jewish family is normally larger than that of the European Jew; the woman's position is less independent and greater physical burdens age her prematurely.

By and large the position of the Jewish woman in Israel is a favorable one. There are no legal discriminations because of sex. On the contrary, numerous special laws and regulations to protect her interests and well-being have been enacted. Sex equality under law is basic in the government principles, universally accepted: "These laws will safeguard full and complete equality of rights and duties to all residents of the state regardless of sex, race, status and nationality."

In the Arab world it is still customary for the male to ride a donkey with the wife or wives following behind on foot while balancing burdensome luggage on their heads; in Israel, the Jewish woman is rapidly progressing to a position of partnership and equality with her husband. Gradually the Arab woman will fare likewise.

Israel, like all pioneering countries, has a larger population of males than of females. In 1955 there were 807,000 Jewish males and 783,000 females. In the most frequent marriageable age bracket, between 15 and 24, there were in that year 118,000 females and 126,000 males. Only in the age group between 65 and 74 do the figures indicate a larger population of females than males: 29,000 to 24,000, a longevity that appears in most civilized countries.

A larger percentage of married women are gainfully employed in addition to carrying on home duties to supplement the income of husbands in order to meet the necessities of life. In 1954 the number of males employed were 63,500 single, 198,723 married and 3,361 widowed or divorced, a total of 265,000. Women employed in the various occupations equaled more than 25 per cent of male workers: 25,635 single, 40,643 married and 8,605 widows and divorcees. Despite woman's equality under law, she does not as yet receive equal pay for equal tasks.

In the food industry, man's average wage is 250 IL per month, woman's 163 IL. In the textile field, man's average monthly pay is 289 IL to 169 IL for women. In clothing and footwear, the proportion is 201 to 140; meat, machinery and electric appliances, 229 to 136; printing and paper, 246 to 154 and chemicals, 253 to 163. While it is true that in some industries women do lighter work and therefore receive less pay, it is equally true that where woman's work is as arduous as that of man's, her wage scale does not equal his.

Woman's participation in every facet of life in Israel is universally recognized. In the Third Knesset, 11 women representing a variety of parties make their voices heard. Among the government employees, permanent and temporary, in 1955 there were 18,731 men and 6,098 women, 2,817 married, 2,359 single, 342 divorcees and 566 widows.

In the teaching profession the number of women almost equaled that of men: 5,786 male and 5,528 female, 3,392 married, 1,640 single and 246 widowed or divorced.

There are 900 women doctors in Israel, almost a quarter of all the physicians in the land. Close to 100 women are lawyers. Gradually, women find their niche in every profession, art and craft. Israel harbors no distinction between the sexes in educational opportunities.

While in the Moslem population in the school year of 1954-55 there were 18,232 boys to 7,115 girls, in the Jewish population no disparity existed. In the field of higher education, too, the progress has been very impressive. In 1955 there were 1,019 female students to 3,269 male at the Hebrew University with 59 to 152 receiving B.A. degrees; 42 to 21 M.A.'s, 17 to 57 M.D.'s and 7 to 47 Ph.D.'s.

In the schools of law and economics in Tel Aviv and Haifa there were 148 women students to 1,072 men. The Haifa Technion numbered 105 female out of the 1,401 students in the day session and 11 out of 240 in the evening. Among the graduate engineers, numbering 189, 13 were women, and 18 received the M.A. degree compared to 274 males. In the Doctor of Science degrees 50 per cent were conferred upon women.

Even the Bar Ilan University, under religious auspices, counted 41 female students to 120 male in 1955. Not only has the Jewish woman become an important factor in the economic, professional, cultural, artistic and higher educational fields in Israel, but she has taken her place alongside men in the military defense of the land. In the army, in the air force and in the outpost settlements, the Israeli Jewish woman is the equal of man in her readiness to protect country and home. The intelligence and independence of women in Israel have augmented the demands for greater social welfare while simultaneously enhancing the quality of self-reliance.

Next to the improved status of woman in a social welfare program, the size of the family and the housing situation are immediate problems. The size of the average immigrant family (excluding those who came as individual units) has been on the increase, primarily with the heavy influx from Oriental lands. In 1952-53 the average size of the immigrant family was 3.3; in 1954, 4.4 and in 1955, 4.8.

Among the natives, too, there has been an increase in size of family. The number of persons per room varies with each locality. It should be noted, however, that the one-room unit means a living and bedroom combination, a small kitchen, a bathroom and small hallway. The lowest urban category is in Ramat Gan with 1.7 persons per room and the highest is to be found in Haifa with Ramle in a close race of 3.5 persons per room.

A movement toward the suburbs is increasing in Israel for the purpose of providing more breathing space for the younger generation despite the inconvenience and cost of transportation.

The landlord situation is not to be envied, with the tenant as the beneficiary of state and municipal regulations. "Key money" is one of the aggravated problems. When a tenant moves he is privileged to sublet his residence for a consideration, thus depriving the landlord of choice of occupant and profit. The government has already partially corrected this inequity by allowing the landlord one-third of the "key-money." Perhaps, in the none too distant future, an adequate solution will be found to the entire problem.

The average income is 2,000 IL per annum for the employed in the various occupations and only slightly higher for the self-employed. Compared to income or wages in the rest of the Middle East this is high, and it approximates the scale in many European countries though it is considerably lower (less than one-half) than in the United States.

The kibbutz—commune—family is differently constituted from the rest of the population. A close relationship between parents and children is woven into the fabric of the group life. In some quarters resistance to the collective raising of children is in evidence and, in the main, the original family theory still prevails in the kibbutz. The traditional style of marriage, however, is regaining favor and the concept of greater sex freedom has been largely abandoned. The parents have accepted for themselves and for their children a code of strict behavior. The radical spirit has spent itself and reversion to the older norm of marriage is on the upgrade.

The children are still practically the wards of the kibbutz. They live in youth houses, cared for during their infancy by nurses, and as they grow older, by kindergarteners, teachers and guides, thus freeing the mothers from child care for the productive labors of the kibbutz, although they are by no means kept rigidly apart from the children. Visits between parents and children are reserved for the daily leisure hours and the days of Sabbath and festival. The adherents of separate quarters for youths and parents prefer this arrangement rather than constant, close contact between the older and younger generations. They insist that the quality of relationship does not suffer when children are raised under a separate roof. They even claim advantages such as specialized child care and economic gain to the kibbutz. Parents are not permitted to spoil their children.

According to the advocates of collective responsibility for the raising of children, most mothers lacking in scientific training are incapable of performing their tasks as effectively as the professional nurse and teacher. As to love and affection, the theory holds that under the kibbutz plan the parents see their children in a festive mood only, without the petty annoyances often occurring when the family lives under one roof. Thus the parents and their offspring learn to know and respect each other under favorable conditions conducive to love and high fidelity for one another. That such mothers relieved of child care become a valuable economic asset to the settlement is self-evident. There is a third benefit derived from the opportunity afforded the younger generation for a cooperative way of life, by learning to share blessings and hardships in the building of a nobler society.

The cohesiveness of the Jewish family has been an important factor in the survival of Jewish life throughout the generations. Faithful marital relationship and respect for parental authority have been the two cardinal principles binding the Jewish family into a powerful bond of unity. Though the Jewish religion always took a liberal view of divorce, there were comparatively few broken Jewish homes in the past.

This tradition no longer prevails in the same degree in modern Israel. The following figures indicate a trend which, while not alarming when compared to other civilized communities where divorce is not prohibited by Church or state, is nevertheless disquieting. In 1948 there were 938 divorces to 7,291 marriages, a ratio of about 1 to 7. In 1949 there were 1,513 divorces to 12,076 marriages, or 1 to 8. In 1950, 2,348 divorces to 16,039 marriages, which shows a similar trend of 1 to 7. The following year, a slight decline in the rate between divorce and marriage is indicated. In 1951 there were 2,373 divorces to 15,556 marriages or 1 to about 6½. In 1952 the proportion was 2,428 divorces to 16,040 marriages, again a ratio of almost 1 to 6½. In the year 1953 the ratio was close to that of the previous year, namely 14,037 marriages to 2,304 divorces. The ratio was 1 to 6 in 1954, *i.e.,* 13,343 to 2,209 and in 1955 there were 13,457 marriages to 2,131 divorces, a ratio of 1 to 6½. In the U.S. the divorce rate is approximately 30 per cent of the marriages.

While Judaism does not consider divorce immoral, it was viewed in the past as a tragedy comparable only to the destruction of the Holy Temple, primarily because of the plight of the children caused by the shattered home. An increase in the divorce rate also spells an added burden to the social welfare problem. However, from close observation it appears that the aggravated situation resulting from the disrupted family in Israel today is only temporary in nature, having been brought about through special immigration conditions.

The largest number of divorces in the past decade occurred among the Oriental immigrant population, of whom the women in their native lands were of inferior status both in practice and law. In Israel the Oriental Jewish woman won her freedom. She promptly rebelled against her marriage, which was consummated without her consent. In numerous instances, a child wife would enter a primary school to gain freedom. The authoritarian manner of the husband, his torrid Oriental temper as well as the wife's unwillingness to seek gainful employment frequently resulted in the break-up of marital relations.

Among the European refugees also the number of divorces is higher than that of Israel's native population. Some of the refugee marriages were prompted more by loneliness than love, and frequently there was a considerable difference in age. Many such marriages ended in divorce in Israel. When the Oriental and European immigrants will have been fully merged into the life of Israel, surely not later than the next generation, the divorce rate will inevitably decline. Only when convinced that dissolution of marriage is in the best interests of all concerned are the parties compelled, the husband to grant and the wife to accept a divorce.

The rabbinical courts to whose jurisdiction matters of the family are referred, before granting a divorce, most frequently employ their influence for a reconciliation.

By law and popular acceptance, the Department of Social Welfare deals with the family as a unit and promotes the mutual responsibility of the members thereof. The social welfare budget, amounting to about 11,000,000 IL, is devoted to the alleviation of hardships and to the rehabilitation of victims of misfortune. In the year 1953-54 the Department of Social Welfare dealt with 60,000 Jewish and 6,000 non-Jewish families totaling approximately 230,000 persons. In the Jewish area there were: 13,000 aged, 11,000 chronically sick, 6,500 seriously ill, 5,200 invalids, 7,800 families with a large number of children, 6,300 cases of absentee mates, 2,600 unemployed because of age, 2,000 cases of disrupted family life and 1,800 persons distressed by lack of or inadequate housing plus 10,000 children's problems consisting of truancy, misbehavior, parental neglect, delinquency and mental retardation. The proportion of boys to girls was approximately 6,000 to 4,000.

All the welfare cases were handled by 700 social service workers of whom two-thirds received their training in the land, the balance abroad, and there were some with no formal training except in the school of practical experience.

Israel now has two schools for social workers, one in Jerusalem sponsored by the Department of Social Welfare and the other in Tel Aviv conducted in cooperation with the municipality. A plan for the organization of a three-year course for social workers at the Hebrew University leading to the B.S.S. degree has recently become a realized fact.

The number of Arab social workers is insignificant. There are only two Arab students in the Jerusalem School for Social Work. These few have to carry a very heavy load of cases of 700 families comprising 6,000 individuals under their care.

In Israel's coalition government, the Ministry of Welfare has been assigned to the minority party of Mizrachi—Religious Group. Thus its leadership has been vested in the religious elements. The large majority of the professional social workers, however, are not identified with the religious party and in no way affect the cooperative relationship between the political heads and the civil servants.

Social service activities began in 1931 in pre-Israel Palestine under the leadership of Henrietta Szold, who infused the workers with a spirit of self-dedication. Since the establishment of Israel, the Department of Social Welfare has assumed the responsibilities which formerly were held under volunteer auspices. The major portion of the budget is spent for direct relief, but as the new immigrants become more self-reliant permanent solution of the problem of the less fortunate will render temporary doles unnecessary.

The Welfare Department in Israel deals not only with individual cases but with voluntary institutions caring for the orphaned, the widowed, the sick and the homeless. Since their major support is derived from Diaspora Jews, they are reluctant to accept the state's supervisory authority. Most of these institutions are well-intentioned, but not always efficiently managed. The department prefers to follow a policy of noninterference unless a bad situation demands corrective measures which are accomplished through public trustees appointed for such purpose.

The work of the Department of Social Welfare is a blending of the scientific approach with the traditional Jewish principle of help for the needy: prevention of pauperism, sympathetic and unhampered, however, by bureaucratic red tape. The old Jewish adage is the guiding principle of the selfless social worker in Israel. Examine the needs of the applicant for aid, but when he is hungry satisfy his immediate needs first and examine him afterwards.

The largest number of needy applicants are the unemployed, those temporarily out of work or those who find it difficult, because of their inability as immigrants, to fit into the economy of the land. The hungry and the destitute look to the Histadrut —the National Labor Union—and to the Saad—the relief agency of the Welfare Department.

In the flood of the modern Jewish movement to the Holy Land, there was a remarkable fulfillment of Jeremiah's prophecy: ". . . and I shall gather them from the uttermost parts of the earth, and with them the blind and the lame, the woman with child and her that travaileth with child together; a great company shall they return hither." Under the present large and unrestricted influx of immigrants suffering from physical limitations and psychological difficulties, it is inevitable that the list of the needy requiring bread and shelter is high. But despite the great demands for relief, the minimum requirements are met.

In health care, there has been a phenomenal advance. A country which for centuries was infested with malaria, trachoma, TB etc. has been converted in the brief span of a generation into one of the world's healthiest. This outstanding accomplishment began with the work of Hadassah—the Woman's Zionist Organization of America—in 1913. First, two nurses for mother and child care were sent to Jerusalem. A half decade later Hadassah took charge of the first American Zionist medical unit consisting of 44 specialists in health and hygiene as well as a contingent of nurses. From these modest beginnings the health system in Israel grew to unprecedented proportions. By the end of 1955, 37 years after the first medical unit landed in the Holy Land, Israel's health guardians numbered 4,064 physicians, 937 dentists, 403 dental practitioners, 897 pharmacists, about 6,100 nurses and 233 midwives.

Israel has a larger percentage of doctors in relation to its population than any other country in the world. But like the situation everywhere else, the doctors are concentrated in the urban areas where the opportunity for a more specialized practice and financial rewards are better, resulting in a shortage of physicians in the rural areas.

The importance of health care in Israel is evidenced by the large number of student nurses. In 1955-56, the number grew to 858. In the decade of Israel's political independence about 1,500 nurses were trained and licensed to practice their profession compared to 1,335 in the previous 30 years. Israel is a leader in the civilized world in the rate of nursing service as illustrated by these figures: in 1955-56 Israel had 3.3 nurses per 1,000 population; Norway, 2.6; Sweden, 2.1; United States, 2.; Poland, 1.3; Yugoslavia, 0.6; Greece, 0.1 and India in 1953, also 0.1.

Health in Israel is guarded by private voluntary agencies under state authority and by the Ministry of Health. The ministry, working on a budget of 22,000,000 IL, maintains a staff of 4,889, of whom 434 are physicians, 2,107 nurses (693 registered and 1,414 practical), 45 pharmacists, 153 laboratory assistants, 32 social workers, 14 clinical psychologists, 133 technical and academic personnel, 681 clerical help, 1,197 general and maintenance workers, 93 drivers, etc. Some 75 per cent of the Health Department staff are employed in hospitals with one-fourth of the budget devoted to hospital grants.

Israel now has 100 hospitals: 33 general, 26 mental, 22 chronic diseases, nine TB, nine maternity and one Hansen's disease. In 1956 Israel maintained a total of 12,300 beds compared to 4,600 in 1948, of which 4,480 were under the direction of the Ministry of Health and the balance were maintained by other agencies: Kupat Holim—the General Sick Fund of the National Labor Organization, 1,915 beds; private hospitals numbering 1,835 beds, mainly for mental cases and other chronic diseases; Malben, 1,524 beds devoted to the treatment of tuberculosis and chronic diseases only; municipal hospitals, 818 beds; Hadassah, 687 beds and other public and Christian hospitals, 959 beds.

Compared to other civilized countries, Israel has done well in the number of beds for the sick in proportion to her population. While the United States for all types of cases, general, tuberculosis and mental, averages 9.8 beds per 1,000 population, with Norway and Belgium close runners-up and Sweden the highest with 10.9 beds per 1,000 population, Israel provides six beds per 1,000. This is considerably higher than most countries, especially when compared to her neighbor, Egypt, which maintains only 1.6 beds per 1,000 population and India among the lowest, 0.6 beds per 1,000.

The efforts invested in the health of the nation have brought satisfactory results. The figures of the past decade indicate a life expectancy of 69.4 years for males and 72.1 for females. The progress achieved in reducing the death rate is excellent: in 1922 the rate was 13.7 per 1,000; in 1948, 6.46 and in 1957, 6.02 per 1,000 of Jewish population. In 1955 over 42,000 Jewish children were born. In the same year there were 8,969 deaths, a proportionate rate of 27.2 births to 5.77 deaths per 1,000. The average rate of infant mortality was 32.3 per 1,000 with the lowest, 18.07, in the kibbutzim and the highest in the ma'barot—transition camps for newest immigrants—of 45.3. The non-Jewish population showed a much higher birth rate of 42.72 per 1,000 as well as a higher death rate of 8.01.

The medical advances in life saving are clear from the gradual reduction of the rate of infant mortality. In 1922 the rate of infant mortality in the Yishuv stood high at 127 per 1,000 live births; in 1948 the rate was lowered to 39.9 per 1,000 and in 1957, 32 per 1,000. Each successive year shows a marked improvement because of the prenatal care which the expectant mothers receive in ever-increasing numbers. Mortality of women at childbirth and during pregnancy has reached a very low level, .08 per 1,000. The growing numbers of births in hospitals, from 85 per cent in 1953 to 95 per cent in 1955, is another factor contributing to the lowering of infant mortality. Postnatal care and mother guidance in proper hygiene and food have also added much toward the decrease of infant mortality. By the end of 1955 Israel had 429 mother and child health stations, of which 206 were maintained by the Ministry of Health, 170 by the Kupat Holim and 53 by Hadassah and Tel Aviv municipality.

Considering the financial limitations of the Health Ministry, much has been accomplished in wiping out many of the diseases which once plagued the Jewish community in Israel.

Trachoma, so widespread in the pre- and post-mandate period, is no longer a major problem. Except for those infected with the disease in their native countries before migrating to Israel, this disease is only a sad memory. Until the swamps and marshes were drained through the heroic efforts of the builders of the new state, malaria was perhaps the severest menace to the health of the pioneers. To this very day a great deal of labor is devoted to antimalarial work, consuming 20,000 work days for the spraying of remaining malaria infected areas. But the results are most gratifying. The decrease in malaria cases has been steady and substantial. In 1950 there were 842 cases, which were reduced to 217 in 1951 with a rise to 403 in 1952 but with a gradual decline thereafter: 275 in 1953, 302 in 1954 and only 91 in 1955.

Tuberculosis, another dreaded scourge, is now gradually disappearing from the land. In 1952 there were 1,519 cases; in 1953, 1,591; in 1954, 1,202 and in 1955, 1,042. The government report substantiates the conclusion that tuberculosis is no longer the fatal plague of yesteryear. "The mortality rate from all forms of tuberculosis among Jews dropped in 1955 to 7.4 per 100,000, one of the lowest rates in the world. The following comparative figures of rates of mortality from this disease recorded in 1954 in several European countries are most instructive: Finland, 40.6 per 100,000 population; France 31.9; Switzerland, 21.4; United Kingdom, 19.0; Denmark 7.7 and Holland, 7.5."

The favorable health situation is due in no small measure to the improvement of the sanitation service and the supervision of food in its preparation and sale, together with the introduction of the pasteurization and sterilization of milk.

Among the yet unsolved health problems remain those of drinking water and adequate sewerage systems. Much attention is being given to their solution. An American firm of consulting engineers at the request of the Foreign Operations Administration is now preparing plans for water and for a sewerage system that will best serve the needs of a growing population. In the field of insect control gratifying progress has been made.

The Ministry of Health is concerned with the well-being of the Arab population as well. Unfortunately, however, gains in that direction do not measure up to the high mark attained by the Jewish community for two reasons. Because of their lower cultural level, the Arab population is less cooperative in observance of the hygienic rules of life. The second difficulty lies in the fact that Arab girls are unwilling to be trained for the nursing profession. There is no discrimination against Arabs in any of the hospitals, schools or health centers of the country. As a special concession, the ministry maintains four clinics for the Negev Bedouins as well as 13 mother and child care stations.

Infant mortality decreases to the extent to which Arab expectant mothers make use of hospitals for maternity purposes. Until recently only 5 per cent of Arab births took place in hospitals. By 1953-54 the percentage rose to 22 per cent. As to tuberculosis, which is more prevalent among Arabs, the ministry, through early examinations and detection of the disease, has already slowed down the death rate from this ravaging malady among them. Much is yet to be accomplished. With public education and patience, health progress among the Arabs is inevitable.

This problem of public education is not limited to the Arab population. The need of observing hygienic laws must be inculcated among the newer Jewish immigrants from the Arab countries as well. Many of them look with suspicion at all the "newfangled" ideas of which their fathers never heard. Sometimes even visual instruction fails to persuade them of the need for proper sanitary living.

The ministries of Education and Health, as well as other agencies, combined their efforts to reach both young and old through health stations, nurseries, kindergartens and primary schools to afford them a better appreciation of the essential sanitary and hygienic regulations for the new life in Israel today.

The accent in Israel is on youth. Through kindergartens and day schools, the Ministry of Social Welfare in 1954-55 cared for 8,500 infants and children up to the age of six, with nearly 1,000 completely institutionalized and almost 300 accommodated in foster homes. Wherever possible the family is kept intact through special subventions to maintain its cohesion and avoid the need of placement of children away from home. Sixteen hundred and fifty between the age of six and 14 in need of the state's aid were placed in various institutions in 1955 due to orphanhood, homes ruptured through divorce, remarriage of one of the parents or physical or mental incapacities.

The number of unwanted children is very small and the numbers who desire to adopt them are very considerable. The Social Service Department scrutinizes most carefully all who apply, with the result that in 1955 out of the 201 applications filed with the court only 70 adoptions were effected.

In cooperation with the Ministry of Education and voluntary agencies, preventive work in the field of child behavior is carried on among 10,000 children of school age who require special social and educational treatment. The mentally and physically defective children are cared for in special institutions. Child guidance clinics are maintained for mentally disturbed children and parents. Sixteen employment projects are maintained for the neglected teen-agers to train them for useful citizenship. A Youth Protective Authority within the Ministry of Social Welfare is set up to deal with the problem of juvenile offenders, while a probation service recommends to the courts the imposition or suspension of sentence. Juvenile delinquency in Israel, augmented by the problem of immigrant youth adjustments, is large enough to receive serious attention but somewhat less alarming than in other countries. This social problem is more fully considered in the chapter on Pursuit of Justice.

How does the social welfare program deal with the major problems of sickness, unemployment and old age? Israel is a new country with limited economic resources and with a burdensome defense budget. Nevertheless, efforts with various degrees of success have been made to afford at least a minimum of security for the average inhabitant of the land. In the area of sick benefits nearly two-thirds of the population are insured by Kupat Holim—General Sick Fund of the Histadrut. With the state's hospital facilities, 37 per cent of the total, plus 16 per cent Kupat Holim, 15 per cent private institutions, 13 per cent Malben and the rest municipal, Hadassah and other public hospitals, the entire population of Israel enjoys the assurance of protection in the event of illness. The sick insurance benefits also cover disability through accident and longer periods required for recovery and care of the chronically ill.

There is no unemployment insurance as yet in Israel but the Histadrut and government are conscious of their responsibilities to the unemployed and are conscientiously trying to fulfill those responsibilities. The National Federation of Labor uses its good offices to see that work is proportionately distributed among all the workers in slack times rather than have full employment for some and none for others.

When joblessness becomes a serious problem, the government initiates public works to relieve the situation. But in any event there is the Saad—the Relief Department of the Ministry of Social Welfare—to whom the unemployed without means of subsistence may turn for help. The country is too young and the economic resources insufficient to initiate an immediate unemployment insurance system. This needed security for the worker will have to wait for more propitious times and circumstances.

The problem of the aged grows as longevity increases. Those with family are in the category of the aged at 65 and with no family at 55. Until the social security law took effect in April 1954, the aged person incapable of maintaining himself sought his food and shelter in the Home for the Aged. This often required a burdensome admission fee with monthly compensation from the Saad. The Malben with its numerous institutions has eased the situation considerably, particularly in caring for the aged of the immigrant class no longer physically capable of gainful employment.

The social security law is changing the picture for the aged. All above the age of 18, except those who reached 67 when the law was adopted, or new arrivals at the age of 60 and over for men and 55 for women, contribute 3.3 per cent of wages or salary toward old age pensions. Old age pension begins at 65 for men and 60 for women, with a somewhat lower age for those in the more hazardous occupations. For those who prefer to begin to draw their pensions at a later age, such as 70 for men and 65 for women, the pensions are increased proportionately. The social security law also provides for motherhood expenses and for support of the widow and the orphan. For an extra rate the insured is protected with workmen's compensation in case of injury, a benefit accorded to the self-employed as well. In case of death of the insured, funeral expenses are provided in addition to a one-year pension for widows and orphans.

Ninety-two per cent of those eligible are insured by the state for the various benefits. In the first two years of the operation of the National Security Law, 61,500,000 IL were collected and 15,000,000 IL were distributed in benefits, with the balance invested for future insurance. Claims for compensation cases in the first year numbered 24,000, in the second year 31,000, and maternity benefits rose from 3,000 to 5,000.

Israel is insurance conscious. Commercial life insurance there is doing well, too. In 1953 there were 91,271 who carried life insurance policies of which 78,284 were written with Israeli insurance companies and the balance with foreign companies.

Social welfare is the state's responsibility, but in the formative years of the program the major burden fell on voluntary organizations. No estimate of the gigantic task of health and welfare in Israel can be complete without some reference to the various organizations carrying the heavy load. International Zionism, contrary to Arab sinister distortions of the term, implies primarily world Jewry's deep interest in the well-being of the Israeli Jewish community. The United Jewish Appeal, the Jewish National Fund and a variety of economic instruments have contributed substantially to the program of nation building, involving immigration, land, housing, etc. But there are other causes as well that have elicited Jewry's interest and support.

Reference has already been made to Hadassah, founded for the "Healing of My People." From the very day it took charge of the first Zionist medical unit in 1918, it began to lay the foundation for a healthy people in a healthy land, with no distinction between Jew and Arab. The Hadassah leadership, from the very outset, recognized the moral and practical principle that health is indivisible. The Jewish community could not assure its own well-being while its immediate neighbors, the Arabs, were plagued by contagious diseases.

Hadassah came to Palestine to fight malaria, trachoma and other tropical diseases, but expanded its activities in behalf of mother and child, school hygiene service, playgrounds, lunches, nurses' training and medical research. In cooperation with the Hebrew University it established a medical center consisting of school and hospital for the training of doctors, nurses, dentists and pharmacists. Youth aliyah—young immigrants—activities and vocational training have become identified with Hadassah, whose annual budget of $12,000,000 is raised through its various branches in the United States. With its policy of investing each local community with responsibility for its own social welfare program, Hadassah has transferred many of its successful endeavors to localities where the service is rendered. Its newest contribution, Bet Mazmil, a community health center dedicated to the principle of treating the family as a unit in all phases of health, diet, leisure and culture, is a model to be emulated. This is Hadassah's major accomplishment, not to multiply or perpetuate organizational enterprises but to show the way, to teach and inspire the Israeli communities to become self-reliant, eventually to assume responsibility for the improvement of their health and social conditions.

Native to Israel is the Kupat Holim—the General Sick Fund of the National Federation of Labor. It has grown out of the needs of the country and through the vision of labor leadership in the land. Kupat Holim came into being in 1912 to promote the cause of public health, Arab as well as Jewish. It accompanied the Jewish pioneers of agriculture to every part of the country. Kupat Holim is now the outstanding voluntary sick benefit insurance organization in Israel. Since 1948 it has grown from 328,000 to 1,050,000 members. Many of the insured are family men. Therefore the total number of insured is approximately between two-thirds and three-quarters of the entire population. Geographically, Kupat Holim covers over 700 settlements, including many in the Negev. Its bed capacity in 1948 was only 500. In seven years it more than quadrupled that number and now has 2,140 beds.

In close kinship with Kupat Holim is the Women's Workers Council, organized in 1920 to carry on a program of cultural, educational and social service activities. With the dual goal of equality for the sexes and health for the population, mainly in the rural areas, the Women's Workers Council has through the years endeavored to educate the women of the country for health, defense and equality in political, economic and other spheres of life. The Women's Workers Council now embraces a membership of close to a quarter of a million, mainly wives of Histadrut members. Since the beginning of the state, that organization has concentrated on the problem of the integration of the new immigrants into the life of the nation by teaching immigrant women to read and write Hebrew, to operate their homes efficiently, to care for their children and to become useful citizens of the land.

Malben symbolizes another forward-looking voluntary social welfare activity in Israel. It was founded in 1949 under the auspices of the American Joint Distribution Committee, organized for overseas relief in First World War days. The word is derived from the initial letters of the four Hebrew words constituting its name: Mosad L'tapel Bo-olim Nechshalim—Organization Devoted to Aid Enfeebled Immigrants. With a budget of over $12,000,000 for constructive relief efforts plus another million in grants to yeshivot—Talmudical academies—Malben contributes much more to the welfare of Israel's population than the substantial financial program would indicate. The warm approach and scientific methods employed by Malben in servicing the health and welfare needs of the immigrants is indeed a tribute to its professional staff and its organizational leadership. It maintains four hospitals for the chronically ill, numbering 500, who are taught self-help and skills for self-support, a tuberculosis hospital, 12 homes for the aged with 1,900 inmates, four infirmaries accommodating 250, two villages for the aged with 2,400 residents, 23 workshops training 600 and 5,000 small loans, including loans with which to start a small business. Handicapped adults and retarded children are taught self-support, with many of their families receiving aid and medical attention. Malben is important in Israel not only because of its work in relieving the government or Jewish Agency of burdensome responsibilities but primarily because of the progressive and humane methods employed in servicing the needy and incapacitated immigrants.

Jewish folklore holds that when Israel becomes reconstituted as a nation, all the institutions established in the Diaspora will be transplanted to the Holy Land. Ort is one of the organizations that fits into the spirit of this folklore. Established in 1880 to serve Diaspora Jewry, it has largely shifted its center of activities to Israel.

Ort—an abbreviation of the three Russian words meaning Organization for Rehabilitation and Training—was first conceived as an instrument to adjust the lives of Jews in their native or adopted lands to their new economic and political environment by teaching them trades and skills, and thus remove from them the stigma of "middleman." The founders of Ort believed that emigration for the Jew from his native land was no solution to his problem. It was, therefore, decided to reeducate the Jew occupationally and vocationally to make him a more desirable, productive and useful citizen in the country where he resided. Fate ordained otherwise.

European Jewry was decimated. The survivors found a haven in Israel. Ort's experience, facilities and means were immediately utilized to prepare prospective immigrants for productive life before they entered Israel or upon arrival. Its large-scale activities in Israel began in 1948. In the first decade it founded 24 schools in 22 localities, training the youth in 25 different trades most needed and useful in the Holy Land. Thus Ort, originally a Diaspora institution, has become a major contributor to the welfare of the younger generation and, through the youth, a builder of Israel's future, although it still functions effectively in Jewish communities throughout the world.

Wizo stands for Women's International Zionist Organization, founded almost three decades before the birth of the state. Its membership and funds are derived from world Jewry outside of the United States where Hadassah has been accorded the exclusive privilege of conducting noncompetitive women's Zionist activities. Wizo's interest in Israel is in providing agricultural and vocational training for women and youth. It maintains babies' and children's homes, day nurseries and kindergartens. Young girl immigrants between 13 and 20 who do not attend school are helped by means of club rooms and similar facilities. Wizo develops home industry, workshops and other areas of employment for elderly women. Like other organizations, it is most concerned with the problems of new immigrants, helping the women to adjust themselves to their new environment and creating bridges between the new and the settled population.

The Mizrachi Women likewise make their specific contribution to the welfare of Israel's population. They have entered into many phases of the social well-being of the Jewish community, emphasizing the religious phases in all of their activities. They maintain a children's village, nurseries and kindergartens for children of maladjusted families, afternoon clubs for children and teen-agers and Hebrew classes for immigrants. The Mizrachi Women also maintain hostels for working girls, distribute food and clothing to the needy, provide scholarships for underprivileged youth as well as summer and day camps for children. The Mizrachi Women, who derive most of their financial support from America, also conduct evening classes for adults in sewing and crafts; they provide family counseling service as well as facilities for religious worship for the newcomers.

The Women's League for Israel, another American-sponsored organization, began its efforts in the Holy Land in 1927, focusing its attention primarily on the immigrant girl. It maintains five resident homes in Israel for single women and a sixth at the Hebrew University campus. During its existence Women's League for Israel provided homes for more than 35,000 immigrant girls in the pioneer houses which the organization has erected and maintained. These homes are not mere resting places for weary girls. They are homes for the spirit as well as the body. The residents are provided with social life and with opportunities to become self-supporting in their new land. They receive vocational training and are familiarized with the cultural life of the country. Through class, library, club and lounge facilities the new immigrant girls find peace and security.

The new-old land is filled with agents of mercy. The welfare and health of the underprivileged is the concern of both the government and the citizenry. The Jewish people in Israel remain true to their traditionally characteristic sympathy for their brethren in distress: "We are our brothers' keepers."

IX. Pursuit of Justice

When the British mandatory government abdicated its rule over Palestine in 1948, renascent Israel was faced overnight with an enormous dual problem, the defense of her borders and the maintenance of law and order.

The hurried British exit was deliberately timed to leave Israel exposed to attack and unprepared for self-rule. Not to be caught in a legal vacuum, however, the Provisional Assembly as a measure of expediency continued in force the British mandatory law by which Palestine had been governed for three decades, abrogating only the prohibitions against Jewish immigration and the sale of Arab land to Jews.

It was left to the future democratically elected Knesset—Parliament—to substitute, change or modify all other laws as needs required. In consonance with this plan, the Provisional Assembly at the founding of the state in May 1948 declared: "The law which existed in Palestine shall remain in force insofar as there is nothing therein repugnant to . . . other laws . . . and subject to such modification as may result from the establishment of the state and its authorities."

The postponement of the adoption of a written constitution placed on each succeeding Knesset session the responsibility for enacting laws and setting up necessary instruments for the implementation of a legal social order. Thus courts, rules of justice and their enforcement began to be instituted in 1949. They were modified by subsequent Knesset decisions for more applicable and effective justice, law and order in the land.

As the Israeli law-makers began to ponder proposed fundamental laws of the new Israel, sharply conflicting views were to be expected. The "Torah True Jews," those adhering to the orthodox philosophy of Judaism, advocated that all Jewish law be derived from and based on halachah as developed in the Talmud and by later commentators and codifiers. The secularists maintained that those laws having remained moribund for many centuries had become inoperative in a dynamic world of change. They therefore insisted that justice in Israel must be based on the principles of modern law derived especially from Western civilization. The moderates held that Israeli law must be rooted in the Jewish past, interpreted, however, and applied in accord with modern legal principles best suited to the needs and people of the new state.

In essence Israeli law has for its basis remnants of the Turkish legal system of premandatory days and British common law as well as halachic principles now included in the training of the legal profession.

The courts of law are well established in Israel, and their authority is unchallenged. Excepting family matters, which are under religious jurisdiction, all judicial questions are vested in the authority of the state and its subdivisions.

The courts in Israel are of three jurisdictions: Magistrate, District and Supreme. Some other inferior courts dealing with municipal regulations and by-laws also function, but all litigation and the protection of individual rights are within the jurisdiction of the three named. The lowest is the Magistrate Court numbering 50 judges who preside in every part of the land and deal with relatively minor complaints and claims. These courts pass on small monetary matters and deal with less important criminal charges as well as with possession and use of real and personal property, including landlord and tenant relations. Much of the magistrate's task is devoted to traffic charges for infraction of motor vehicle regulations.

The District Court is of higher jurisdiction, presided over by 25 judges. It reviews appeals from the magistrate's decisions and considers all matters beyond the magistrate's authority such as arson, burglary, treason and spying.

The District Court not only tries cases beyond the magistrate's powers and hears appeals against his decisions but also acts on appeals from quasi-judicial verdicts rendered by administrative officers.

The highest tribunal in the land is the Supreme Court, consisting of nine judges. They represent the final authority of the law against whose decisions there are no appeals. Jerusalem is their official headquarters. They do not all sit on the same case, the normal number of judges being three and never more than five.

The Supreme Court is available to all who seek justice not administered in other courts. Neither personal interest nor bias has ever been charged against the Supreme Court's rulings since its inception. It is vested with the responsibility to hear or deny appeals against decisions of the District Court. It also has authority to revise the judgments of the religious courts and guide the civil court appointees charged with the duty of implementing judgments of the religious judicial authorities.

But above and beyond these functions the highest court has become the guardian of human rights and freedoms in the land. It is the natural tendency of a government to seek power over its citizenry and to discourage opposition from its critics. This may, as it often does, lead to abridgment of the citizen's right to freedom of the spoken or written word. The Supreme Court in Israel has watched over these rights zealously and effectively. It is ever ready to correct abuses of power exercised by higher officials to the disadvantage of their subordinates; to prohibit the unlawful withholding of licenses to conduct commercial or industrial enterprises; to void illegal elections and prevent encroachment against the interests of the individual by his fellow citizens or by the state, regardless of origin, religion or social status.

The high caliber of Supreme Court judges is due in no small measure to the method of their selection. They do not attain their position as a reward for political service or loyalty to the party in power. They are chosen by a Statutory Committee consisting of the chief justice and two of his associates, two cabinet members, two members of the Parliament and two members of the bar. The names of the nominees are presented to the president of the state, who formally makes the designations. He has no choice in the matter for he has no power of veto. The appointment is for life and the office is immune from political pressures. The salaries of the judges are determined by the Parliament's Finance Committee, thus minimizing the government's possible influence through material considerations.

The nonpartisanship of the judges in Israel is not left to mere chance. The Basic Principles of Government Program adopted by the Knesset in 1955 clearly states: "Civil and rabbinical judges qualified for their task by the state and receiving salary from the State Treasury or from that of local authorities will not be allowed to participate in election campaigns or to carry on party propaganda."

So well established is the conviction in the land that the judges are beyond political and partisan influence that the Board of Elections is usually presided over by a Supreme Court judge. To illustrate the scrupulous observance of the prevailing nonpartisan practice, the chief justice on an inquiry from a political party regarding an election law refused to pass judgment unless the representatives of all parties participated in the inquiry of the issue involved. Similarly, he would not be present at a reception in honor of a president of the Zionist Organization of America visiting Israel lest he be considered as sympathetic toward any party in Zionism. Although the Supreme Court judges in Israel are not well compensated materially, between 350 and 500 IL basic salary per month, they are otherwise rewarded by the high esteem in which they are universally held throughout the country.

There is no jury system in Israel. The court rules both on questions of law and fact with one to three judges participating, depending on the importance of each case.

The jury system has not been instituted in Israel for two reasons. Because of the limited size of the country, members of the jury might be familiar with either complainant or defendant and thus be prejudiced either for or against them. Secondly, judges by reason of their training and experience are better able to determine the value of testimony than laymen, who are easily swayed by lawyers' tactics and oratory.

Lawyers constitute the second important element in the administration of justice in the land. Approximately 1,600 are members of the legal profession. When their numbers were proportionately fewer, economic rewards were more satisfactory. As a result of the lower compensation due to the increase in numbers of lawyers, not all who are licensed to practice enter the legal profession. Some seek careers in various branches of the Civil Service or accept governmental employment through political appointments. Others enter a variety of fields where their legal training might be advantageous in the pursuit of their respective occupations.

Legal training may be obtained either at the Hebrew University in Jerusalem or at the Tel Aviv Law School. Since Israel's legal system is heir to British mandatory law, it follows that the legal studies are very broad, covering principles and practice of common law, halachah—Jewish law—and some elements of the Turkish code which the mandatory government retained on assuming power in Palestine. The legal regulations and precedents established during the three decades of British rule in Palestine also have been retained.

Lawyers to be admitted to practice on completion of their legal studies must serve a clerkship of two years and require a favorable recommendation by a special character committee before they are licensed. Those who study abroad, in addition to clerkship and committee recommendation, must also equip themselves with the special knowledge of the branches of law essential for practice in Israel. Practicing lawyers of other countries who desire to enter Israel's legal profession may have their clerkship dispensed with or shortened.

The number of lawyers grows annually. Every year many are licensed and added to the roster of the legal profession. In 1949, 35 lawyers were accredited for practice; in 1950 there were 47. The numbers grew to 123 in 1951 and 114 in 1952. Since then the increase has continued: 222 in 1953; 261 in 1954 and 327 in 1955. Law libraries containing 16,000 volumes, of which 1,400 are on United States law, are in constant use for the advancement of legal knowledge.

All members of the bar, irrespective of experience or erudition, are eligible to practice in any court. In the Supreme Court there is dissatisfaction with such procedure, since the younger lawyers often lack the legal acumen and experience needed to conduct important cases.

Malpractice is almost completely absent in the Israeli legal profession and "ambulance chasing" is rare. In the year 1955-56 there were 110 complaints of malpractice in law. Of these only one lawyer was recommended for disbarment and 12 others were found guilty in lesser degrees with short-term suspensions. Neither petitioners nor defendants are required to employ legal counsel; nevertheless, except for minor litigation in lower courts, the services of attorneys at law are engaged in most disputes that come before the courts.

The attorney general constitutes a third element in the administration of the law in Israel. He is the official advisor to the government and is charged with the duty to pursue the cause of justice without favor to person, party or government. He may appeal on behalf of his office to the Supreme Court against a decision of the lower court if he is convinced that the judgment is either too lenient or too harsh.

The attorney general combines in his office the dual function of public prosecutor and public defender. His right to appeal from decisions of lower courts, if he believes that justice has miscarried, is very likely a relic of British mandatory practice.

When the mandatory government found lower court rulings not to its satisfaction, its Justice Department instituted appeals to the higher courts for a more favorable consideration. But whatever the origin of the practice, the attorney general's power in Israel to intervene has proven its worth. He is clothed with authority to advise the government on the laws of the land, help prepare statutes for enactment by the Knesset and enforce the military draft laws. He also presides over the Law Council, whose duty it is to supervise the education of future lawyers and to take disciplinary measures against unethical practices in the legal profession. Finally, it is his duty to provide legal aid for those who cannot afford it.

The minister of justice, a government appointee with Cabinet rank, supervises the Magistrate and District courts and determines their number. He is also responsible for the establishment of special tribunals for the prevention of profiteering or speculation deemed harmful to the economic welfare of the country. The selection of judges, however, for the regularly constituted courts is left to the Statutory Committee with the president's formal approval.

In the first years of the state's existence, the minister of justice if politically motivated could have employed favoritism in judicial appointments, but since 1953 such possibilities were completely eliminated by law. The courts are a separate and independent entity within the Ministry of Justice. In addition to the one Supreme Court consisting of nine members, there are three District Courts, 17 Magistrate Courts, four Municipal Courts and a number of Juvenile Courts.

The courts are inadequately housed and devoid of architectural embellishment or attractive appointments. There is no uniformity as to dress or costume and other equipment within the courts. Some judges sit with covered heads, others maintain a completely secular atmosphere. The predominance of the Hebrew language, however, in all courts lends them a distinct Israeli flavor. The lawyers, too, vary with regard to the covered head depending on their religious practices. Litigants, witnesses and visitors differ in dress, manner and language.

There is no uniformity to the swearing in of witnesses, each acting in accord with his own conscience. The strictly religious litigant takes no oath because such practice is opposed by his traditions. The irreligious object to any oath on the Bible. Only the religiously neutral person takes the oath with his hand on the Holy Scriptures obligating himself to tell the truth. The Christian swears on the New Testament, the Moslem on the Koran and the Druze, whose Holy Writ is his own private domain, pledges only his word of honor.

The absence of a formal oath does not imply that liberties are taken with the truth. Perjury is severely punished by Israel's laws.

Courts in Israel do not make a complete record of the proceedings of a trial. The presiding judge takes down in longhand whatever he considers pertinent. Often the interrogation of a witness will be interrupted to afford the judge an opportunity to write down a certain testimony or legal argument. The official reason for the absence of stenographic reports is economy. The court's budget does not provide for this special service. This seems to be false economy. If the judge were free from taking notes the testimony might be expedited at a saving of time, which of course implies economic saving as well. Justice too would be better served by the judge's closer attention to the proceedings, undistracted by paper work. Facial expressions more often reveal an untruth or distortion of fact than do the words of a witness. Furthermore, stenographic records would be more reliable for review purposes than sketchy notes of a presiding judge. Some prefer the present method of recording testimony not for economic reasons but for the advantage of conciseness, relevance and brevity inherent in the judge's longhand notes.

The dispensing of justice in Israel is of a very complex nature. While the procedure is less formal and therefore less cumbersome than elsewhere, the knowledge of law and its interpretation is more complicated for judge and lawyer alike. The difficulty is due to two factors: first, the many sources from which Israel's law is derived, and second, the international character of the population with the necessity of taking into account the laws of the disputants' country of origin.

As previously pointed out, Israel fell heir to the legal code of the British mandatory government, which in turn retained a considerable part of the legislation of the Ottoman Turkish Empire. Add to the common and Turkish law, specific mandatory enactments as well as religious laws, Moslem, Jewish and Christian, primarily in matters of family and estates, and the complexity of Israel's judicial system can be readily seen.

The international complications are equally evident. Two illustrations will suffice. The husband is born in one country, the wife in another. Their dispute concerns their rights to premarital property, the husband claiming it to be his under the laws of his native land, the wife insisting it is hers under her country's laws. It is therefore incumbent upon the judge to familiarize himself not only with the merits of the claims but with their validity under the respective native laws of the claimants. Or, consider this even more involved situation: the husband appeals from a District Court's decision imposing alimony for a wife who he claims abandoned him. They were married civilly in Poland where the husband refused a religious ceremony. Under these conditions they are not subject to the jurisdiction of the religious court in Israel. The court in sympathy with a wife who justifies abandonment on the ground of her husband's extreme cruelty finds it difficult to reconcile the law of the foreign country with the Israeli law.

Particularly the lack of an official constitution is a contributing problem in Israel's judicial system. The postponement of a formal constitution serves the cause of Jewish unity. The delay has avoided conflict on basic religious issues. But the courts are deprived thereby of any veto power over hastily enacted legislation inimical to the best interests of a freedom-loving people. The only fundamental legal principles rooted in Israel are those expressed in general terms in the original Declaration of the State of Israel: "Freedom, justice and peace as envisaged by the prophets of Israel; it will ensure equality of social and political rights to all its inhabitants irrespective of religious conscience, language, education and culture. . . ." This is more akin to a constitutional preamble than to a national fundamental law.

So lacking is the element of stability that the Knesset in the 1956-57 session debated the question of eliminating the principle of precedent in judicial considerations with the majority of Israel's bench and bar averse to a precedentless court. They argued that this would leave each case to the whim of individual judges. Lawyers would not be able to advise their clients whether their cases had any merit before a court of justice.

For the present the courts in Israel follow precedents scrupulously, not only those originated in Israel but in the highest courts of England and the United States as well.

Despite their shortcomings, Israel's courts are of the highest caliber. The written opinions of Israel's Supreme Court judges are comparable to the best in the Anglo-Saxon world. They represent profound erudition, clarity of expression as well as adherence to the highest legal principles.

Israel's judicial system has taken over from the Anglo-Saxon law the principle of search and warrant. The courts will not admit evidence illegally obtained. They tend to give highest credence to evidence obtained through examination and cross examination in open court. Less direct evidence of questionable character, obtained, for example, through the aid of a bloodhound, is given only the slightest measure of importance. Circumstantial evidence in cases of homicide, not admissible in the religious law, is admitted in Israel's courts but is not given the same weight as testimony presented by eye witnesses.

The death penalty is traditionally abhorrent to Israel's conception of justice. The popular view is opposed to "a life for a life" reprisal principle, no matter what the crime. In the past two years Parliament considered the question of the death penalty for treason. Even if such a law were adopted it would be difficult to find a Jewish executioner.

Family issues and matters of estate by choice of litigants are under the jurisdiction of the religious courts under state authority. Should the question of jurisdiction on a given matter be in dispute between the religious and civil courts, a special tribunal designated by the Supreme Court would determine the judicial authority. Though in theory the religious courts are equal to their civil counterparts in their limited field of jurisdiction, in practice the Supreme Court is the over-all authority. It may in various degrees and for good reasons modify the decisions of the religious courts. It also exercises authority through appointment of the officers needed by the religious courts for the enforcement of their decisions. Those courts are also held in check by the threat of Knesset legislation to curb their authority if they go beyond their limited jurisdiction. Subject to these limitations, the religious courts carry on in matters of marriage and divorce. If the litigants in an estate dispute so agree, they may also have the ecclesiastical court resolve their claims in law and equity.

Because Israel recognizes the right of its citizens to their respective religious convictions, religious courts have been established for each of the three major faiths: the Rabbinical Court for the Jewish inhabitants, the Sharia for the Moslem population and Canon Law Court for the Christians. The last, however, has separate courts for Protestant, Roman Catholic, Greek Orthodox, Melkite and Maronite.

The ecclesiastical courts are those of the first instance, where suit is instituted, and the higher tribunals are those to which appeals are taken from decisions of the lower courts. There may be appeals to the Supreme Court on administrative matters but the law itself as construed by any of the religious denominations is not reviewable.

The government's legislative power may in the long run influence religious courts' decisions. For example, the Rabbinical Court may rule against intermarriage between Jews and Karaites on the ground that they, the Karaites, have rejected the oral—Talmudic—law. Should Parliamentary regulations oppose such views, the religious courts will very likely yield to such a decision. So far there has not been any head-on collision between the ecclesiastical courts and the government. From all indications, the future augurs well against serious clashes between the legislative body and the judiciary of the religious courts.

To give the religious courts an equal footing with the civil courts, dayanim—religious judges—receive compensation similar to that of the civil judges. In recent years the training for their positions has been much improved. Candidates take examinations for judgeships in the religious courts and are designated in accordance with their standing after having successfully passed the tests.

All together there are 60 Rabbinical Court judges. Each Rabbinical Court consists of three judges selected by the Chief Rabbinate. In the main the rabbinical judges are men of venerable mien, extensive erudition and cognizance of the vital problems of the modern age.

The Rabbinical Court, less formal than the civil court in procedure, is equally thorough in behalf of justice. Any deficiency in decorum is made up by the opportunities afforded to litigants, witnesses and counsel for free expression unencumbered by rigid rules of procedure. In the absence of attorneys, who are not required in the Rabbinical Court, the judges delve into the heart of the matter to insure justice for all the litigants. While women, in accordance with Jewish traditional law, do not act as witnesses, rabbinic judges avail themselves of expert knowledge and advice from female social welfare workers and others to help solve family problems under their jurisdiction.

The religious courts frequently look to civil authority for

the enforcement of their decisions. To illustrate: in a divorce proceeding, according to Jewish religious law, the husband unilaterally divorces his wife. The court is powerless to act without his consent. When, in the judgment of the court, the wife is entitled to a divorce whether the husband agrees or not, no authority can be substituted for his will. Under such conditions, at the recommendation of the religious court, the civil court may incarcerate the husband until such time as he changes his mind and consents to divorce his wife, making her free and eligible to marry another man. At times, the ecclesiastical court may render a decision requiring enforcement by a civil officer but the civil court may refuse to so act on the ground that the case was not within ecclesiastical jurisdiction or that the decision was contrary to natural law. It may be seen from the foregoing that the ecclesiastical courts are circumscribed in their authority, even in their limited field of jurisdiction, by the higher civil courts.

Close to 14,000 cases were entered in the Rabbinical Courts in 1955. Of this number 12,000 were adjudicated, leaving approximately 2,000 pending cases. However, because of previous accumulations, the Rabbinical Courts have nearly 7,000 cases still pending.

Family problems assigned to religious courts are becoming more numerous. Marital dissensions, separations, divorces, payment of alimony and support of children have increased beyond the proportional growth of the general population.

Though the Jewish religious attitude toward divorce has always been liberal, both in the distant and recent past, the broken home was the rare exception. Even in the Orient where the position of the Jewish woman was on a lower level than that of her sister in the Western World, there were comparatively few divorces.

The Oriental Jewish woman suffered her lot, believing that destiny ordained it so. She sought no freedom from an unhappy marriage, since she was aware of her husband's mastery over the situation. After reaching Israel, the Oriental Jewish woman learned the possibility of improving her lot through the religious courts. Thus family litigation multiplied. The Sharia Court (Moslem) dealt with 1,782 cases in 1955 with but eight undecided. The Moslem religious law does not require formal legal action for divorce. The procedure is completed by the husband's repeated statement to his wife: "Leave my house." In the Greek Orthodox Court, 193 cases were placed on the docket; in the Melkite Court, 55 and the Roman Catholic Court handled 37 cases in the same year. Through the ecclesiastical courts' jurisdiction over problems of the family, the various religions in Israel play important roles in the individual lives of their adherents and maintain considerable influence in other areas throughout the land.

Both the civil and ecclesiastical courts are conducted on a very high plane. The character of men presiding over the courts, their legal equipment and their complete integrity augur well for the equitable dispensation of justice. Only to the extent, however, that the punishment meted out acts as a deterrent against lawlessness, and that the confidence of the populace is merited by fair decisions, do the courts succeed in influencing correct social behavior within the community of Israel. The degree of conflict with the law, in the final analysis, lies with the inherent will of the people to abide by the laws of the land.

The early Zionist propagandist ascribed Jewish criminals in the Diaspora to their hostile environment. Once a Jewish national home is established, crime among Jews in their own land will vanish, they argued. In the premandate days, this fact was cited: "Tel Aviv municipality has a prison but no prisoners. When Jews live in a normal environment they need no courts, judges, police or detention houses." Today's heirs to the early Zionist propagandists ascribe the rise of crime in Israel to those who came from abroad with proven criminal tendencies. Undoubtedly considerable numbers of lawless elements in the Holy Land have come from other countries. They were undesirables in their native lands and were not reformed in Israel.

Four factors must be taken into consideration to explain the present situation. Due to a more concentrated public opinion and the easier detection of criminal acts, the rural population is freer from crimes than the urban sections. The rapid growth of the city inevitably brought a corresponding increase in law-breaking. Secondly, a distinction must be made between halutzim—early pioneers—and olim—the more recent immigrants. The former were motivated by the ideal of nation building and the latter by improvement of individual status. Certainly the idealists who uproot their lives for the sake of national aspirations are less likely to come into conflict with the law than those who are primarily concerned with their personal fortunes. Thirdly, some of the comparatively recent immigrants came from countries of lower standards of human behavior. Fourthly, the far-ranging heterogeneity of the newcomers caused distinctions which fostered antagonisms.

Fortunately, the older settlers live by the practice of the principle, "We are our brothers' keepers." Much is being done to raise the social attitudes of those who originate from countries of lower standards of human behavior and even more so to fuse all the newcomers into one household of Israel. With the complete adjustment of the newcomers, there is good reason to believe that law and order in Israel will be insignificantly disturbed.

However, despite the huge immigration of multiple origins, the general attitude toward the law has been relatively good. In the four years between 1952 and 1955 the population increase was considerable, but the number of offenses against the law did not grow in the same proportion. The total number of such offenses in 1952 was 41,070; in 1953, 40,169; in 1954, 43,441 and in 1955, 45,426. Homicide, the most heinous of crimes, showed a decrease: 62 in 1952; 67 in 1953; 58 in 1954 and 32 in 1955. When one deducts from these figures the murders committed by Arab infiltrators or by homicides within the Arab community in Israel through feuds, one must conclude that Israel's rate of homicide is the lowest among the civilized nations of the world.

Attempted murder, too, has shown a decrease: 111 in 1952; 118 in 1953; 110 in 1954 and 90 in 1955. Similarly, in the number of unintentional or accidental homicides the decline was marked: 151 in 1952; 129 in 1953; 144 in 1954 and 125 in 1955.

In the area of physical assault there has been a substantial enough increase to warrant some alarm. In 1952 there were 3,543 such cases; in 1953 the number grew to 3,797; in 1954 they increased to 4,746 and in 1955 there were 6,340 cases of assault.

Robbery and attempted robbery were few in number: 161 in 1952; 137 in 1953; 94 in 1954 and 69 in 1955. Housebreaking and thefts constitute the majority of criminal acts in Israel. In 1952 there were 6,322 housebreaking acts and 17,706 thefts; in 1953, 5,921 and 15,691; in 1954, 5,607 and 16,755 and in 1955, 5,348 and 16,284.

There are two major reasons for the large number of cases of housebreaking and thievery: one, in tropical countries there are more open doors and windows in the average home than in the countries of colder climate. Unlawful entrance is thus made easier. More careful window and door guards might decrease the crime of housebreaking. Two, Israel must fit the punishment to the crime. Thievery and housebreaking would be more readily discouraged by the infliction of more severe penalties against the guilty. Both house robbery and acts of thievery are numerous in all Mediterranean countries with the exception of Saudi Arabia, where punishment is the harshest and often most cruel. No one in authority in Israel approves of Saudi Arabian barbaric forms of punishment, but more severe treatment of thievery might deter many from the crime of theft.

Receiving and possessing stolen goods has been cut in half in the last four years. There were 1,073 such cases in 1952; 710 in 1953; 567 in 1954 and 539 in 1955. Professional fences in Israel are becoming very rare.

However, the crime of arson and damage to property is troubling Israeli authorities. The present situation is not a happy one. In 1952 there were 1,435 arson and damage to property cases; in 1953 there were 1,429. In 1954 the number jumped to 2,142 and in 1955 to 2,454. The legal punishment for this type of crime has been made more severe as a deterrent against such acts.

Offenses against morality are comparatively few. There were 599 in 1952; 757 in 1953; 859 in 1954 and 928 in 1955. Considering the increase of population, the higher figures between 1952 and 1955 are not at all alarming. Sex crimes in Israel are very few for the Jewish population but fairly high among the Arab residents.

There is no legalized prostitution in Israel, although this moral offense does exist in various degrees in different locations. Haifa, being a port city, leads in that unsavory business, with Tel Aviv in second place and Jerusalem trailing far behind.

Fraud and forgery, mainly in Israel's world of commerce, are well under control. There were 608 such cases in 1952; 700 in 1953; 807 in 1954 and 794 in 1955. Offenses against a "dangerous drugs" ordinance are comparatively rare: 98 in 1952; 83 in 1955; 153 in 1954 and 141 in 1955.

Illegal acts of trespassing and squatting are natural in a new pioneering country with many claimants demanding legal recognition of their property. As ownership titles become more clarified, the number of trespassers and squatters decreases. In 1952 there were 1,020 claimants of property rights; in 1953 there were 637; in 1954, 347 and in 1955, 313.

Miscellaneous and less significant offenses increased in each successive year: 7,396 in 1952; 9,086 in 1953; 9,859 in 1954 and 10,508 in 1955.

Gangs of the milder type are also to be found in Israel, with a limited amount of card gambling. Pool, dice, races and the "numbers" racket are unknown in the land. The betting instinct finds sufficient expression through the government sanctioned lotteries, the profits of which go for the advancement of education.

Injury to self is considered a criminal act in Israel. In the category of suicide or attempted suicide the following figures tell the story. In 1952 there were 110 suicides; in 1953, 150; in 1954, 147 and in 1955, 162. Attempted suicides showed larger numbers: 233 in 1952; 308 in 1953; 362 in 1954 and 500 in 1955. These figures in no wise reflect a normal situation. They are mainly due to the large numbers of broken or nearly broken lives, distraught with torturing memories, that were brought to Israel in the recent waves of unrestricted immigration. Many of these lives were rebuilt and made whole again; others remained shattered, too far gone to be reinspired with new hope.

The venturesome, pioneering spirit of the land makes life in Israel absorbing although rigorous. Nevertheless, stamina is needed to meet the hardships involved in the struggle for bread and in the program of defense. Some too weak in spirit, unprepared to accept the hazards of a new land striving heroically for survival, succumb to desperation and weakness before the eventide of their life.

The teen-ager problem in relation to conflict with the law is reflected in the following figures. In 1955 there were 2,163 Jewish youths, 1,843 boys and 320 girls, who were referred to the Youth Probation Service for various offenses. In the same year 972 Arab youths, 828 boys and 144 girls, were apprehended for various acts of lawlessness. Considering the size of Jewish in proportion to Arab population, the former represents a smaller percentage of juvenile delinquents.

Offenses committed by Jewish youth were primarily against property. Only 227 out of 2,163 were involved in offenses against persons or in immoral acts. Of the youths apprehended for alleged violations of the law only a small percentage has been sentenced to detention or correction houses for punishment or rehabilitation. The courts annulled the accusations against 419 of the Jewish offenders and 224 of the Arabs. Of those that stood trial, 102 Jewish youths and 76 Arabs were acquitted of wrongdoing. Two hundred and ninety-two Jewish youths and 27 Arabs were released with a reprimand and warning. About 500 Jewish and Arab youths were subjected to fines paid by their parents or guardians. Suspended sentences or probation were given to 260 Jewish youths and 40 Arabs. The actual number of detention cases referred to various educational-correctional institutions were 19 for the Arabs and 121 for the Jews. The balance of those accused in 1955 represent cases still pending.

No age group represents a more acute problem than any other in the commission of crimes in Israel. Juvenile delinquency has somewhat increased but not alarmingly so. In 1953 the delinquency ratio was 105 for every 100,000 population. In 1954 the number increased to 130 per 100,000 and in 1955 to 155. With the speedier integration of the growing immigrant population, a decline in the rate may be justifiably expected. The older age groups do not indicate disproportionate numbers for any category. For the year 1954 both Jews and Arabs in conflict with the law between 17 and 19 years of age numbered 1,922 persons; those from 20 to 24, 2,898; between 25 and 29, 2,057; between 30 and 39, 2,551 and those of 40 and over, a total of 3,408.

Both the detention and correction houses for the youth as well as the prisons for the adult violators of the law are conducted on humane principles with the goal of rehabilitation and are devoid of the objectives of punishment or reprisal.

Court sentences are intended to act both as deterrents against potential offenders of the law and to rehabilitate the criminal. But the institutions of correction deemphasize the first motivating factor and concentrate on the training of the inmates to become useful and productive members of society on the termination of the period of their incarceration. Many of them are sentenced for short terms up to six months, affording little time for the Correction Department to help rebuild the prisoners' lives. Of a group of 3,000 legally detained in a fixed period, about 2,100 received sentences of six months; about 250 between six months and a year; 225 between one and three years; 50 from three to 10 years; a dozen for more than three years and 25 for life imprisonment, with the balance detained pending trial.

The total number of life prisoners consists of only 50, 19 of whom are Jews, 31 Arabs, five of whom are infiltrators. Those who are detained for a long period are afforded the opportunity to learn various trades such as agriculture, building, carpentry, shoe repairing, plastics, etc. They are paid for their labors. Their leisure hours are devoted to entertainment, cultural and educational courses. However, despite all the efforts in behalf of those sentenced for crimes and the advanced methods to train them, too many are recidivists. In the year 1953 out of a prison population of 14,227 almost a third had served prison terms before. The proportion was even larger in 1954. Out of 12,836 prisoners there were 4,765 recidivists, 2,755 Jewish and 2,010 Arab. In 1955 the number of recidivists declined considerably.

In all, taking 1955 as the average of previous years, there were 45,426 offenses against the law, felonies and misdemeanors, detected by Israel's police force and brought to the various courts for disposition. This number does not include contraventions such as illegal sale of intoxicating liquors, trade and industry ordinances and traffic law infractions. The last, considering the increase in all types of vehicular traffic from year to year, indicates a tolerable situation as indicated by the table of comparative figures of accidents between 1952 and 1955 inclusive. In 1952 the total number of traffic accidents was 5,036 resulting in 228 deaths, 1,293 seriously injured and 3,515 slightly injured. In 1953 the total remained almost the same: 5,056. Fatal cases appreciably decreased: 174 deaths, 1,175 seriously injured and 3,707 suffered minor injuries. While in 1954 the number increased to 5,915, the proportion of deaths rose only slightly, 182, with the other categories being 1,306 to 4,992. In 1955 the total climbed again by about 8 per cent above the previous year, rising to 6,432, but the number of deaths declined again: only 134 with 1,306 seriously injured and 4,992 slightly hurt.

The police force in Israel has a personnel of 6,000 of whom 300 are women. There are 350 officers. It is a national body and is divided into districts, sub-districts, stations and posts. The force is charged with administrative, organizational and investigative duties. The detection of crimes is effective in cases of homicide. About 90 per cent of all murder cases have been solved and the accused found guilty. But in thefts, the percentage has not been so high. The smaller success in this area may be ascribed to the fact that the civil population does not fully cooperate with the police in support of accusations. Jews themselves throughout the ages have suffered so much from "informers" that they are instinctively reluctant to assume this role even against guilty parties.

New countries, always characterized by the aggressive "race to the swift and battle to the strong," ordinarily are beset by greater and more serious lawlessness than the older, better organized and longer stabilized lands. Israel, a new country permeated by the rugged pioneer spirit and burdened with the enormous problems of adjustment from within and defense from without, has nevertheless succeeded in establishing law and order equal to the best in the civilized world.

Israel's system of justice, the law-abiding attitude of its people and the high quality of men administering law and order are in consonance with the prophetic admonition: "Justice shalt thou pursue."

X. The Builders

The status of labor is a true measure of human progress in any country. In Jewish tradition both work and worker are held in high regard. Beginning with the Biblical command, "Six days thou shalt labor," the Jewish people held the welfare of the laborer as a sacred obligation. His person was protected under the law and prompt payment of wages was guaranteed. In theory and practice the Jewish worker was treated as a human being and never as a beast of burden.

Unlike the Greek concept that work befits the slave and leisure the free man, Judaism teaches, "Love labor and hate lordship." Even Torah study, so preciously sacred in Jewish life, Israel's sages maintain, is worthless unless coupled with a useful occupation: "All study of the Torah without work must in the end be futile and become the cause of sin." In Jewish tradition the laborer is not a mere commodity as conceived in the industrial age. Labor neither defiles a man's lineage nor does it lower his dignity. "Man must toil with both hands and God will prosper him in his efforts."

Beginning with the Middle Ages up to the Industrial Revolution the Jewish conception of manual labor was ignominiously distorted. Because of the prevailing racial and religious prejudices, Jews were excluded from labor guilds. To survive economically, they were compelled to become middlemen, money lenders and traders. These, because they were considered to be the lowest types of human endeavor, were the only areas of livelihood left open to them in order deliberately to degrade them.

Necessity became a virtue. They learned to adjust themselves to their new situation which evolved three advantages: a lesser degree of competition, a portable type of wealth for their enforced wandering from country to country and greater leisure for their most cherished avocation—Torah study. Thus they found "the soul of good in things evil."

At the beginning of the Industrial Revolution many Jews became "hired hands" together with other sections of the urban population. When laborers became more conscious of their organized strength through their guilds, the Jewish workers provided their share of effort and leadership to wrest from their economic exploiters more equitable rewards and improved labor conditions. While many continued as middlemen, the new industrial age absorbed a large number of Jews, affording them not only gainful employment but an opportunity for service in a high cause: to strive for a just social order for the laboring class.

But as labor's struggles became intensified the Jewish workers involved in the conflict paid less attention to the problem of their survival as Jews and more to their aspiration for economic gains. To counteract the Jewish laborer's indifference to his group survival, Labor Zionism was brought into being with a fusion of two ideals: the establishment of a Jewish national home to solve the problem of the Jewish homeless and the creation of a just social order, a society without exploiters or exploited.

The Socialist-Zionists (Poalai Zion) presented their program in 1907 at the Eighth World Zionist Congress in the Hague where they received official recognition as a party in the Zionist Organization. The platform was a combination of two philosophies, one advanced by Ber Borochov (1881-1917) emphasizing the Marxian concept of class struggle, and the other advocated by Dr. Nahum Sirkin (1868-1928) exalting the ideals of prophetic social justice over dogmatic Socialism. The Socialist-Zionists, while primarily motivated by the problem of a Jewish homeland for the homeless established on the principles of justice and equity, also included in their platform the vision of a reconstructed world through the triumph of the Socialist ideal. Thus the new party carved out for itself the dual task of nation building and world rehabilitation.

Almost simultaneously with the development of the Poalai Zion there appeared in numerous places organized groups of the Hapoel Hatzair—the Young Worker—dedicated to the purpose of combining Zionism with Socialism and the added ideal of personal redemption through work on the soil. Aaron David Gordon (1856-1922) by word and personal example became the spiritual father of this movement, making himself immortal in the life of the yishuv—the Jewish settlement in Palestine. Less concerned with class struggle than the Poalai Zion, the Hapoel Hatzair, besides its major dedication to labor on the soil, championed the revival of Hebrew as a language and a cultural program.

In the Diaspora, Labor Zionism had to contend with opposing forces. The international Socialists maintained: "The world is our fatherland and Socialism our religion. Why be concerned with the Jewish problem affecting a small minority of the world's population when Socialism is destined to solve the ills of the entire human family? Why create another nation when present lines of division between nations should be obliterated?" But the Socialist-Zionists maintained that the national and class struggle, far from being mutually exclusive, were two branches of the same tree. To them, "internationalism" did not spell the erasure of national boundaries. On the contrary, the very meaning of the words "between nations" implies national coexistence, in peace and security, irrespective of size or power, all nations contributing to the welfare of humanity.

Another rival movement among the Jewish laboring classes was Jewish nationalism regardless of territory, aimed at maintaining everywhere a Jewish minority status with the preservation of the Yiddish language and culture as a major goal. The Socialist-Zionists countered by blaming all Jewish woes on their people's minority status. The cure of the Jewish problem would therefore be a territory with a Jewish majority willing and able to fulfill the Hebraic prophetic vision of a happy mankind. That territory was Palestine, waiting to be restored by Jewish hands. The language and culture had to be Hebraic to rejuvenate the Jewish spirit of the ages and to unify Jewry's scattered remnants in the far corners of the world into a national entity.

From the very beginning the Socialist-Zionists played a leading role in World Zionist congresses. Though a minority party in World Zionist affairs during prestatehood days, they displayed considerable influence in the shaping of Zionist policies.

Beginning with the second aliyah—immigration wave—(by later standards a mere trickle), the Socialist-Zionists became the backbone of haluziut—pioneering in Palestine—winning respect and admiration even from opponents of their economic ideology. They carried the full load in the conquest of the soil. They overcame inhibitions, centuries old, against working on the land. Inch by inch they reclaimed the barren, rocky ground on which they settled. Arab attacks did not discourage them nor did their meager diet make them shrink from their determination to build a country and establish a nation.

Life was rugged but hope was high and they persevered. The halutzim came to Palestine in the spirit of the popular song which they authored: "To Build and to Be Rebuilt." While forging ahead with their program of creating a nation, they succeeded in their aim to refashion their own lives, from trader to laborer, from middleman to man of the soil. Because of their selfless labors, their cheerful acceptance of the most onerous, backbreaking tasks, they gained cooperation from Zionists not necessarily in sympathy with their Socialist aspirations, among them Weizmann, leader of the General Zionists, an opponent of Marxism since his early student days.

The Socialist-Zionists' influence became more pronounced in later World Zionist congresses, not only because of the chaluziut tasks they accomplished, acknowledged by all Zionists as the foundation upon which the projected Jewish state would be built, but also because of their organizational skill and effort in electing to the World Zionist congresses large numbers of delegates, beyond their proportional membership in the Diaspora. Anyone paying the Zionist tax of a shekel, 50¢ in U.S. coin, had the privilege of voting for delegates to the World Zionist Congress. While the Socialist-Zionists, appealing as they did to the laboring class, were not as successful as the General Zionists in raising the larger funds necessary for settlement activities in Palestine, they eventually became the most proficient in securing shekel payers in behalf of their party and program. (The shekel system of representation is to be modified at the 1959 World Zionist Congress. Israel will be limited to 40 per cent of the total, while the American Zionist movement's delegation will increase from 23 per cent to 30 per cent.)

At congresses, therefore, Dr. Weizmann and his followers frequently aligned themselves with the Labor Zionist delegation in order to win a majority vote for General Zionist policies, acquired through an exchange by support of Zionist-Socialist goals which were at times in conflict with the principles of a free economy upheld by other Zionist parties and factions.

In Palestine the Socialist-Zionists, from the very beginning of their career, made headway under the dynamic leadership of Ben Gurion and Ben Zvi in close collaboration with Berl Katznelson, the movement's high priest and prophet. In theory and practice, they set up the Jewish worker as the foundation stone for the Jewish state of the future: a labor commonwealth. To them the Talmudic sentiment, "Read: not banayich—*thy children*—but bonayich—thy builders," was not a mere play on words.

When they reached Palestine they found the first aliyah settlers, aided by the Baron Edmund de Rothschild Pica—Palestine Jewish colonization movement—working the soil with cheap Arab labor. Without prejudice against the natives but with the firm conviction that no land or nation could be built by hired hands, they set in motion the principle of Jewish self-labor. This ideal clashed with the personal interests of the small Jewish landowners who preferred low-cost Arab labor to the higher demands of the Jewish worker. It was also opposed by the Arabs themselves, who were thus deprived of the opportunities offered by Jewish employers, which were better than those afforded them by their more affluent native brothers.

To educate and persuade Jewish immigrants to till the soil; to compel the Jewish employer to engage Jewish laborers and secure for them a minimum standard of working conditions, became the immediate goal of the Socialist-Zionists in Palestine. They were prompted by the ideal of a Jewish state normalizing Jewish life by lifting it from a minority to a majority status in a planned economy in which labor would play the dominant role.

The dream of a society unhampered by inequities and oppressions saw the beginning of its realization in the organization of the first kibbutz—collective agricultural colony—of Degania in 1909 and in the first moshav—cooperative agricultural colony—of Nahalal in 1921. Thus began the era of organized and cooperative labor in Palestine, constantly and consistently striving for the improvement of the lot of the Jewish worker, for the rebuilding of his own life while building a land and a nation and for the creation of a classless society, with Marx as a guide but with prophetic principles as the ultimate goal.

In the main, three major forces are responsible for labor's favorable status since the inception of the state: Histadrut, Mapai and the Labor government. Because of their close interrelationship it is not feasible to delineate the parts played by each, but for the sake of clarity it is well to consider each of the three forces as entities, leaving the account of their interdependence to a few implied or explicit references.

Histadrut first started with the agricultural settlements and the hired workers in the citrus groves. In 1912 the Agricultural Workers' Federation was founded. Actually Histadrut (abbreviated from the full Hebrew name: Histadrut Hak'lalit shel

Haovdim Haivrim B'eretz Israel—The General Federation of Labor in Israel), which included both urban and rural laborers, did not come into existence until 1920, preceding the founding of the state by nearly three decades. Three years later Histadrut adopted a formal program which eventually embraced every phase of the workers' needs and aspirations, personal as well as national.

Through its central body, Hevrat Ovdim—Workers' Cooperative Association—Histadrut carried on the economic institutions and established other agencies for the advancement of health, welfare, education, culture, local and national politics, defense, immigration, etc. It also engaged in such major services as labor exchanges, unemployment relief, funds for protection from other emergencies and old age.

Israel's General Federation of Labor differed radically at least in one major respect from its counterpart in America. The American Federation of Labor was composed of national and local trade unions, each autonomous in membership and administration. The individual worker's affiliation was with his local trade union only. In Israel the worker applies for membership directly to Histadrut. Following his acceptance he is assigned to the local branch, which lacks the power of rejection. In brief, while in America the national federation is the sum of its component parts, in Israel Histadrut is the all-controlling central power. Once Histadrut has conferred the privilege of membership on an applicant, the trade union to which he is assigned automatically concurs.

Israel's labor federation is open to all men and women of 18 years and over. Unlike other labor organizations, the self-interest of the constituted membership is not paramount. All persons meeting the qualifications of skill and the willingness to abide by Histadrut rules and regulations are eligible for membership even if the labor supply is greater than the demand. To maintain the labor organization and to be entitled to the benefits thereof, each member is required to pay dues amounting to 3 to 4½ per cent of his wages, depending on his income and the benefits derived.

The kibbutzim are part of Histadrut in their collective capacity. Their membership, however, is subject to their own jurisdiction. Unlike the rules governing all other workers, no member of Histadrut can be forced on a kibbutz for acceptance, since this involves the problem of compatability, of living together and sharing the cumulative possessions and services of the group. The kibbutzim recognize Histadrut's supremacy in all matters that do not violate their autonomy. Their financial obligation to Histadrut is determined by their economic capacity. The older and better established kibbutzim pay a higher rate than the more recent collective settlements, to minimize financial strain on the new groups. On the same principle, unemployed workers are allowed reductions from their insurance premiums for sick and other benefits.

Histadrut's membership grew from 175,000 in 1948 at the birth of the state to 500,000 in 1957, including wives of members. This represents about 75 per cent of all workers and close to 90 per cent of all organized labor in Israel. The remainder consists of the self-employed or proprietors of small workshops, too few to warrant the expense of organizing them.

If within the framework of Histadrut were also included the dependents of members, children, housewives, the aged, etc., then Israel's labor federation could accurately claim an overall influence touching on more than 50 per cent of the total population.

Women comprise almost one-third of the entire membership. They are gradually becoming the equal of men as assets in the economic, educational and political life of the country.

This is the comparative marital status within the Histadrut membership: of the male members 69 per cent are married and 29 per cent single with 2 per cent widowed or divorced. The female membership consists of 53 per cent married, 36 per cent single and 11 per cent widowed and divorced.

The labor force is divided into the following categories: agriculture, afforestation and fishing about 105,000—18 per cent; industry, mining and quarrying 127,000—22.3 per cent; construction and public works 53,000—9 per cent; electricity, gas and water 7,000—1.8 per cent; commerce and banking, 63,000—12.4 per cent; transporation, storage and communication 38,000—6.2 per cent; health, education, social welfare, public and personal service 172,000—29.4 per cent and the balance, a fraction of 1 per cent, are in miscellaneous fields.

Histadrut, the largest single organized force in the country, exercising a powerful impact on Israel's entire population, requires a vast machinery for administration. Though complex in its organization because of the great variety of interests and activities represented, Israel's labor federation employs entirely democratic forms. Despite the vested interests of some and the lust for power by others, in essence Histadrut is democratically governed, from the grass roots to the highest ranks. To begin with, each plant elects a workers' committee whose members in turn constitute both the local labor councils as well as the national trade unions, numbering thirty-three, in accordance with the various occupational categories promulgated by Histadrut.

From plant committee, local council and trade union embracing the various shades of economic and religious philosophies, Histadrut's democratic processes have evolved the main governing body. Selected at the General Convention, this body consists of a General Council of 291 members in whose hands are entrusted the policies of Israel's labor program. Since this number is too cumbersome to administer the detailed activities of so large an organization, the General Council elects an Executive Committee of 91 who in turn appoint an Executive Bureau with authority to administer the daily affairs of the federation.

The religious workers, under the auspices of Hapoel Hamizrachi and Poale Agudat Israel, numbering close to 15 per cent of Israel's labor force, were until recently separate entities. They joined Histadrut without forfeiting any of their distinctive religious attributes. Under Histadrut's democratic procedure their autonomy is preserved and protected. Similarly, the General Zionist workers, who do not share in the Socialistic tendencies or the planned state program of Histadrut's majority, have joined the General Labor Federation. Even the Arabs, who until 1953 were distinctly segregated from the Jewish labor movement and maintained two labor unions of their own, one Communist dominated and the other independent with slight Histadrut links, have with the exception of the Communist element become part of the General Labor Federation.

The various elected bodies, whether their function is policy making or managerial, are made up by proportional representation from the various parties constituting the General Convention, as evidenced by these figures. In the 1955 General Convention, Mapai had 58 per cent of the delegates; Ahdut Hoavodah and Mapan, the two other Socialist parties, combined, 27 per cent and the balance of 15 per cent was divided between the General Zionists, Progressive, religious parties and Communists. This proportion is reflected in the inner Executive Bureau of 13 members charged with the management of Histadrut's day to day affairs; eight from Mapai, four from the other two Socialist parties and one from the Progressive Zionists.

The leadership as a whole, is very close-knit. Those who held positions of importance in Histadrut's early development continue at the helm, unless they were transferred to government or Jewish Agency posts. Some of the highest executives serve in two or even three capacities, as do members of interlocking directorates of large corporations. This may prove to be ill-advised on two counts: one, Histadrut's continued progress in numbers and influence requires the ablest of the younger generation in its leadership if its development is not to stagnate. Two, should Histadrut's inner circle find no room for the most ambitious and talented in the lower strata of the present structure, the labor movement will suffer the consequences of fragmentation and paralysis from within. The younger elements, disillusioned in their quest for positions of leadership, will justify their dissensions and secessions on differences in ideology, when in reality they will be motivated by legitimate aspirations for place and power now monopolized by the "old guard."

What are Histadrut's major achievements in its program for improving the laborer's lot in Israel? The average worker is concerned first with wages and next with physical labor conditions, such as hours, speed-ups and the plant's facilities. In each of these areas there has been marked progress. The sweat shop does not exist in Israel, speed-ups are hardly known and the wages are relatively good.

The comparatively higher wage of the Israeli worker is due largely to Histadrut's efforts to establish and maintain a minimum wage standard. No minimum wage law has as yet been enacted by the state. This has made Histadrut's task more difficult but not less successful. The worker's average daily income approximates $3.90. Multiplied by six, his take is $23.40 per week, which, except for the American standard, is high compared to that of other countries.

Many economists, professional and amateur, believe even these wages are too high for a pioneering, resource-limited country like Israel. On the basis of the low standards of most undeveloped countries, Israel's wages are generous, but not generous enough to make ends meet. The average income ranges from about 1,800 IL to 3,600 IL per annum, depending on the category of employment and the sex of the worker. The average for the self-employed is 1,793 IL. The wages in agriculture and fisheries average 1,879 IL. In industry and craft the worker averages 2,037 IL; in building, 2,130 IL; in transport and communication, 1,793 IL and in the wholesale commercial field, 2,642 IL. The highest pay for workers is to be found in the rubber industry, in which they receive as much as 307 IL per month; stone and cement 297 IL per month, while the clothing worker nets about 200 IL per month. Despite the trend in Israel to make woman the equal of man, she has not as yet reached equality in wages, the difference at times being substantial.

The hours of labor per week, between 45 and 48, excluding overtime, are not excessive considering the still primitive conditions of the land and the need for larger production to compete in the world market against goods produced in countries where a lower scale of wages prevails.

The worker enjoys two breaks per day, one for breakfast and the other for lunch, the first necessitated by the early start of the workday in order to finish in time to avoid the hot sun of the middle afternoon. Workers in commercial enterprises rest between one to three or four P.M., making up lost time in the late afternoon to afford the population additional shopping time.

The farm laborers adjust their hours to suit the needs of the seasons. The communes, in the main, follow the industrial workers' day, with two modifications: during the spring-summer season they labor one hour longer per day, which begins at sunrise and concludes before the hot midday.

Next to wages, hours and other labor conditions, the worker is most concerned with the problem of tenure. Here too, the worker is indebted to Histadrut for stability of employment, now fairly well established throughout the land. The assurance of no dismissal without cause and the guarantee of seniority in employment affords the worker a sense of security in his struggle for a better life. Management, of course, prefers complete freedom of hiring and firing, both for the increase of production and to quell the rebellious spirit of employees. But with such an undisputed right, the slower laborer, whether because of his lack of capacity, age, sickness or indolence could be summarily discharged and the more productive worker hired. This unlimited power of management has been curtailed through Histadrut efforts. No organized worker can be dismissed without a hearing.

The federation has become the great "father" of the worker in another respect. When, for economic reasons, lay-offs become inevitable, Histadrut intervenes in behalf of equitable proportionate distribution of employment among all the workers without favoritism.

Perhaps the most contentious problem vexing the relations between Histadrut and management is the question of "last hired, first fired," in time of lay-offs. Efficiency of production demands that the most willing and energetic worker be retained irrespective of his seniority of service. Since Histadrut insists on retaining the principle of "last hired, first fired," it would seem that management has to fight a futile battle to be rid of the less efficient worker who becomes a drag on productivity. This is not necessarily so.

Both in private and public industry three causes for dismissal are considered valid. One, contraction of business, when it becomes necessary to reduce the roster of employees due to a curtailed demand for goods produced. The number of dismissals is not questioned. However, the union's demand that the last hired be first fired is the problem. On this issue there has been considerable conflict. Some day a modus operandi will be found acceptable both to labor and management for the solution of this difficulty. Two, proven inefficiency. Once the inefficiency of a worker is established and severance pay is granted, the employer is given the right to discharge. Three, indolence. An impartial committee is designated to determine the truth of the charge. If proven, the worker loses his right of tenure.

In brief, even with the principle of tenure, the employer has the right on proven complaint to dismiss workers for indolence, inefficiency and other valid causes, subject to severance pay in proportion to time employed. The principle of severance pay has become generally accepted to the extent that now many employers carry severance pay insurance as a legitimate business expense. Under such an arrangement the cost of severance is covered by tax reductions with little extra burden imposed on management.

Through Histadrut additional benefits have been conferred

on the workers, such as annual holidays. Vacations for working men and women with pay for 12 working days to a month, depending on length of employment, have become established practice. When both husband and wife work they may arrange to have vacations simultaneously. Even day workers are allowed a limited vacation through payments made by employers into a special fund.

Some conflicts of interest between labor and management are unavoidable. Especially in a new country like Israel, the differences may at times be acute. It is to the credit of Histadrut that conflicts have been held to a minimum. These comparative figures indicate the growing cooperative spirit holding labor and management together: in 1949 there were 53 strikes involving 5,193 workers, causing a loss of 57,436 man days of labor, with each worker losing approximately 10 days of gainful employment. In the succeeding years, the population mounted rapidly with no marked increase in loss of time due to employer and employee strife. Nineteen fifty witnessed 72 strikes involving 9,100 persons, each losing about six days of labor. In 1951 there were 76 strikes involving 9,715 workers causing a loss of about 12 days per individual. In 1952 the number of strikes rose to 94 involving 14,010 men with an average loss of four days' work per man. In 1953 the number of strikes was reduced to 89 involving 8,804 men with a loss of four days per worker. In 1954 there were 82 strikes embracing 12,128 men with an average loss of 5½ work days per employee. In 1955 there were 87 strikes in which 9,861 participated with an average loss of 4½ work days per worker.

As an indication of Histadrut's policy to avoid open conflict between labor and management wherever possible, the experience of 1955-56, fairly representative of other years, tells the story. The year 1955-56 registered a total of 1,369 disputes involving 7,095 workers. Three hundred and seventy-eight labor-management disputes were arbitrated, 754 were mediated and 237 were settled by intervention. In addition there were 450 applications from labor or management or both for guidance to avoid conflicts or threatened strikes. Thus many of the disputes that might have resulted in strikes with concomitant loss of wages and profits were avoided for the good of labor and management as well as for the country's stability.

The causes of friction between labor and management throw additional light on their mutual relations. Taking the 1955 experience as representative of other years as well, six strikes were called on account of wage rates; 12 concerned wage rates and general conditions; 22, general working conditions; 24, irregular payment of wages; five, recruitment of workers; seven, dismissal of workers or unfair distribution of work and 11, miscellaneous causes.

The clashes, short lived, did not end in complete victory or surrender for either side. The principle of give and take was applied by both. Forty-one disputes were settled by compromise and withdrawal of demands. Thirty-seven strikes resulted in a capitulation to labor and nine proved fruitless, the workers returning with no gains.

The labor-management picture is further clarified by labor's turnover situation. This is reflected in every field of endeavor. In 1949, dismissals on various grounds involved 5.7 per cent of employees while there were 7.43 per cent of new job placements. In 1950, dismissals decreased to 4.6 per cent as against 5 per cent new placements. In 1951 the proportion between dismissals and new employment was 4.3 per cent to 4.6 per cent. In 1952 the discharges remained the same as the previous year but the new placements fell to 3.4 per cent. In 1953 and 1954 the ratios were 3.4 per cent to 3.9 per cent and 3.5 per cent to 3.8 per cent respectively. The year 1955 showed 4 per cent of discharges as against 4.03 per cent new workers.

It is a source of embarrassment to the federation when one of its own enterprises is threatened with a strike. Equally difficult is the problem of dismissing the indolent and the less productive worker in Histadrut ventures. The organization cannot afford to become a model of efficiency with workers' tenure and security in jeopardy. It must find a synthesis between humaneness and efficiency. So far, whenever it was necessary to intervene in any of its enterprises threatened by conflict, its methods of conciliation resolved the difficulty.

In one particular labor owned and managed venture, Histadrut succeeded in dismissing almost 300 out of 950 employees as inefficient workers without any real dislocation of its dual function of employer and employee.

Three other substantial benefits are conferred by Histadrut on workers: labor exchanges, relief aid and sick benefits. The first was brought into being and maintained by the federation long before the establishment of the state, but is now largely financed by the government. The second, both in the form of insurance and direct support in time of distress, is still a major Histadrut responsibility, though the state has recently initiated under its own auspices the service of old age pensions. The third, sick benefits, through an advanced system of medical care and hospitalization known as the Kupat Holim, is a great humanitarian enterprise which extends beyond the confines of the laboring classes. It serves the entire country with distinction.

The federation maintains and conducts a network of 60 labor exchanges throughout the land. It is estimated that on the average the labor exchanges serve 32,000 workers per month. Until such time as the government takes over the task of locating job vacancies for equitable distribution among applicants, Histadrut continues to perform this difficult function. Considering the human imperfections involved in such a sensitive area as finding jobs for the unemployed, the federation, despite occasional criticism, has carried on this activity effectively.

Criticism and tensions in the distribution of jobs are inevitable. Applicants not fortunate enough to receive employment of the kind they seek will indicate their dissatisfaction sometimes with ill-tempered vehemence, stirring up feuds and rifts. That in some instances labor exchange authorities may favor particular friends or party members is believable. But as a general rule the labor exchange performs its function with a minimum of favoritism or partisanship. Available jobs are distributed among all workers irrespective of party affiliation.

Hapoel Hamizrachi and more recently Poalai Agudat Israel, the religious workers' parties, joined hands with Histadrut to make job distribution the joint responsibility of united labor. The applicant's needs are the primary considerations for priority in employment. Duration of unemployment, size of the family, health conditions and how many other members of the family are gainfully employed are the criteria. While the labor exchange is a Histadrut agency, the benefits are conferred on members and nonmembers as well.

In 1956 the federation's General Council recommended that the labor exchange service become a government function. Israel's Parliament after studying the question recently adopted a law embodying the recommendation subject to the provision that the agency to be set up is to have exclusive control of all applications from management and labor alike and that the service is to be rendered impartially, irrespective of political affiliation, religion, race, sex and age.

The unemployed worker, whether he be a victim of seasonal hazards or illness, needs aid to tide him over the period of economic distress. Histadrut is the organization to which he turns for help. Once a member is employed for two months he becomes entitled to up to 90 per cent of his wages for a period of eight months in time of unemployment. This aid accorded to union members out of work is derived from Histadrut funds set aside for the purpose, augmented by other sources made available for unemployment aid.

As an example of the efforts to make funds available for the unemployed it is worth recalling that following the Sinai Campaign, when unemployment became more aggravated, many workers turned in their vacation pay to the union for distribution among the unemployed. However, the major fund from which the unemployed are aided is derived from a system of insurance paid jointly by the worker and employer to Histadrut's Provident Fund. Part of the fund is also used for retirement purposes. Perhaps some day it may become a regular practice to utilize surpluses from the Provident Fund to supplement the income of old age pensions under government auspices.

In the area of medical care and hospitalization, through the Kupat Holim—the Workers' Sick Fund—Histadrut's contributions to the welfare of its union members in particular and to the public in general are the greatest organized form of benevolence in the country. It cares for those who are affiliated with Kupat Holim in sickness and old age from the cradle to the grave.

Its "health department," Kupat Holim, maintains nearly 900 clinics, 14 general and special hospitals plus a number of invalid homes as well as over 2,200 beds, the most modern medical equipment plus a staff of doctors, nurses and attendants. During 1957, Kupat Holim rendered aid to approximately 1,200,000 people. The expenses involved are in the main covered by workers' dues, from the 3 to 4½ per cent of their income, of which almost half goes to the Workers' Sick Fund.The government contributes 8 per cent of the Kupat Holim budget to help defray the deficit.

A less spectacular but nonetheless significant contribution is the Histadrut program in the field of education and culture in behalf of Israel's workers. In addition to governmental educational efforts, Histadrut carries on a cultural program for adults from beginners' Hebrew for the new immigrants to courses in vocational training, foreign languages, social studies, physical sciences, Bible and cognate subjects. The federation contributes from its budget substantial sums for scholarships to enable young people to receive a high school education. It publishes newspapers and periodicals. It encourages the theater and promotes sports on a large scale.

The Israeli worker is a willing and loyal member of Histadrut. He is fully aware of the many advantages he derives from his labor federation. Throughout his life he is dependent on it for his welfare. He finds his job through a labor exchange. He is assured of tenure and some financial assistance in any emergency that may arise. In time of sickness he can rely on Kupat Holim to afford him the necessary medical service. In old age he may expect additional aid to supplement his meager government pension. He may even be assured of care in case of disability with the burdens of the family lightened in the event of his death. Histadrut has brought to the worker a large measure of security and has given him a position of dignity in the land.

Few are the voices in Israel that are critical of Histadrut's distinguished role improving the lot of the worker through a fair living wage and decent working conditions. But the opposition in certain quarters is often vociferous and bitter in respect to its manifold industrial activities and capitalistic interests. Within the federation itself there are now ominous whispers questioning the wisdom of labor's widespread octopuslike control of the land's economy.

In agriculture, industry, commerce, finance and services, Histadrut plays a leading role. Not inclusive of the citrus groves, the collective and cooperative settlements affiliated with it produce 75 per cent of all the crops of the country. The 725 industrial enterprises which it developed during its existence are responsible for 23 per cent of the country's total industry.

The agricultural produce is marketed by Tnuva, a Histadrut cooperative organization which also distributes about 70 per cent of all bottled milk. Through the Hamashbir Hamerkazi—the Central Purchasing Cooperative—with its network of local consumer associations, Histadrut very likely supplies the needs of almost half the population.

The building industry, in all its allied branches of the federation, through Solel Boneh employs upwards of 50,000 workers. Through another cooperative it controls all passenger bus transportation service and has a substantial interest in Israel's airlines and shipping industries. Add to all these ownership, control or investment in various manufacturing enterprises, oil, chemicals and water distribution, and Histadrut's stature appears colossal. It is estimated that its ownership and control of agriculture and industry is valued at two billion IL. It is the biggest employer in the country, directing the destinies of almost half of all the employed. No wonder labor's economic empire looms so formidable in the eyes of many who see in it a real and present danger to individual initiative and private enterprise which they regard as essential for the state's growth and development.

Histadrut's present leadership disclaims any monopolistic character. According to recent authoritative statements it participates only in such enterprises as it believes are necessary for the economic well-being of the country and which do not attract private initiative because they involve risks to capital investments and offer too little profit.

There is recognition within the federation that not all is well with the organization. Bureaucracy is one of its major ills. Some ventures can be better handled by government or private entrepreneurs. Bus transportation is an example. But it is not fair to apply to the federation the frequently heard observation that "power corrupts and absolute power corrupts absolutely."

However, the fact that the leadership is aware of the shortcomings is a good omen. But two elements militate against immediate correction: ideology and vested interests. In the first instance, Histadrut was founded not only as a labor union to improve working conditions but to create a labor community, that is, a planned society, a perfect welfare state. The stout adherents of this ideal are not ready to abandon or modify their original program even in the face of practical necessity. Others in the seat of authority fear that concessions to the pragmatic needs of the country will force them to become "displaced persons" in any new setup. Their vested interests will not permit them to accede to change.

There is no doubt, however, that Histadrut has been a constructive force in the development of the country. Although founded in behalf of the laboring class, it serves the whole people. It has not set itself up as group against group, to strive for its own advantages irrespective of the common good. The Marxian principle of class struggle and Socialism in our day has been toned down. The federation, for the most part, is blessed with an enlightened leadership devoted to the ideal of nation-building above and beyond class interests. In its broader policy it has come, at least in theory, to recognize the mutuality of interest between labor and capital. It knows that the failure of the latter means unemployment with consequent ills to the workers as well as to the country. Therefore, for labor's sake, industry and commerce are encouraged and helped to operate at a profit.

In a number of instances Histadrut has utilized its welfare fund for the extension of loans either to save a business or industry from going under or to help them expand their facilities. This policy of aid and cooperation has also been applied to new enterprises for the purpose of creating new avenues for additional employment. Recognizing that new undertakings may not be able to compete with the efficient management of older establishments, the federation permits a lower wage scale up to 10 per cent to give the new venture a competitive chance to succeed.

Histadrut has also earned public approbation for its nonpartisan attitude in larger national areas, such as its support of the unified school system. Until 1953 political parties stressed their respective programs in the elementary schools under their aegis. This led to the consequent training of children to believe that party allegiance takes precedence over loyalty to country. Histadrut's support in behalf of the unified school system eliminated that evil.

For the country's good, the federation voluntarily decided to transfer the labor exchange to the government. While relinquishing this responsibility will lighten Histadrut's burdens, it will also considerably reduce its influence and power in the workers' ranks. But as in the area of education, its leaders expressed a willingness to part with this all-important function for the public weal. Likewise there are definite indications that the federation would be ready under certain conditions to turn over to the government the direction of Kupat Holim, the largest private health agency in the country.

All authorities in Israel are agreed on the importance of the project to conciliate the Arab population of the state, to endeavor to fuse them into Israel's life and influence them to become loyal citizens of the land. The task is still a distant goal. But whatever advances have been made in the direction of affiliating the Israeli Arabs have been due largely to the efforts of Histadrut. As members of the General Federation of Labor they have scored gains in wages, fringe benefits and the acquisition of better skills in agriculture and industry.

The nation is indebted to Histadrut for accomplishments in other fields as well. From early Zionist days it strove for increased immigration, playing a leading role in the sad but heroic chapter of bringing in "illegal immigrants" in defiance of the inhumane and shameful tactics of British authority. In defense of country, Histadrut served in the forefront during World War I, in the War for Independence and throughout Israel's statehood.

Aware of the need to advance the agricultural activity of the country, it initiated a "back to the land" movement of its own, resulting in the transplantation of 5,000 city and town workers to life on the farm in a period of three years.

The impartial observer is impressed with this distinguished organization's contribution to the welfare of the worker by making manual labor an honored occupation. It helped the worker to earn his bread with less sweat and fewer tears. And more than bread, it helped him to aspire to cultural attainments. But above all, it inspired the laborer with a sincere patriotic spirit transcending party and class interests. In a word, Histadrut lifted the worker to a status of human dignity. It made him a nation-builder.

The second vital force next in importance to Histadrut in the reshaping of the workers' lives is undoubtedly Mapai, the major Socialist party in Israel. Mapai in essence has been the yeast in Histadrut's phenomenal operations, particularly in projecting the program of cooperative ownership, marketing and purchasing. To be sure, Mapam and Ahdut Hoavodah, the more to the left Socialists, also made their contributions to these notable successes, but because of Mapai's wider influence, it is singled out to symbolize the political forces that helped make Histadrut great. In nearly four decades of that far-ranging organization's existence, Mapai has maintained a majority in the federation's elections, with a very perceptible increase in the last three elections: 53 per cent in 1945; 57 per cent in 1949 and 59 per cent in 1956.

Mapai, a union of the Poalai Zion and Hapoel Hatzair forces founded in 1930, began to prepare for statehood at its very inception. Its aim was the establishment of a labor commonwealth. It recognized that in the capitalist system the worker was not all-important. He was deemed primarily as a commodity to be bought or sold. In the struggle for a better life, capitalism placed property above human rights. Occasionally it relented and chose a position of neutrality: let the fittest survive. At best, paternalism, pity for the underdog, was the policy of the more enlightened, but they would not permit the laborer to be a partner in the economic and political life of the state.

Mapai set out with the goal of becoming the government, with power to make labor's voice dominant in the Jewish commonwealth to be. From the start it won the confidence of the Yishuv and continued to hold it throughout the British mandatory period. It linked its destiny with Histadrut, advocating and advancing many of the functions and activities which in time made the General Labor Federation the most powerful single force in Israel. While it was committed to the principle of a Socialist state, Mapai did not insist on a dogmatic implementation of its ideology. With a choice between unproven social theories and practical results, it frequently chose the latter.

At the inception of the state, the Yishuv's largest vote of confidence was conferred on Mapai. Though insufficient to command a one-party government, it nevertheless had the largest representation in Parliament and was summoned to head a coalition rule.

Thus was formed a famous triumvirate: Histadrut, Mapai and the government's Labor Ministry, united to help the worker improve his lot and become a more devoted and efficient builder of Israel. Through legislation the Labor Ministry enacted the regulation of hours of work, limiting it to 47 hours per week with overtime only by permission of the ministry. It established by law the principle of vacations with pay for all workers, temporary laborers receiving it in the form of extra pay. By state authority the ministry introduced new regulations governing working conditions for the youth intended to protect their health and moral development. It also organized apprenticeship courses to help the youth acquire a competence in various trades of their choice. Since the founding of the state 200,000 youths, immigrant and native, have been trained and retrained in a variety of trades and skills, thus adding substantially to the productive labor forces of the land.

The Labor Ministry is also to be credited with the enactment of the 1954 law prohibiting night work for women and granting maternity leave. Under its auspices, both day and night courses in vocational training for adults have been established. These have been especially helpful to the immigrant working contingent. In the first seven years of the state's career about 75,000 took advantage of these courses.

In 1955 the government also organized Maskit, the instrument by which immigrants are afforded the opportunity to be gainfully employed at home through various forms of handicraft. With Histadrut the Labor Ministry co-sponsors and helps to finance the 60 labor exchanges in existence. It renders aid in settling or avoiding labor disputes. In every phase of the worker's life, the Ministry of Labor is responsive to his needs.

The dreams, plans, efforts and attempts to make Israel a labor community are there. It would be erroneous, however, to conclude that the Israeli worker lives in a worker's paradise. While without Histadrut, Mapai and the Labor government his life would be much harder, it is still no bed of roses. His wages are comparatively high, but living costs are equally high. Seldom can a family be adequately supported by one breadwinner. Many of the comforts and luxuries enjoyed by the American laborer are unknown to his Israeli counterpart. But the Israeli workers are not less happy. They are conscious of themselves as nation-builders. Israel's success is as important to them as their own self-interest. They derive an incalculable and unpurchasable measure of satisfaction from the day to day visible progress of their people and their land.

The worker in the reborn state is the "servant in the house" of what, he believes, is destined to be a wonderful new temple of humanity.

XI. Zion and Diaspora

Will Israel's statehood lead to a divided and fragmented Jewish people, one segment in Israel and the other in the world outside of Israel?

If the present unrealistic attitudes are to continue to be intensified and congealed into dogmatic, watertight compartments, the concept of Jewish peoplehood may fade into the mists of illusion, and the trinity of Israel, God and Torah which the centuries have welded into a sacred unity as the raison d'être of Jewish life may be dissipated.

Both for the viability of the State of Israel and a significant Jewish life the world over, the mutual relationship and responsibilities of Israel and Diaspora Jewry must be sharply clarified and thoroughly understood.

There will always be Jews beyond Israel's territorial confines. No nation comprises all her nationals within her geographic boundaries. Long before Judea yielded her independence to the sledgehammer blows of Roman conquest there were large numbers of Jews who for economic and other reasons migrated to neighboring countries.

In Alexandria, Rome and other communities they settled in large groups, survived and even flourished in those places for many generations. They were accepted as citizens of their new lands of residence, retaining, however, a deep and abiding spiritual interest in their ancestral homeland. They rooted themselves economically in their adopted countries. Politically, also, they were consolidated into their new environments. Culturally, too, they accepted much from their new friends and neighbors. But because of their common origin and religion shared with fellow Jews in the Holy Land, they remained in sentiment closely affiliated with Judea. Thus they continued to draw inspiration from their motherland while rendering her every possible support consistent with obligations to their adopted lands.

The most amazing thing about the Jew of history is that he was able to adjust himself to every type of environment, clime, language, people and country on the face of the globe. Yet, against all odds, in spite of the blandishments of assimilation as well as of the pressure of persecution, he maintained his Jewish identity.

What were the contributing factors that enabled Jews to survive as minorities in various, far-flung locales in ancient as well as modern times for a much longer period than any other migrant group?

The non-Jewish immigrant transferring to a new environment had only to shed his previous social and political coloration and learn the language, local manners and customs of the land to become absorbed by it. Being not far removed from his new friends in religious and cultural character, he found himself at home with them in public worship, in the celebration of festive days and with a minimum of barriers to intermarriage.

Not so the Jew. While economically and politically he became adjusted almost overnight, he was compelled, because of his different religious heritage, to live under the regimen of two cultures, that of the new environment and his Jewish birthright which conflicted in various spheres. Observing as he did a religious calendar of his own, he necessarily set himself apart from the holy days and holidays of the rest of the community. His diet, governed by rigid religious regulations, served as a barrier against more intimate social contact. As his mode of worship required a knowledge of Hebrew, his Hebraic religious education and that of his children had to be continued. And out of fear of losing his Jewish identification he more consciously and vigorously opposed intermarriage.

Pressure of assimilation caused large numbers of Jews to

forsake their minority and exposed status to become completely absorbed in the non-Jewish community. Large numbers might have been absorbed and lost as Jews if assimilation had been a one-way avenue. However the majority population in most lands, to put it mildly, did not always entertain a cordial attitude toward the Jewish group. Discrimination, whether it be economic, political or social tends to discourage defection from the Jewish ranks. The weaker one falls by the wayside, but the stronger character develops a stouter resistance through resentment against prejudice, generating a more intense determination for a positive self-identification.

Historically the Jew acquired a larger capacity to persist under storm and stress than under favorable conditions. In the modern free world the Jew survived both, paradoxically, because of the prejudices which confined him to his own milieu and because of the more liberal attitudes which tempered religious distinctions. Whether cultural pluralism will ever become a dominant force in the free world, time only will tell, but certainly religious pluralism, too, appears to have taken root in modern free society. Since Judaism connotes a spiritual-cultural complex, Jewish minority survival, despite individual defections in the free world, seems assured in the foreseeable future.

Assuming the new Israel's continued existence together with Jewish life in the Diaspora, what will the attitudes and relationships be between the two? No racial kinship unites them. Except for some isolated groups in the backward, undeveloped world, racial purity is nonexistent. This fact is self-evident in Israel, the center of the "ingathering of the exiles," where every type of physiognomy and color, from the white to the very dark-skinned and from the blond to the black-haired, is to be found.

But there is a racial memory plus historic force which helps bind Jewry into a unity. It is more of a kinship of common ancestry than of blood and is a factor to be reckoned with for an understanding of the mystery of Jewish cohesiveness.

Though Jews differ in their physical characteristics from one another no less than they differ from non-Jews, their historic memories, like a centripetal force, tend to hold them together to such an extent that misfortune to one segment is felt by the rest of world Jewry. A common tradition of religion and culture is the tie that binds them.

Due to the dispersion and its concomitants, lack of a common territory, political sovereignty, military defenses, etc., the term nation as applied to other peoples was not applicable to Jewry. But Jews through the centuries have constituted a peoplehood with common traditions, symbols, ceremonies and a unity based on the one God idea, a galaxy of great historic figures, heroes, martyrs, scholars, saints and the common hope of restoration to the Holy Land with God as the acknowledged ruler of the universe. Throughout the Exile, Jews never ceased to be, spiritually, a nation.

Some Jews, thinking wishfully, misinterpreted the spiritual concept of Jewish oneness which, for lack of a better term, was labeled Jewish nationalism. In order to avoid suspicion of dual loyalties, they preferred to emphasize their difference from the non-Jewish citizenry of their adopted land as religious only, disclaiming other ties with world Jewry. To sever religion from Jewish peoplehood or dissociate the concept of Jewish nationhood from Judaism is as feasible as to detach the flame from the wick without destroying the light they jointly produce.

These Jewish religionists, known as liberals or reformers, however, who underscore their aloofness from "Catholic Israel" are haunted by fears of prejudice and possible rejection by their non-Jewish neighbors. The traditional, religious Jew deeply rooted in faith and practice finds it incongruous, in fact impossible, to deny his oneness with his people.

Judaism to the traditional Jew means, if nothing else, an affirmation of the threefold concept: God, Torah and Israel are one and indivisible. Jewish unity is best expressed by Israel's sages. When one limb is hurt all the others react sympathetically. The converse is equally true. The renewed energy and progress of one community of Jewry must inevitably invigorate the life of the entire Jewish people.

The Provisional Assembly selected "Israel," meaning protagonist or prince of God, as the name of the Third Jewish Commonwealth. The historic background of the designation as well as its euphonious sound met with almost universal approval. At first the selection of that name caused some confusion among Diaspora Jews. Through the centuries "Israel" denoted a nonpolitical characterization of the Jewish people. As a political entity, "Israel" did not exist after the fall of the Northern Kingdom of the Ten Tribes in 721 B.C.E. at the hands of Assyria. Thereafter "Israel" became vested with only a religious connotation as in the Biblical term, "Children of Israel," and symbolized Jewish peoplehood.

To illustrate the confusion created by the name "Israel" for the Third Jewish Commonwealth: the formula of the presentation of the wedding ring at a marriage ceremony concludes with the phrase "in accordance with the law of Moses and Israel." This surely does not mean the "State of Israel" but the "Children of Israel"—a religious and not a political appellation. By this time, however, it has become clear that an Israeli is one who is a citizen of the State of Israel and that all others of the faith of Israel wherever they reside, are properly known as Jews.

The founders of the Third Jewish Commonwealth had no intention to categorize all Jews as Israelis. All Jews are of the Jewish people but not all are Israelis, although there are and will always be many ties that constitute a universal Jewish unity. The relationship between Israel and world Jewry has been succinctly expressed by Ben Gurion: "I am a Jew first and an Israeli only afterward, for in my conviction Israel was created for and on behalf of the whole Jewish people."

Every Jew who lives outside of Israel is a citizen of his country, required to do his duty and entitled to his rights like any other citizen. But every Jew, wherever he may be, belongs to the Jewish people. There is a historic national cohesion of the Jews of the world, a cohesion based on a common heritage, common aspirations and common destiny.

Hardened Zionist opponents accuse the new state of arrogating to herself the political adherence of all Jews. This is a groundless assertion prompted by prejudice and ignorance. Not only are Jews of other lands considered by Israel as citizens of their respective countries, but citizens of other lands who come to reside in Israel are not recognized as citizens until they voluntarily become naturalized by signifying their wish to become citizens. Otherwise they remain ineligible for military service or public office and are not subject to taxes, money exchange, etc. Since the birth of the state, 39,414 residents declared their intention to retain the citizenship of their respective native or adopted lands. From the Israeli laws and actions it is amply evident that the new state has in no wise attempted to impose a political status on Diaspora Jewry.

Nevertheless it is important to point out the basic factors which represent a positive unity between Israel and world Jewry.

The principle of the "ingathering of the exiles," Israel's open door policy, definitely invites any Jew anywhere in the world to enter the land at any time. This solicitude for the Jewish immigrant has moved some American zealots to seek the U.S. State Department's intervention against this Israeli policy on the ground that it sets up a dual allegiance and that this special consideration of Jews infringes on their rights as Americans.

Does the "ingathering of the exiles" challenge the citizenship rights and duties of Jews in the Diaspora? Without spelling it out explicitly the United States has for some time maintained a more favorable policy toward Anglo-Saxon immigrants. Does this in any way affect the citizenship status of Anglo-Saxon peoples? The Israeli special immigration consideration is based on human needs, on providing a home for the homeless, a fundamental Zionist principle.

Now that Zionist aims have been realized, shall not Israel keep her doors wide open to all Jews who wish to enter for whatever reason—to escape religious or political persecution; to improve their economic status; to take advantage of desired educational opportunities or join creative forces in the building of people, land, culture and religion? The fact that there are free Jews, first-class citizens who need no open door policy, does not minimize the validity of the principle of the "ingathering of the exiles." History has placed a moral as well as historic obligation on fortunate Jews to help keep Israel's gates open for all their brethren who have abandoned hope of a better life in their native lands.

While Israel's doors are open primarily to the downtrodden, she nevertheless looks also for immigrants from the free world. Israel is anxious to receive increasing contingents of newcomers from the Western World, but not for reasons of territorial expansion. Israel's current borders are more than ample to contain additional sizable numbers of immigrants. The desire for a larger mass influx is based on three factors: uninhabited land is used as ammunition by the neighboring Arab states by affording them the invidious argument to justify within the United Nations a reduction of Israel's territory to the pre-armistice lines. Therefore, the greater the population and the more occupied the land, the less effective become the Arab contentions for the curtailment of Israel's territory. Another factor is of a strategic nature. To meet the danger of the growing military power of the Arab world, Israel needs a larger population from whom to draw manpower for stronger defense forces. Thirdly, to counterbalance the large number of unskilled immigrants from the Oriental countries, the Western immigrant possessed of the "know-how" is essential both for the economy of the land as well as for higher cultural standards.

In recent days a Zionist was defined as one who settles permanently in the Holy Land. All others may be friends or supporters of Israel but not Zionists, co-partners in the historic processes of making Israel a viable state and nation. Diaspora Zionists dispute this definition. The Basel Program adopted at the First World Zionist Congress stipulates that "the aim of Zionism is to create a publicly recognized, legally secured home for the Jewish people in Palestine." The word "people" is to be underscored. While the Zionist program looks to individual men and women to build the Jewish national home, it in no way implies that only those who established themselves in Palestine are Zionists. It does mean that everyone who furthers the cause of Zion rebuilt is a Zionist, each serving the cause in accordance with his special capacity and means, no matter where he resides.

The history of Zionist achievement argues in favor of maintaining this classic definition of a Zionist. Israel needs all the friends and helpers it can muster whether they be Zionists or not, but a basic distinction remains between them and the Zionist. The former are motivated primarily by humanitarian sympathies; the latter in addition aspires toward a Jewish national status in the Holy Land with all that it implies—political sovereignty, economic self-sufficiency, and religious cultural creativity.

Furthermore, for Israel's sake, single-minded Zionists in the Diaspora are most important as the yeast in the formula of a growing friendship for the new state. For the maintenance of the historic ideal of Jewish peoplehood, Zionists beyond Israel's borders are as important as Israeli Zionists. For the Diaspora Zionist entertains even a broader view of Jewish people and life than does the provincial Israeli nationalist who claims all Jewry for the state's future and sees eventual doom for Diaspora Jewry.

According to Ben Gurion, "The Zionist organization has lost its soul and all its Zionist significance," and therefore he implies that its dissolution might be desired. Ben Gurion ignores the inherent vitality of the Zionist organization to keep world Jewry's deep interest in Zion alive. While Israel's friends are moved by good impulses to aid, Zionists are possessed by an inner urge to serve even in politically adverse atmospheres. Without world Zionism there might have been no U.N. Palestine decision. Without a virile Zionist organization Israel's position in the free world might be less secure.

To add potency to the argument for Jewish mass migration from the free world to Israel, proof is offered for the inevitability of Jewish dissolution in the Diaspora. This is the inexorable law of history according to these pseudorealists. As anti-Jewish pressures are relieved and social discrimination diminishes, Jews tend to lose their identity and become absorbed in the general population. Denmark, Norway, Sweden and Finland are cited as examples of this tendency. To avoid the dangers of assimilation threatening Jews in the free world, they are urged to settle in Israel to become true partners in the thrilling adventure of the reborn nation.

The objective observer cannot deny the uphill struggle for Jewish survival in the Diaspora lands. The truth is that while many of the weak ones fall by the wayside, the general trend is a substantial increase in synagogue affiliation, religious education and philanthropic institutions, and this trend does not spell doom for the Jewries of the free world.

The precise content and form of Jewish life of tomorrow in the free world cannot be predicted. But judged by historic precedents, Jewish survival even under favorable conditions is quite feasible. Judaism endured in the past not only under stress but under fortunate circumstances as well. Jewish life in Alexandria and the Golden Age period in Spain testify to that fact.

The present-day experience of the northern European countries is not applicable to America and other parts of the world where the majority of Jews reside. Two underlying differences distinguish the former from the latter. The northern European lands have never had more than a very limited Jewish population, incapable of maintaining the necessary institutions and trained professional leadership for the advancement and the deepening of the Jewish spirit. Secondly, the social barriers which characterize discrimination against Jews elsewhere have broken down in those northern countries, thus creating a more favorable atmosphere for intermarriage on a broader scale.

In America, England and elsewhere, where the Jewish population is considerable and is chiefly concentrated in the larger cities, there is no serious lack of institutional instruments and professional leadership for the preservation of Jewish life. The social barriers which have almost been obliterated in northern Europe still prevail in North America as well as in other sections of the free world as a constant whiplash to the Jew, forcing him to live with "his own kind."

With few exceptions, not only is the Jew an unwilling "victim" of intermarriage but the gentile resents it as well. While it is indeed easier to live a full Jewish life in Israel than in the Diaspora, it is not a foregone conclusion that the Jew in the free world does not have the will or capacity to be a faithful heir to his Jewish historic past, even adding to its spiritual treasures.

The fact that it is more difficult to thrive under the aegis of two civilizations than of one is no reason for the abandonment of hope for the continuity of Jewish life in the Diaspora. Those who predict the eventual liquidation of a creative Jewish life in the Diaspora may as well revise their prophecy of doom. History has proven Judaism's astounding capacity for adjustment to new conditions in a changing world. It has flourished under freedom as well as under pressure.

The unprecedented Nazi atrocities cannot happen in a democratic world. Jews in America, England and elsewhere are not alarmed by the prediction of a Jewish blackout in their respective lands.

Only they are really in exile who by force are transplanted

to an unwanted land with no freedom of exit. This does not apply to Jewry in the free world. Jewish history has always distinguished between galut—exile—and hutz la-aretz—voluntary domicile beyond Israel's borders.

What of the future? Are the Jewish people safe even in a democracy like America, the home of the largest unit of Jewry?

Anti-Semitic destruction of Jewish life cannot happen in the U.S. As far as it is possible to predict, while Jews may suffer some form of individual discrimination in various phases of American life, official anti-Semitism, degrading the Jew to second-class citizenship or, even worse, wholesale physical persecution, is neither probable nor possible in America.

Despite anti-Jewish prejudices in the economic, educational, political and social spheres of American life, no governmental policy of drastic anti-Semitism can be fostered in America so long as America remains a democracy in fact as well as in theory. Both the principles upon which American democracy was established and the practical experience of nearly two centuries negate any prophecy of the decimation of American Israel.

The United States is a land of multiple races and religions. The population of America is heterogeneous, a blend of all the racial strands of the peoples of the Western World. While racial descents and national origins will gradually be merged, religious differences will continue as constitutionally protected natural rights for all majority and minority groups.

Unlike Hitler's Germany, where a program of fiendish anti-Semitism was possible because of the racial homogeneity of its Teutonic population, America is a pluralistic and not a monolithic society, affording all people of different racial origins and all religious persuasions the right to live together peacefully and harmoniously despite their differences. If one religious minority is oppressed all others would be in equal danger and in self-interest would unite to oppose such oppression. Therefore, irrespective of the party in power, the Jewish minority need have no fear concerning its future position in the U.S. The American Constitution, which cannot easily be amended, is a further guarantee of Jewish security and equality of status.

But what if another world war with consequent upheaval could lead the United States to dictatorship and abandonment of its Constitution? Should an atomic catastrophe strike the world, extinguishing the light of freedom in the United States, darkness would descend on all mankind with no safety for Jewry anywhere, not even in Israel.

Wishful thinkers and alarmists might as well face it. Large numbers of Jews in the free world will not be persuaded to uproot themselves from their native lands to settle in Israel either because of the need of building up the new state more securely or to avoid eventual extinction in their present lands, either by the threat of persecution or the force of assimilation.

In fact the Exile ceased when the new Israel was born. Zion redeemed is the unanswerable refutation of the cruel and wicked calumny of Eugene Sue's "Wandering Jew."

Jews remain in the free world by choice as the full exercise of a moral right. But even in the Communist countries where the freedom to emigrate is universally abrogated, the concept of galut does not apply. There is always the hope that in a fast-changing world some way will be found or a new miracle will happen affording the Children of Israel the opportunity to leave their modern houses of bondage. If and when that happens the new Israel will stand ready and eager to welcome them.

Does this imply that no Jewish immigration from the free world to Israel is possible? A number of Jewish immigrants from the Western World to the ancient homeland is both desirable and feasible; desirable not only for Israel but for Diaspora Jewry as well. The oneness of Jewish peoplehood everywhere will be considerably enhanced as Jewish families from various groups and communities of the free world are physically as well as spiritually bound up with the life of Israel. They will serve as living links between Diaspora Jewry and the Jewry of

Israel; a two-way unofficial ambassadorship of substantial mutual understanding and good will.

What are the possible sources of immigration to Israel from the free world? The general motivating factors for settling in Israel are four: persecution, economic improvement, nationalism and a new social order. If emigration flows from the hunger for bread, for freedom or both in backward lands, then the Jew of the free world is not a likely candidate for settlement in Israel. Therefore the Zionist idealist and nationalist Socialist uninfluenced by material considerations but eager to become actual partners in the building of the land are the most likely prospects in the free world as settlers in the Holy Land.

But if the idealists with means and experience who in addition are more than romanticists are to be attracted to Israel, they must receive greater encouragement and assurance from her government for the safe investment of their capital and their useful labors in that land.

Zionist idealists are not lacking among the self-employed and the laboring classes as well. To encourage the pioneering spirit of the latter, Israel's government must afford them the assistance it so readily lends to those who flee from oppression. It is roughly estimated that the Jewish Agency for Israel spends and invests $10,000 for every refugee family settling in Israel. They, of course, deserve priority. They who are the victims of inhuman persecution should receive first consideration. But it is important to give a helping hand also to the prospective immigrant from the free world and to offer him worthwhile concessions, for through his skill he will help raise the standard of living of all Israel. The self-employed with capital of their own, as well as the less affluent, must be given aid and counsel for sound investments, profitable to them and to the state's economy.

In addition to the idealists, another group of prospective immigrants from the Western World might be attracted to Israel, such as retired persons with pensions, social security or other forms of modest incomes. Many of these, though elderly, have skills and talents that could well be utilized. These elements would bring a twofold benefit to Israel: American dollars and links with their families and friends abroad, and thus help create additional ties between Diaspora and Israel.

The greatest contribution to Israel's growth can be made by those who have been trained in technology and the various sciences. If larger numbers of them could not be induced to transplant themselves permanently to the Holy Land they might be persuaded to give a few years of their "know-how" to projects of special interest in their chosen fields. Some who may be willing to come on a temporary basis, enamored of a people's magnificent dedication to the rebuilding of a nation, might well feel "the call" to throw in their lot with the new state permanently. The returnees would most likely become messengers of good will in behalf of Israel.

The idealists, the retired and the specialists would not register a mass migration to Israel from the free world, but they could provide sufficient numbers to be advantageous to the new state and effective for the spiritual rejuvenation of Diaspora Jewry.

Israel and the Diaspora are intrinsic parts of a greater whole, the Jewish people. Their relationships must be sound and mutually helpful for the good of each and for the good of Catholic Israel.

In the early days of Zionism, that movement was the cause of divisiveness in Jewish life. It comprised at first a small group of Zionists with a considerable background of inactive sympathizers and with opposition from many circles of Jewry.

The extreme orthodox condemned Zionism as secularist and contrary to the traditional concept of a Messianic redemption of Israel, prior to the rebuilding of Zion.

The reform movement, abandoning every hope and desire for the rebirth of Jewish nationhood, ascribed to Jewish dispersion the allegedly divine plan of spreading the mission idea in the world, and they claimed that a return to Zion spelled a reversion to tribalism. Jewish laborers saw their salvation either in union movements or in striving toward the fulfillment of Marxian Socialism. Territorialists, Diaspora nationalists, Yiddishists (advocates of Yiddish as a language and culture) and other opponents strove against Zionism with more or less ferocity.

With the consummation of Zionism Israel has become the great unifying force in Jewish life. Except for a small but vociferous group, the American Council for Judaism, all Jewish movements, parties and organizations now look to Israel as the symbol of Jewish solidarity. Israel as an ideology provoked antagonisms; Israel as a reality has evoked universal Jewish sympathy.

Two recent major historic events closely following each other proved to be irresistible forces of cement that reestablished Jewish unity. The blazing heat of Hitler's insensate and revolting atrocities against the Jews rekindled their spirit of kinship. It sparked a longing for togetherness among all camps of Jewry.

This was a kinship not limited to mere passive sympathy but to open hearts and willing hands eager to throw a lifeline to those caught in the unprecedented human tragedy. This spirit of unity was further confirmed and intensified by the electrifying event of the rebirth of the State of Israel. The Jewish people were brought together as partners in distress and then, with closed ranks, marched forward as brothers of one great hope.

The fulfillment of that hope for the revitalization of an economically and spiritually flourishing Zion will justify the faith that the six million martyrs of our day did not perish in vain.

Free world Jewry is vitally interested in Israel's well-being and in the maintenance of binding ties between the two. The new state is included as a subject of study in the curriculum of the Diaspora religious school. In the houses of worship the ancient prayers for Zion rebuilt, with God's spirit dwelling therein, have taken on new meaning. The interest in Hebrew as a full-fledged living language and literature has received a powerful impetus since Israel's rise to statehood.

Visits to the Holy Land have increased considerably. Articles of handicraft, particularly of a religious nature, made in Israel exercise a strong appeal to Jews in the Diaspora. The financial help through the United Jewish Appeal and Bonds for Israel is a fabulous outpouring of Jewish generosity. When one also takes into consideration the monetary aid given to specific causes like Hadassah, Labor Zionist, Mizrachi, United Fund for Israeli Institutions, Jewish National Fund, Hebrew University, Haifa Technion, Weizmann Institute and large numbers of Talmudic academies as well as eleemosynary institutions, the huge amounts contributed by Diaspora Jewry to Israel are fantastic.

To this Herculean record must be added the help rendered by individuals to their impoverished relatives and friends in Israel. This unprecedented generosity is yielding a rich return to Diaspora Jewry in terms of a reawakened interest and pride in an affirmative Jewish life.

This spiritual quid pro quo is reflected in the Jewish folklore tale of the two travelers in no man's land who were overtaken by inclement weather. When one was in danger of freezing to death the other massaged him to accelerate his blood circulation for warmth, and thus through the effort to keep his fellow traveler alive he, by his vigorous effort, saved his own life from the threat of the wintry blast.

All the campaigns in behalf of Israel with the accompanying lectures, conferences, meetings and public dinner events frequently addressed by Israeli representatives result not only in an enormous volume of vital aid to Israel but help to stimulate Jewish survival and revival in the Diaspora as well.

While Diaspora interest in Israel continues unabated, the reverse is unfortunately not true. Israel's eagerness to welcome new immigrants and receive substantial funds with which to enable the settlers to be "at home" in the new land is evident enough. But her interest is in the gift, not the giver. This is no exaggeration.

The natives known as sabras—born in Israel—on the long road to Jewish independence lost 17 centuries of Jewish history. All that happened in the Galut—Exile—since Jewish expulsion under Rome until the birth of modern Jewish nationalism is of little interest to them. The lives and spiritual achievements of the scholars, saints and martyrs of past generations and their historic importance make scarcely any impression on them. As Ben Gurion put it: "I have no special longing for the near or distant past of the Diaspora. My profound and basic attachment is to the period of our ancient history—from the Patriarchs to the early Hasmoneans."

In a sense he accepts the Toynbee verdict of Jewish history that it ceased to exist beyond the Biblical era, except that the modern historian strongly believes in the resurrection of the Nazarene only, while Israel's prime minister accepts as real only the national rebirth of the Jewish people. His leap from Bible days to the 20th century is most perilous to Jewish continuity, an integral element in the concept of Jewish peoplehood.

The younger Israelis discount even the significant contributions of Diaspora Jews to the fulfillment of the Zionist dream. They are not familiar with the distinguished names of Diaspora leaders. Few of the younger generation in Israel have any adequate knowledge of the Zionist accomplishments of such notables as the late Justice Louis D. Brandeis of the United States Supreme Court, Dr. Stephen S. Wise, Dr. Abba Hillel Silver, Louis Lipsky, Emanuel Newmann, Judge Julian W. Mack, Rev. Z. H. Masliansky and other important figures in the history of American Zionism. Israeli teen-agers are unaware of the renowned activities of Jews in the Diaspora, distribution of their population, their religious interests, their cultural progress or the countless problems in their complex program of living in two civilizations.

Were it not for the much-needed funds it provides, Diaspora Jewry might be completely written off from the life of the Jewish people by the Israeli community. Courses of study in contemporary Jewish life the world over are either completely lacking or very limited to the "Jewish consciousness" study in Israel's educational system. The most frequently repeated question which challenges the tourist in Israel is not, "How do you live as a Jew in your country?" but, "How soon will you settle here?"

This ignorance of Diaspora Jewish life and the unconcern with regard to it is a curious phenomenon throughout the land. The newspapers and magazines in Israel neither report adequately Jewish world events of vital importance nor discuss in any detail the difficulties with which Diaspora Jews have to cope.

Undoubtedly there are in Israel educators and other leaders of Jewish thought who are dissatisfied with this attitude toward Diaspora Jewry, but much effort has to be invested to enlighten public opinion in Israel to an understanding of the truth that the Jewish people is greater than any of its parts, including Israel.

That revolutionary thought was recently voiced by Ben Gurion. But if it is not to remain a voice crying in the wilderness, the official leadership must see the light and reverse its wishful belief in the inevitable disappearance of Diaspora Jewry, whatever the climate, under favorable skies or under storm and stress.

To further the present remarkable devotion of Diaspora Jewry to Israel, the Israelis must foster genuine sympathy for and understanding of Diaspora Jewry. It is no longer a choice between one and the other. Rather it is both or neither. In the former days of Zionist propaganda it was necessary for Zionists to minimize the importance of Diaspora Jewry in order to emphasize the urgency of the cause of Zion rebuilt. In answer to many who contended that the Jewish problem could and should be solved in the lands of Jewish dispersion, Zionist propaganda endeavored to prove that Jewish life in the Galut was neither feasible nor desirable. To further that argument the Zionists made no distinction between the Exile and Diaspora. In one the Jewish body, in the other the Jewish spirit is oppressed, they contended.

The old arguments have to be reversed. They have lost their potency and validity. Israel is no longer a theory but a fact: a home for the homeless Jew and a spiritual fountainhead for world Jewry.

In Israel, too, they make a distinction in the "law of return" between the pressured Jew in benighted lands and the emancipated Jew in the free world, as expressed in the Basic Principles of the Government Program: "The bringing of Jews from countries where they are distressed and encouragement of immigration from other countries." Encouragement does not and should not imply liquidation of all Jewry outside of Israel. The survival of one depends upon the other. Israel and Diaspora need have no conflicting interests, either in ideology or in practical programs. They are interdependent. Thriving Jewish communities in the free world will continue to aid Israel morally and financially. Diaspora Jewry will gain much in unpurchasable values through a resurgent Jewish national life in Israel. In the idiom of the day, everything must be done to achieve fusion between Israel and world Jewry and to avoid fission in Jewish peoplehood.

The gravest danger threatening the relationship between Israel and world Jewry lies in the different emphasis on Jewishness, the former stressing the national cultural and the latter the religious cultural aspects.

Israel, on gaining national sovereignty, naturally had to focus her attention on defense, diplomacy, police, taxes, commerce, industry, education, public utilities and the like. Diaspora Jewry has no direct responsibility or concern for any of these instruments of state. Therefore, these alone cannot build the bridge to link Israel and world Jewry into one Jewish peoplehood.

Neither Israel's internal nor external political affairs can advance the cause of world Jewish unity. Other forces, mainly spiritual and cultural, must be the common denominator through which mutual relationships can be maintained between Israel and Diaspora. What, then, are the basic requirements for a lasting wedlock between the two?

Jews are brothers of equal rank the world over. This attitude must continue to be emphasized, though there may be no gainsaying the claim that Jews in Israel have made greater personal sacrifices for the establishment and maintenance of the state than their brethren in the Diaspora. There must be a mutuality of interests with high regard for each other's accomplishments, each willing to help the other materially and spiritually according to ability and need.

Israel's political policies, form of government, economic system or foreign affairs are the concern of her citizenry, not to be challenged by Diaspora Jewries. Yet, Israel, though a sovereign state, in her foreign relations must reckon with the fortunes of Jews in the Diaspora. With no obligation to consult Diaspora Jewry, nevertheless, if Israel's position is to be morally supported in the chancelleries of the world by Jewish leaders in their respective countries, that position must be internationally defensible. Furthermore the State of Israel must be circumspect in her decisions and actions in order not to undermine or adversely affect Diaspora Jewries.

Israel has the right to expect sympathetic understanding and support for her policies from world Jewries, but not at the price of conflict with the laws of their respective lands. The new state must not look for help from the Diaspora which might in any manner jeopardize the citizenship status of any Jew outside of Israel. Under all circumstances, Jews in Israel and everywhere else must foster the spirit of a mutually constructive brotherhood based on the threefold principle that God,

Israel and Torah are one, and that therefore they must be considerate of each other's best interests.

It is of the greatest importance that a more positive attitude toward the principle of Jewish peoplehood be fostered in Israel through the classroom, public platform, press and book. The Israelis must become more conscious of Diaspora's contributions to their material well-being together with a greater awareness of the problems confronting the Jews of the world in their striving for a better Jewish life in their own native countries which they call home.

The Jews in Israel, for example, have no comprehension of the problem of anti-Semitism. To them all the efforts of Jewish self-defense groups in the Diaspora seem trivial. They who live as members of a Jewish majority are not cognizant of the various problems of Jews who live in a minority status. And yet, with all the environmental differences, all Jews are brothers, members of one people though different in political allegiances.

Furthermore, cultural ties must be strengthened to give the Jewish peoplehood idea greater reality. For the large communities of Jews outside of Israel, Hebrew will remain the sacred tongue for prayer and study, with the vernacular as the instrument of daily usage. However, despite the limited use of Hebrew in the Diaspora, the revival of Hebrew in Israel with an extensive literature of general and religious character is destined to afford new spiritual ties with Diaspora Jewry. Since secular Hebraic culture is bound to be less stressed in the Diaspora, Israel's strongest rapprochement with world Jewry must come through the area of Torah, Jewish law and lore. To paraphrase the sentiment of an Israeli religious spokesman: we as a nation have the power to withdraw our army from Sinai but we cannot withdraw from the law of Sinai.

Israel's burgeoning arts—song, dance, drama, painting, sculpture and all other esthetic forms expressive of the new Jewish life—can serve as tangible links uniting Israel and the Diaspora.

Exchange of students and teachers with an ever-growing

number of tourists will unquestionably forge additional ties. It must be made certain, however, that the students encouraged to visit the Land of Israel to draw inspiration from its fascinating victories of brain and brawn are not influenced to depreciate or negate Diaspora Jewish life. On the contrary, they should be made to feel that Jewish life in their respective homelands is both desirable and feasible and that their sojourn in the Holy Land is intended to instruct them to become more effective leaders for the survival and further advancement of the Jew and Judaism in their native lands.

The professional Jew, to be successful in his leadership and activities, must be "home grown." But he will gain in stature and usefulness by spending a year of study and observation in the Holy Land. He will then also serve as an unofficial carrier of good will to Israel and on returning will bring back the inspiring revelations which he will have gathered during his "pilgrimage" to the Holy Land.

For a considerable time to come there will be a scarcity of trained Hebrew and religious teachers in the Diaspora. For the mutual benefit of world Jewry and Israel a "teachers' lend-lease program" might well be established. Israel could send forth some of her most proficient teachers for a two-year period to serve the spiritual needs of the communities to which they are assigned. The radiations of their influence will carry healing strength to both countries. They will bring with them the rejuvenating spirit of renascent Israel and on their return will sympathetically reinterpret Diaspora Jewish life to the people of the new Zion.

Important as is the philosophy of peoplehood and culture for the spiritual marriage of Israel and Diaspora, the all-important factor remains religion. If the danger of dichotomy, two separate, if not separated, Jewish peoples, one in Israel and the other in the Diaspora, is to be averted, Jewish religion, belief and practice must be the ineluctable basis for Jewish unity.

In Israel the situation is contradictory and confusing. On the one hand, large and influential groups live by secular philosophies. They consider religion as the outworn trappings of the Exile to be discarded by free men in a free land. On the other hand, there are the zealots who will tolerate no deviation from or reinterpretation of Jewish law and practice for cryingly needed adjustments to the demands of the new life.

When liberal elements from Diaspora Jewry settle in Israel and are forbidden to practice religion in accordance with the dictates of their conscience, they find the situation frustrating while their outraged sensibilities set in motion reverberations of sympathy from their coreligionists in their homelands. The bonds are also damaged among other communities of world Jewry when tourists have to search in vain for a kosher restaurant in Tel Aviv or Haifa or find no place of worship or a Holy Scroll in many of the kibbutzim.

A fast-growing awakening to the failure of secularism has led to the introduction of "Jewish consciousness" as a subject of instruction in the school system of Israel. The type of teaching and the caliber of the individual home will be the determining influence in the effort to inculcate Jewish traditions in the life of the average Israeli. While the dynamics of Jewish life in Israel may not produce a revival of past Jewish religious experiences, it is certain that Jewish kinship and esprit de corps in Israel must be based on some well defined form of religious philosophy and practice.

Israel may not yet know it, but she is desperately in need of a continuing vigorous Jewish life in the Diaspora not alone as a reservoir from which to continue to draw sustenance but because it is spiritually closely allied to her striving toward the fulfillment of her national aspirations. This alliance should be primarily religious, cultural and esthetic.

Jewish nationalism in its political phases must of necessity be limited to the borders of Israel. Therefore it is both logical and historically essential that every effort be expended in Israel to make her religious life fruitful not only for her own sake but for the sake of world Jewry.

The greatest obstacle against the execution of such a policy can be spelled out in the single word: rigidity. The official religious leaders must recognize the need for more tolerant and flexible attitudes and a reinterpretation of Jewish beliefs and practices in the light of the revolution that has occurred in Jewish life. The secularists influenced by Marxist philosophy must relax their harsh opposition to what they term Galut Judaism.

Both the extreme right and the extreme left must learn that the new life requires a new Jewish consolidation based on the Jewish past with aspirations transcending the idea of just another "nation among the nations." The Israelis must become a spiritual people united with Jewry everywhere for the advancement of Jewish nobility of soul capable of contributing to the welfare of mankind.

In essence, the new Jewish state must learn to live spiritually, and encourage world Jewry so to live, to the blessing of each other and the world.

XII. Arab and Jew

When the argument was raised in the early Zionist days, "What of the Arabs?" the wishful answer was: "They seem to be more of a problem to the anti-Zionist in the Diaspora than to Palestine itself. Are they not cousins of the Jew racially and linguistically? Besides, to live as kindred is for the common good of both peoples. When they realize the benefits from material advancement which Jewish immigration with Western know-how is destined to bring them, they will welcome the new-comers as brothers." Fortunately for Zionist leadership, they did not foresee the hard realities of the Arab problem while the cause of restoration of Zion progressed. Otherwise, the will and ardor for reconstituting the Jewish state in the Holy Land would have been considerably dampened.

In distant history Arab-Jewish relations were less strained than in the modern era but, contrary to some popular misconceptions, there were other periods as well when Arab animosity threatened the Jewish remnant. An Arab-Jewish "Golden Age" did exist in the Spanish period of the 10th and 11th centuries. Individual Jews held political and economic positions of trust in Moslem lands. Jews became adept in the Arabic language for daily use and literary activity. They became the cultural intermediaries between the East and the West. It is doubtful, however, that the Moslem masses were at all conscious of a Semitic kinship with Abraham's descendants.

Palestine became a dominantly populated Arab country in 638 C.E., four years after Mohammed's death, as a result of conquests by outside Arab caliphates. The decisive war which resulted in the surrender of Jerusalem to Caliph Omar helped save the Jews there from the cruel hands of the early Christian zealots. But Mohammed himself, though at first friendly to the Jews whose monotheistic beliefs served as a basis for his new Islamic religion, did not hesitate to employ ruthlessness against them in Yathrib, subsequently named Medina, for their refusal to accept him and his newly founded faith. The Jews were not spared the fate of the "infidel," while in a number of instances he treated his prospective non-Jewish converts benevolently, permitting them even to retain some of their pagan practices instead of employing the sword to force adherence to Islam.

The conquest of Palestine by Mohammed's followers was made easier by the fact that for centuries preceding the battle between the Christian and Moslem armies at the bank of the Yarmuk which led to the surrender of Jerusalem, Arabs had migrated to the Holy Land in considerable numbers. Jerusalem was officially barred to the Jews by the Romans in 135 C.E., but there is historic evidence that the Holy City was never without Jews.

During the three centuries of Christian control of Palestine between 320 and 635 C.E. Jewish life continued there underground. Beginning with the Mohammedan conquest of Palestine the lot of the Jews alternated between persecution and toleration. To be sure, this was an improvement over their treatment by the Christian rulers, but by no means was it due to a sympathetic understanding of Jewish adversity. The new conquerors did not hesitate to do violence to Jewish property and to sacred Jewish traditions. In 691 C.E. Caliph Abd el Malik erected the Mosque of Omar on the very site where the Holy Temple once stood.

Living conditions for the growing community of Jews continued to be precarious because of many local wars and plunderings, but on the whole the situation in Palestine became more bearable. In the four centuries up to the time of the Crusades, Palestine under Moslem rule afforded new hope for Judaism. Liturgical poetry developed. The Masorah—the final determination of the Biblical text—was completed, including the Hebrew vocalization as well as the system of accents for Bible reading and study. New schools of learning were established or transplanted to Palestine from neighboring lands.

Between 1098 and 1191 C.E. the Christian Crusaders brought to Palestine nothing but chaos and destruction. In their third onslaught they took possession of a few coastal plains together with Acco, which remained in Christian hands until 1291 and became the most important harbor in that area for trade with Europe.

During that century, Jews were permitted to live in Acco and to benefit from the upsurge of its commerce. Thereafter, until the conquest of Palestine by the Ottoman Turks in 1517, the country as a whole experienced various stages of deterioration, although there were breathing spells for the Jewish community under Egyptian conquest and especially under the Mameluke rule. The Arabs served their Turkish masters subserviently, but they had no sympathy for the Jews who came to the Holy Land out of religious conviction and fervor. They displayed active antagonism against the new Jewish immigrants who came later, inspired by the hope of building a Jewish national home as a refuge for the persecuted and the oppressed. But all their continued opposition to Jewish settlement in Palestine up to the beginning of the 20th century had no relation to Arab nationalism, which was nonexistent—unless resentment against immigrants of other faiths can be construed as an expression of nationalism.

There was no Arab nation in Palestine between 70 (C.E.) and 1948. Ethnically, they were remnants of 14 conquests forced to accept Islam. In the early decades of the 20th century only 150,000 Arabs with more than fifty years of history in the land resided in Palestine, the rest were of nomadic origin. Furthermore, the country never enjoyed sovereignty. Either it was a captured territory or the province of successive empires.

The Arabs held sway over Palestine from 635 C.E. to

1098 C.E., when the Crusaders invaded the Holy Land. The four and one-half centuries of more or less uninterrupted Moslem domination did not spell out an organized Arab nationalism in Palestine. They had no national cohesiveness during their occupation of the land before the Crusades nor during the in-between period up to the conquest by the Turks in the beginning of the 16th century. Also, during the four centuries of almost continuous Turkish sway over Palestine between 1517 and 1917, the Arabs in the Holy Land remained equally apathetic to national aspirations.

While Palestine was under Turkish sovereignty, despite frequent local Arab pillage and plunder, life for the Jew in various periods proved to be a blessing. Such was the case under the reign of Selim I and Suleiman II. Even thereafter, despite the imposition of heavy taxes to enrich the Turkish treasury, considering the situation in which the Jews found themselves elsewhere in the world, a world of destructive prejudice, persecution, confiscation, forced conversion and expulsion, the burdens in Palestine were not impossible to bear. A limited number of Jews managed to enter the Holy Land, augmenting the Jewish remnant there.

Judaism in many spheres of activity in Zion revealed signs of spiritual genius. In the 16th century, Palestine produced two great Jewish luminaries: Joseph Caro, born in Spain in 1488, migrated to Jerusalem in 1536, died there in 1575 and, while there, compiled the Shulhan Aruch—Jewish ritual code—and Isaac Luria, born in Jerusalem in 1534, died in Safed, Palestine in 1572. He was the founder of Cabala, a system of profound insights into the nature of the divine, based on an esoteric, mystical interpretation of the Scriptures.

Additional Jews settled in Palestine in the 17th century following the Ukranian massacre under Chmielniki in 1648-49 and the fiasco of the Sabbatai Zvi messianic claims on his return to Jerusalem in 1665.

In the middle of the 18th century larger numbers came from

Tunisia and from Eastern Europe, mainly Hasidim, followers of a new movement in Judaism which emphasized its emotional and mystical aspects above the legal and intellectual phases. They were later joined by Mithnaggdim, opponents of Hasidism from Russia and Poland.

For nearly two centuries there was comparative peace for Jews in Palestine, broken by the abortive expedition of Napoleon into the Levant in 1799, when the Jewish community remained loyal to Turkey. The four post-Napoleonic decades were a disturbed period in Palestine, particularly for the Jews because of the ceaseless moves and countermoves to conquer the land. In each such struggle the Jews were the first to suffer loss of life and property.

By 1840 Turkey, with the aid of European powers, was once more in full control as the result of an agreement that Palestine together with neighboring Syria would be governed with equal rights for all. Thus by the middle of the 19th century European influences began to penetrate into the Holy Land.

Between 1850 and World War I in 1914 there were two major developments in Palestine: one, the activity of the Christian Church and the other, a stream of new Jewish settlers motivated by a reawakened nationalism. At the same time various European governments, in order to establish a foothold in the Holy Land, encouraged missionary expansionist programs of their respective churches through pilgrimages for the avowed purpose of promoting health and education among the Moslem population. Under the influence of the churches with the protection of the consulates of their respective governments, the Jews in Palestine gained greater security for themselves and settled primarily in the cities, Jerusalem, Safed, Tiberias and Hebron, to avoid the dangers of the open country.

Palestinian Jewry depended almost exclusively on halukah—philanthropic aid received from their coreligionists the world over. Attempts at productive labor, establishment of urban settlements and agricultural colonies, hindered at first by corrupt

Turkish politicians, Arab opposition and malaria, eventually materialized because of a variety of historic pressures.

The Russian pogroms of 1881-82 hastened the birth of Hibat Zion—the Lovers of Zion movement—which now acclaimed their ancestral land as a home for the homeless Jews.

The Dreyfus affair in France galvanized Herzl's thoughts, out of which organized Political Zionism emerged at the First World Zionist Congress in 1897 as the solution of the problem of anti-Semitism. Because the new assimilationist tendencies threatened Jewish life in the free world, many Jews now focused their attention on Palestine as the only possible cultural center of Jewish life. The renascent Jewish nationalism, accelerated by the sad plight of Russian Jewry, Western "higher" anti-Semitism and the aspirations for a central cultural power house, gave rise to the first organized Jewish settlements, which became the foundation of the eventual Jewish national home in Palestine. These settlements were materially aided by the princely contributions of Baron Edmond de Rothschild who, although not committed to Political Zionism, was a lover of his people and the Holy Land.

By 1850 there were approximately 12,000 Jews in Zion. In 1882 the numbers grew to 24,000 and by 1914, at the outbreak of World War I, Palestine numbered 85,000 Jewish settlers. The Arabs, though still nationally dormant, by and large continued to be hostile to Jewish immigration into Palestine. They made no distinction between "Lovers of Zion" and Political Zionists. They opposed all Jewish settlers with equal truculence.

There were, of course, Arabs not unfriendly to Jewish immigration who sold their land to Jews. The major tensions stemmed from three sources: Turkish misrule, resulting in almost complete anarchy in the land, with no safety in town or on highway; the tradition of Bedouin pillage, finally overcome by Jewish self-defense; and after World War I the awakened Syrian nationalism, prodded by the French, which laid claim to Palestine as part of a greater Syria. The Anglo-French rivalry, in turn, encouraged the large landowning family, the Husseinis, to exploit the situation, gaining for Amin El Husseini the office of mufti. The mufti became the prime mover for an independent Arab nationalism in Palestine.

The stubbornness of the soil, which meant near starvation for the early settlers, coupled with Turkish corrupt rule was easier to tolerate than the hardships inflicted by Arab harassment punctuated by pitched battles threatening the existence of each new colony established. The first attacks on a larger scale, centered on the northern settlements of Tel Hai and Kefar Geladi, were French financed and supported by Arab tribesmen from Syria to embarrass the British in the hope of annexing the territory to their country. While the impoverished Arab masses stood to gain many advantages from an augmented Jewish immigration, their leaders publicly spurned all benefits that might accrue to their people from increased opportunities for gainful employment and wider demands for agricultural products. For themselves, however, the Arab leaders, who were also the landowners, did not hesitate to profit from the inflated prices of land caused by increasing Jewish needs for agricultural development.

Arab antagonism in the early Zionist days, accompanied by assaults, led to the founding of the Hashomer—the Jewish Watchmen—who took over from Arab guards the task of protecting Jewish life and property. This effective unit, dissolved under Turkish order during World War I, was merged with the newly formed Haganah organization in 1920 to protect Jewish historic rights to Palestine reinforced by the Balfour Declaration.

The liberation of the Arabs from Turkish rule stirred an awakened nationalist spirit among the more educated Arabs. This event opened up a new and sharply defined Arab hostility to the fulfillment of Zionism. The Arabs were aware of British reluctance to risk their hostility by releasing a proposed declaration in behalf of a Jewish national home in Palestine. They were also aware of the Sykes-Picot Agreement which in effect set up divided British-French spheres of influence. They claimed that a McMahon (British high commissioner to Egypt) promise was made to Husein, grand sherif of Mecca, to grant independence to the Arabs for their revolt against Turkey. McMahon, in a letter to the London *Times* in 1936, denied that Palestine was ever envisaged in his negotiations with Husein of Mecca to become a part of Arab national sovereignty. Husein's son, Feisal, who led the Arab delegation to the 1919 peace conference, never claimed Palestine for the Arabs, ceding it to development toward Jewish national independence. But the Arabs nevertheless employed every other means at their command, fair or foul, to block the issuance of the Balfour Declaration and to nullify it after its publication. Even when the League of Nations, fifty-two in number, refused to recognize Arab claims to Palestine by embodying the Balfour Declaration in the mandate to Great Britain, the Arabs continued their resistance.

Despite all opposition, the British government publicly announced their historic pledge to "favor the establishment in Palestine of a national home for the Jewish people and will use their best endeavors to facilitate the achievement of this object. . . ."

Sympathy for the plight of the Jew and his historic association with the Holy Land most likely influenced the Allies' recognition of Zionist claims, but there were other considerations. As Lloyd George stated two decades later: "The Zionist leaders gave us a definite promise that, if the Allies committed themselves to give facilities for the establishment of a national home for the Jews in Palestine, they would do their best to rally Jewish sentiment and support throughout the world to the Allied cause. . . ."

This the Jews did in much greater measure than the Arabs in their promised revolt against Turkey. Of the 1,200,000 square miles liberated from the Ottoman Empire by the Allied Powers less than 10,000 square miles within the Palestine boundaries were included. This was indeed an insignificant allotment for a Jewish national homeland, but the Arabs would yield no ground to the Jewish people despite world recognition of their historic claims.

McMahon's statement that "It was never intended by me in giving this pledge to King Husein to include Palestine in the area in which Arab independence was promised," was of no avail. Likewise, the promise of the Emir Feisal to Dr. Weizmann in the presence of Lawrence of Arabia pledging Arab cooperation with Jews, as well as his letter to Felix Frankfurter professing racial kinship and sympathy with Zionist aims, had no effect upon the Arabs. The land area of Palestine was sufficient for both peoples but the Arabs were determined to destroy all Zionist efforts.

A number of factors encouraged them in their opposition to the Jewish national home: French-English rivalry in the Middle East, Christian missionary opposition to Zionist aims, the Vatican's withdrawal of its endorsement of the Balfour Declaration and the lack of sympathy for Zionist objectives by the military administration of Palestine up to the final peace settlement with Turkey.

After attacking a number of Jewish settlements, the Arabs in 1920 proclaimed Feisal as the king of Syria and Palestine and incited rioting in the old city of Jerusalem. The military government closed its eyes to Arab riots while it restrained Jewish self-defense and imprisoned those Jews who dared to obey the natural law of the struggle for survival.

British concessions to Arab demands brought no peace in the Holy Land. The appointment of Amin el Husseini (Nazi collaborator in World War II), a fugitive from justice, as mufti of Jerusalem provided official leadership for Arab resistance. Churchill's separation of Trans-Jordan from Palestine to make it an Arab puppet state did not lessen the tensions. His White

Paper limiting Jewish immigration satisfied no one. All measures of appeasement failed. In 1921 the Arabs again resorted to violence, hoping thus to forestall the League of Nations grant of the Palestine mandate to Great Britain on July 24, 1922.

The intent of the Balfour Declaration was clear: "The establishment of a national home in Palestine." Great Britain chose the road of compromise, the only outcome of which was to stimulate Arab appetite for further resistance at the expense of Jewish rights under the declaration.

Only during Lord Plummer's administration of Palestine (1925-1928) was Arab resistance fully checked. The plunder and destruction of Jewish lives and property ceased. Lord Plummer was a soldier, not a politician. He refused to yield to any appeasement policy.

Later, however, Arab violence increased with each advance of the Zionist program. The Arab flare-up in 1929, causing 133 deaths and twice as many wounded, was the answer to the formation of the Jewish Agency for Palestine. The Arabs feared that a united world Jewry would hasten the establishment of the Jewish state. The British government was not concerned with the blood bath. It took no resolute or undaunted stand. A new commission was appointed and a White Paper issued, in line with their appeasement policy.

However, neither Arab terror nor British duplicity was able to block the historic processes eventuating in the creation of the Jewish state.

The Arab riots in the early thirties proved even costlier to the Arabs than to the Jews: 2,287 Arab casualties to 450 Jewish plus 140 British. The Jewish settlers courageously stood their ground and wisely harnessed the Haganah (now numbering 25,000) to a policy of havlagah—self-restraint—in the interests of the new torrent of Jewish immigration precipitated by the Nazi life-and-death challenge to world Jewry in the middle and late thirties.

Arab hostility with weapons of violence and boycott continued in unison with Hitler's horrendous threats. Great Britain, with a temporizing policy, or no policy at all, for the fulfillment of the Balfour Declaration, resorted to delaying tactics by a variety of commissions, conferences and recommendations, some rejected by the Arabs, others by Jews as well. Because of Arab demands, British warships blockaded Palestine against any possible "illegal" Jewish immigrants fleeing from Hitler's all-consuming madness.

The British pledge after World War II to abide by a United Nations solution of the Palestine problem was not kept. But the Arab plans to deal with the Jews as they pleased were frustrated. Destiny decided the issue. The Arab all-out war against Israel immediately after the new state's Declaration of Independence May 15, 1948, ended in an armistice with Egypt, Lebanon, Jordan and Syria in July 1949. It left the new state territorially enlarged beyond the boundaries assigned by the U.N. Palestine Resolution of November 29, 1947.

The signatures were still drying on the armistice agreement when the Arabs launched raids against the new Israel's borders, destroying life and property. Their attacks were calculated to accomplish three things: one, terrorize Israel into an acceptance of Arab demands; two, provoke Israel to wage further war, and thereby suffer U.N. condemnation; three, damage Israel's existence by constant threats of war, necessitating the maintenance of large, costly defense forces.

These tensions were also designed to discourage tourist trade, so essential for foreign exchange currencies. To wreck Israel's economy the Arabs refused innocent passage of Israel's shipping through the Suez Canal and Gulf of Aqaba. They also launched a world-wide boycott against the new state, not only to prevent Arab states from trading with Israel but also to force many international firms to do likewise.

The Arab states thus went beyond the confines of Israel to inflict economic sabotage. They refused to deal with Jewish-owned business concerns anywhere in the world or even those having directors of the Jewish faith on their boards. To be certain that all their business contacts would be Judenrein—clear of all Jews—the Arab League sent this questionnaire to business corporations throughout the world:

1. Have you any commercial connections with Israel? Do you sell your products to the Jewish state? What is the name and address of your representative in Israel?
2. Do you import any material from Israel needed for the manufacture of your product?
3. Do you own a factory in Israel or do you have a personal interest in any of Israel's factories?
4. Is any of your capital drawn from Israel and to what extent?
5. Do you employ any Jews in your factory? If so, how many and in what positions?
6. Do you have any Jews on your governing board?
7. Is one of your executives of the Jewish faith? If so, give his name.
8. Is one authorized to sign for your firm a Jew?
9. How many Jews do you employ in your factory and office?

(signed) Arab Bureau for the Boycott of Israel.

The questionnaire concluded with a warning to give true information and calls for two copies of the answers.

The Arab states, defeated on the battlefields, arrogantly and with chicanery justify the cold war and their attacks against Israel's borders on the ground that a state of belligerency still exists between them and the new state, there being no peace treaty. As for the armistice, they signed it only to dishonor it. This position coincides with neither logic nor the quest for security in the Middle East.

What does an armistice mean if not an agreement to terminate hostilities? Infiltration, local skirmishes, economic boycott and prohibition of passage through international waterways do not indicate a desire to end warfare. While an armistice does not mean a settlement of all outstanding issues or a compulsory program of cooperation, neither does it mean the provocation of incidents which rupture amicable relations and engender fear and hatred on a scale that makes peace or even conditional peace spelled out by the armistice impossible. The Arabs accepted an armistice but rejected peace, hoping, conspiring and planning for a second round that would blot Israel from the map of the Middle East. They were never even rebuked by the U.N. for their defiance of its expressed will.

Israel's Arab problem is twofold in nature: external and internal. While the two phases are not completely separate, it is well for greater clarity to treat them apart, leaving their interrelation in the background.

First, the external problem that menaces Israel most: tension between the Arab states and Israel continues unabated. The armistice set up lengthy and vulnerable borders: 591 miles of land, 158 miles of water boundaries, Lebanon on the north, Syria on the northeast, the Hashemite Jordan kingdom on the east and Egypt on the south and west. Israel covers 70 miles at its widest point and 12 miles at the narrowest, north of Tel Aviv.

The recognition of Israel's existence and her repeated overtures for peace were persistently rejected unless four prior conditions were met: 1) The Arab refugees from Palestine, numbering close to a million according to their estimates (a much inflated figure, 750,000 being a more realistic approximation), must be permitted to reoccupy their lands and homes in Israel before any conversations for peace could be initiated. (Only 457,000 actually left the territory that is now Israel. The balance consists of natural increase, Arabs who infiltrated into U.N.R.W.A. camps and nonregistered deaths to maintain relief ration cards.) 2) Israel must agree to accept the borders originally assigned by the United Nations on November 29, 1947. 3) Jerusalem must be internationalized. 4) Israel must close her doors to additional Jewish immigrants and abandon her alleged ambitions for expansion into Arab territory. Without these four prerequisites the Arabs would consider no peace negotiations with Israel.

However, despite the uneasy armistice, continued Arab intransigence, insecure borders and the risk of another war, Israel, though vitally needing peace and fervently desiring it, rejected the four Arab prior conditions as the price for a round table, face to face conference.

How does Israel justify her position?

First, the Arab refugee problem. In the words of the secretary of the Higher Arab Executive shortly after the first truce in the war for liberation: "The fact that there are these refugees is the direct consequence of the Arab states opposing partition and the Jewish state. The Arab states agreed on this policy unanimously." What was left unsaid is equally important.

The Arabs of Palestine accepted the role of refugeeism at the behest of their leaders to ease the task of their military forces, *i.e.,* not to be encumbered by a civilian population in their plan for anticipated swift destruction of Israel. Many Arabs fled because of the fear instilled in them by their leaders that the Jews would drive them into the sea. Others did so because of the threat that they would be stigmatized as renegades to the cause of Arab nationalism and still others relied on the promise that after certain victory they would return to their homes to repossess their property and become heirs to the Jewish wealth left behind in flight from conquering Arab armies. As explained by one Arab dignitary: "We left our homeland in reliance on the false promises of corrupt military officers of the Arab countries. They assured us that our exile would last no more than two weeks and would be akin to a hike, and that at the end of this period we would return. We are the victims of you, the Arab leaders."

That the plight of the refugees is most serious, all agree. The heart of the question is this: How can their problem be solved without fomenting greater difficulties?

First it must be remembered that the United Nations Palestine Resolution embodied a twofold stipulation: The creation of the Jewish state as well as an Arab state with an economic union for both. What happened to the contemplated Arab state? Part of that territory remains in Arab hands. The number of refugees this territory can absorb is as yet undetermined, but that it can and should accept Arab refugees is undisputed.

What is the actual number of refugees? To create a more favorable public opinion for their plight, the Arab states have been very generous in their count. The U.N. relief "hand-out" has undoubtedly attracted many Arabs unrelated to the Palestine problem, and in the decade of unconstructive aid the refugee problem was aggravated by a natural birth increase.

Why do not the Arabs and Jews get together to solve this human problem which blocks the road to peace in the Middle East irrespective of original responsibility for the problem of refugeeism? A former official of the United Nations Relief and Work Agency diagnosed the uncooperative Arab attitude as politically motivated: "The Arab nations do not want to solve the Arab refugee problem. They want to keep it as an open sore, as an affront against the United Nations and as a weapon against Israel."

But what of Israel? Why doesn't she open the doors to the uprooted Arabs? Israel disclaims both obstinacy and enmity. She bases her position on the ground of self-preservation. Of Israel's present population of 2,000,000, 200,000 are Arabs, 48,000 of whom have been readmitted since the birth of the state with the possibility of the resettlement of an additional sizable number of refugees to be agreed on at the peace table. Israel formally offered to readmit 100,000 now. But for Israel to readmit the majority of the homeless Arabs would spell national suicide. The refugees, embittered by their sad experience, would certainly pose a threat to Israel's security, internally as well as externally.

For years prior to Israel's restoration, the Arabs in Palestine were taught to look upon Jews as their enemies. This hate has been inflamed since then, with the younger generation trained and conditioned by their parents and teachers to avenge their national disgrace. Therefore the Israelis contend that a mass refugee return would constitute a dangerous fifth column threatening the existence of the Jewish national home. Economically, too, a large influx of Arabs would involve a precarious situation for the country.

What then is the solution of this complex problem? Surely not the status quo of U.N. relief to which the Arab states make no contribution. The Israelis properly point out: If the refugees were our kindred we would aid them irrespective of the cause of their misfortune. The Arab states have vast stretches of land waiting for cultivation. Why not settle the refugees there? Of the million newcomers to Israel since her acquisition of statehood, 400,000 have come from Arab countries. Their vacated places could now be occupied by the so-called displaced Arabs. Were the Arab states really concerned with the fate of the refugees and not in their use as pawns on the chessboard of Middle East politics, the very substantial sums spent by U.N.R.W.A. for mere subsistence could have been successfully employed for their permanent resettlement and rehabilitation in the lands of their brethren.

It is logical to conclude, Israel maintains, that while the uprooted from Palestine have a natural desire to return to their native land, they could not be as happy under the new conditions there as they would be in Arab countries where they would share with their kinsfolk a common religion, language, literature and culture. Israel's new democratic institutions, industrialization, dominant Hebrew culture and Judaism as the religion of the majority, could not offer to them the equivalent of "home."

Concerning compensation for property left behind and cost of resettlement in Arab lands, the Israelis do not deny their equitable obligations. Some time ago Israel, as a first step, released $12,000,000 of frozen accounts. While the young state may be incapable of providing unaided the huge resources that would be required for a large-scale resettlement project, the money question could be solved through world Jewry's philanthropic contributions, international loans and the cooperation of a free world. $200,000,000 will be available from U.N. funds for resettlement. Many Arab countries with extensive uncultivated fertile areas are short of manpower. The only land available in Israel is in the Negev, which requires pioneer efforts unattractive to Arab refugees lacking in will and purpose to make the necessary sacrifices. Furthermore, 70 per cent of Israel's soil never belonged to the Arabs. It was crown land to which Israel fell heir. Of Israel's cultivated land only 13 per cent belonged to the Arabs who fled the country in the War for Independence.

Israel maintains a custodian's office for abandoned Arab property with accurate records and fair evaluation commensurate with assessed values of Jewish-owned adjoining property. Israel, however, insists that the compensation bookkeeping should have both a debit and a credit side. In a final settlement, consideration will have to be given to Jewish losses sustained in the war, including the value of Jewish properties confiscated in Arab lands as well as to Arab properties under Israel's jurisdiction. Such a settlement, determined by standards of equity, would meet with Israel's approval.

Of the three tried and proven methods of dealing with this problem, emigration, repatriation and resettlement, the last seems to be the most logical, equitable and practical for the Arab refugees. They could naturally be merged into the life of the Arab nations. Those states occupy 10,000,000 square miles of land compared to Israel's 8,000 square miles. There is ample "lebensraum" for them among their own people who speak their language, practice their religion and share their culture. Israel has given a graphic and inspiring demonstration to the world that this proposed resettlement project, however difficult it may appear, can be consummated. All that is needed is Arab good will plus good faith and the problem can be solved.

The second Arab demand, withdrawal of Israel to the pre-armistice borders, is, on its face, unrealistic. The boundaries fixed by the U.N. Resolution were predicated on economic union with the U.N.-projected new Arab state. Otherwise, with the limited territory thus proposed, the Jewish state could not be viable economically. Since no Arab state in Palestine came into being, the U.N. decision calling for an economic union did not materialize. No territory was allotted to the Arab states outside of Palestine by the 1947 U.N. decision. The territory they captured in western Jordan and Gaza Strip is illegally held by them. No demand on their part that Israel cede territory (to them) is accompanied by an offer to withdraw from western Jordan and Gaza. Under these circumstances, plus the Arab unilateral failure to honor that decision, the original U.N. territorial assignment for Israel no longer has practical merit or legal status and the Arab demands are untenable.

In recent months, the Middle East geopolitical situation has changed radically: Egypt and Syria have become a united republic, Yemen is hanging on its coat tails; Iraq and Jordan first joined forces and then disbanded, thus presenting a new alignment neither contemplated by the U.N. nor foreseen at the armistice.

Iraq's revolution, Lebanon's rebellion and Jordan's perilously unstable situation are additional factors making absolutely inequitable any demands for Israel's return to the status quo of 1947.

In any dispute before a tribunal of justice it is axiomatic that the plaintiff must come into court with clean hands to plead his case. The Arabs are unable to do so. Because of their illegal war of aggression, the United Nations Resolution, violated by that act, became ineffective. They who are guilty of having repudiated the U.N. decision cannot in all fairness now come to resurrect it for their particular advantage. In addition, Israel holds that the new borders purchased by her blood should not be returned to those who by violence precipitated the bloodshed. To do so would be to reward them for betraying and nullifying the U.N. Palestine Resolution.

Time does not stand still. A lot of water has passed under the bridge in the last 11 years since the United Nations drew up Israel's boundaries. History may have a way of repeating itself but never gives us a "throw-back" as in fantasy. Some modifications of the borders between Israel and her neighbors may have to be made at the peace table, but Israel rejects a preconceived, ironclad, unilateral surrender of territory as the price of discussing terms of peace. As a matter of fact, the armistice agreement signed by Israel and the several Arab States specifically spells out the understanding that no territorial changes could be effected without the mutual consent of the parties.

The third condition, the internationalization of Jerusalem, has no ring of sincerity or conviction. The Zionists at the U.N. session acceded with misgivings to this phase of the Palestine Resolution in order to assure the necessary two-thirds vote on the proposal to establish a Jewish state.

Those who favored Jerusalem as a separate enclave under international control deemed it best for the impartial protection of all holy places. However, the Arab war on Israel resulting in a Holy City divided between Jews and Arabs radically changed the Jerusalem situation. While the other Arab states have been loudly demanding the internationalization of Jerusalem, Jordan as well as Israel decisively opposed it.

The Arabs are not interested in safeguarding the holy places, most of which are under their control in the Jordan sector, but what they seek is to injure Israel, whose scrupulous and reverential care of everything sacred to the Moslem and Christian world in the Holy Land is recognized by all.

It would be a political and economic disaster for Israel to agree now to the internationalization of Jerusalem. There is no need whatever for such a procedure for the purpose of protecting the holy places. Out of 39 holy places, only three are in the Israel sector of Jerusalem, two Christian and one Moslem. Israel has offered U.N. supervision of these three sites but sees no justification for international control of its capital city. It should not be forgotten that when in 1948 seven Arab states together strove to overwhelm and destroy the new Israel, Jewish soldiers went out of their way to protect and safeguard Christian as well as Moslem shrines from Arab attack.

Israel cannot and will not part with the Holy City. To do so would be tantamount to severing the heart from the body. Jewish religious-historic associations with Jerusalem are too strong to be obliterated by resolutions or demands. The difficulties of such an act are apparent. Surgery of that sort would leave a wound that would never be healed and could only be aggravated under international auspices. Jerusalem's 150,000 Jewish population would be in no man's land, with their inviolate ties to Israel severed by a coerced pledge of allegiance to an alien state of international character.

Nor could Israel afford for economic, military, religious and cultural reasons to give up so important a segment of her population whose qualities of leadership and influence so far transcend even their numbers.

Language, money exchange, post office, transportation and public utilities are only a few of the problems that would bedevil an internationalized Holy City. In addition, the U.N. Resolution on Jerusalem envisioned a ten-year experiment, with a plebiscite at the end of that period to determine the final political constitution of the city. At the birth of the state the city's Jewish inhabitants exceeded 60 per cent of its population. In 1959 the city is almost completely Jewish. In such a plebiscite the vote would have been an overwhelming NO!

In the decade of Israel's existence the scheme of subjecting Jerusalem to U.N. control has become a dead issue. While the Arab nations still demand it only to make the attainment of peace more difficult, Jordan rejects it and Israel for all practical purposes has made Jerusalem as a "fait accompli" its capital city religiously and culturally as well as politically.

Perhaps the loss of the Old City with its Wailing Wall is

significant of the new Israel destined not for weeping, of which she has had more than her share, but for the joy of constructive and world inspiring enterprise.

The favorite Arab demand, to freeze the Jewish population, is on all accounts unacceptable to Israel. Such demands violate national sovereignty and the most basic of Zionist principles: a home for the Jewish homeless. The Arab states need have no fear of Jewish designs on their lands to accommodate a Jewish population expanding through immigration or natural growth. While there may be some ultra-nationalists who see visions of a Jewish state on both sides of the Jordan, the State of Israel categorically denies any expansionist encroachments on Arab areas.

Israel is not land hungry. As a matter of fact her immediate need is more people and not more territory. The development of the Negev at an accelerated pace is completely dependent on additional immigrants. Nor should the future disturb Arab equanimity. The Negev is 60 per cent of Israel's land surface but contains only five per cent of her population. With the advance of technical sciences in the development of the Negev, there will be room in Israel for a population of additional millions. Scientific advances in agriculture and industry and the eventual peaceful use of atomic power will adequately provide for Israel's present and augmented population. Israel does not want more "real estate." She wants peace and the opportunity for a fuller life within the limits of the land she now occupies.

Israel's internal Arab problem, though less acute than the external one, nevertheless requires patience, tact and sagacity. Fortunately these qualities have not been lacking in the leadership of the new state.

To begin with, the Arabs within Israel find themselves in an anomalous position. Only yesterday they constituted a majority; today they are in a minority status with the natural reaction of insecurity common to all minorities. They are bewildered and confused to see the Jewish "upstarts" as rulers of "their" land.

They long to be reunited with the vast Arab majority outside, but unlike the infiltration between East and West Germany, they do not cross the borders to the Arab states. They prefer the higher standards of living and the democracy in Israel to the backward, feudal or police state rule of Jordan, Syria or Egypt.

At the end of 1956 Israel's 209,000 Arabs, 10 per cent of the general population, represented three major divisions: 140,000 Moslem, 50,000 Christian and 20,000 Druze. The Druzes were most friendly to the Jewish state and joined the Israeli army in the War for Independence. At the end of that war the number of Arabs in Israel was approximately 140,000. In less than a decade the state accepted and reunited 48,000 Arab refugees with their families. The balance of about 35,000 resulted from the natural birth increment.

Geographically, 128,000 of the Arabs remained settled in the rural areas with little change in their primitive mode of living from past generations, 35,000 in towns and 22,000 Bedouins in constant search of pasture for their flocks. The majority of the Israeli Arabs in 1956 were concentrated in three localities: 65 per cent in Galilee, 18 per cent in the Little Triangle bordering on Jordan, 8 per cent Bedouins in the South and the balance, 9 per cent, scattered throughout the land.

Israel's basic laws guarantee equality of citizenship irrespective of sex, race, national origin, language, culture, economic or social status. "The State of Israel will guarantee complete equality of civil and political rights to all inhabitants irrespective of religion, race and sex. It will guarantee freedom of religion, conscience, language, education and culture." More specifically the government's platform of 1955 states: "The Arabs and all other minorities shall enjoy all the rights of citizens and share their duties . . . involving health, education, welfare, equal pay, taxes, Arab language and culture."

For obvious reasons a policy of "respect and suspect" had to be the government's attitude toward the Arab minority. Almost 85 per cent of the Arab population are in close proximity to the borders of the Arab states. This fact naturally requires Israel to be on guard lest its Arab citizenry be tempted or pressured to aid the Arab states in time of political or military danger. Israel's Basic Principles take cognizance of this anomalous situation: "Arabs living in border areas where security measures are essential as a result of the refusal of the Arab states to make peace with Israel will be restricted to actual and vital security requirements alone which shall not unnecessarily infringe on the civil rights and the freedom of movement of inhabitants in border areas."

While in all other respects the Arabs within the state enjoy equal rights, it is inevitable for Israel's government to control the movements of the Arab population until peace with the Arab states is established. In recent years the limitations on such movements have been considerably relaxed. Arab residents in Galilee are no longer required to obtain permits to go to Nazareth, Afula or Acre. There has also been an easing of the night curfew in the "triangle" area. Military control has been limited to border security with no authority in civilian affairs. Also for reasons of security, Arabs in Israel are exempt from military service. In this, the government is also motivated by the desire to avoid for the Arab citizenry the problem of double loyalty. Israel endeavors to inculcate a patriotic spirit in the upgrowing Arab generation. When this is accomplished, complete freedom will prevail and military service will encompass the entire citizenry as it does the Jewish and Druze population.

In all other phases of Israeli life, the Arab minority does well. Politically, eight Arabs were elected to the Third Knesset —5 Mapai, 2 Communists, and 1 Mapam—with full freedom to vote and to speak in their own language. In the 1955 elections there were 77,000 eligible Arab voters of whom 91 per cent of the men and women above the age of 18 went to the polls. In deference to the Arab minority, whenever a Parliamentary committee is designated to call on Israel's president, one of the Arab members is included in the delegation. They have not as yet shown the capacity or will to govern themselves locally in their villages, but while progress in that direction is still slow, it is nevertheless certain.

Their economic advance has been substantial. One hundred and twenty thousand Arabs live on agriculture. They cultivate 1,250,000 dunams of their own and 100,000 dunams leased from the government. Israel has helped them agriculturally by introducing them to new and scientific methods of farming, relieving them of their past backbreaking labors. The growth of the Jewish population has provided a profitable market for their increased production, estimated at sixfold since the birth of the state.

The Bedouins, particularly in the Beersheba area, are no longer shackled to a life of wandering in search of grazing land for their sheep because of the new water resources developed and distributed by the state. The Arabs in Israel have been aided in establishing cooperative outlets to suit their needs.

Arab labor conditions have also improved. While the ratio of unskilled labor is still high, five to one, the vocational training provided for them is beginning to show good results.

Mortality figures indicate the type of health and social services rendered by the Israel government to her Arab population. From the first American Zionist Medical Unit, under Hadassah direction starting in 1918, the Arabs in large numbers have benefited. The Zionist health program recognized that health, like peace, cannot be reserved for some to the exclusion of others. The following figures tell an important story. In neighboring Egypt the infant mortality rate is one of the highest in the world, 280.4 per thousand births, which is a staggering figure. Among the Israeli Arabs the rate is 65.37 for the Moslem population, 62.58 for the Druze and 58.58 for the Christians. Infant mortality among Israeli Arabs might be even further reduced if the prospective mothers were more willing to give birth in hospitals instead of homes. It is also important to note that despite the larger infant death rate among the Arabs the net increase in population is now proportionately higher among them than among the Jews, due not alone to their higher birth rate but to their generally improved health conditions. The natural increase for the Moslem Arabs is 41.05 per thousand; 35.23 for the Druze and 27.84 for the Christians, while the Jewish increase is only 21.45 per thousand.

The lot of the Arab woman has immeasurably improved. In the eyes of civil law she is no longer a chattel. If her progress continues she may soon become a free person in all the walks of life.

In the field of education Israel has made an earnest effort to eliminate illiteracy and encourage cultural interests among the Arabs. Under British mandatory rule only 48 per cent of Arab children attended elementary schools with some regularity. Since the beginning of the state the attendance of children of elementary school age has increased to 71 per cent. A higher percentage will materialize when the Arabs recognize the importance of schooling for girls. A sizable number of Arabs also attend intermediate schools and nearly 100 are enrolled at the Hebrew University and Haifa Technion.

Israel officially recognizes the Arabic language in Parliament, courts, all legal documents, inscriptions on coins, currency and postage stamps. An Arabic daily newspaper plus eight weeklies and seven other periodicals are published in Israel. The radio, too, carries Arabic programs of dramatic, cultural and religious content.

Religiously the Arabs in Israel enjoy full equality. Their Moslem religious organization, consisting of 130 clergy and advisory councils compensated by the state, has a free hand in the performance of its duties and services, including matters of the family, marriage and divorce. Religious worship is conducted in almost 100 mosques.

The Christian community, mostly Arab, one-third the size of the Moslem population, maintains 160 churches and chapels representing every Christian denomination in the world, with a clergy exceeding 1,000 including monks and men of a large variety of orders. The Druzes, who withdrew from the Moslem religion in the 11th century, constitute about one-ninth of the Moslem population. They also enjoy religious autonomy and receive Israel's financial support as do the Moslem and Christian communities.

The public and private attitude toward the Arab population ranges from indifference to warmth. The majority of Jews do not have frequent or intimate contacts with the Arabs, who are much closer to one another geographically than to their fellow citizens of the Jewish faith. There are still unpleasant memories of Arab riots and looting from the mandatory days as well as the suspicions that have generated since the War for Independence. In the communes there is a conscious effort to cooperate with the Arab agricultural workers and to be of aid to them in attaining increased production and better marketing. As a whole, the Jewish population is mindful of the necessity to live cooperatively with their Arab neighbors and be at peace with the Arab world.

In sum: in every phase of life the Arabs are equal under the law. It is Israel's policy neither to isolate nor to assimilate them. They are given every opportunity to live their lives freely and develop themselves economically, politically, religiously and culturally to their advantage and the well-being of the state.

Peace is now the big question mark. Can it ever be established between the Arab states and Israel? We cannot know what the future has in store for the Middle East. But if reason and logic are criterions, three conditions are prerequisite to the establishment of peace: improvement of the world situation, stability within the Arab world and Jewish cooperation.

Israel's sincere desire for peace is universally recognized. But the groundless fears of the Arabs block the road to peace.

Israel's internal development has been growing at a phenomenal pace. The doors are wide open to additional immigrants, not only to provide a haven for the oppressed but to augment Israel's manpower for any contingency.

Israel's gates will always be open to the persecuted, homeless Jew. But as world conditions improve the number of such Jews will decline. Fear begets fear and engenders suspicion and hate. Israel's proud boast of her ability to counter any attack makes her appear dangerous to the Arab world. While Zionist propaganda in the pre-state days proved very effective, Israel's public information activities have not brought the desired results. Arab fears of Israel's alleged expansionist policy have not been sufficiently deflated. It is of course difficult for Israel to influence public opinion in the Arab world where the spoken and printed word is government controlled. Every method of public relations must be employed to convince the Arab peoples that Israel has no ulterior designs on them.

In recent months the state has unfrozen Arab funds sequestered during the War for Liberation. This is a step in the right direction. Other steps may be taken to allay fears regarding compensation for Arab property. During the past decade 4,000 or more Arab refugees per year were reunited with their families in Israel. This should be a continuous process as an expression of good will. The disclaimer of guilt in the refugee matter and assertions of incapacity to meet Arab demands may well be justified. But peace requires the assuming of obligations that go beyond legal stipulations. Israel's generous intentions must become known and acknowledged throughout the Arab world.

There was a time when the absentee effendi—landlord—dominated the Arab world, with the poor fellahin as his submissive slave. The Western Jewish immigrant looked upon these exploited ones as beasts of burden, which in reality they were. Arab nationalism has revolutionized the process of thinking, if not as yet the conditions of living in the Middle East. Israel's leadership is fully aware of the stirrings for a better life in the Arab world. It must be made crystal clear that the Jewish state will enhance Arab national aspirations for the better life and not deter them. Arrogance will not help; flattery will be of no effect. Since only acts of cooperation will eventuate in a better understanding, many authentic voices in Israel readily profess this to be the policy accepted by the vast majority of the Jewish population. None can deny that sincere cooperation with the Arab world is the hope and aim of Israel. But this must become more clearly articulated to be heard and believed in the right places.

There are also those in Israel who consider conciliatory attitudes as appeasement which the Arabs will interpret as signs of Jewish weakness. They point to the many Israeli gestures of friendship rejected by the Arabs who, Pharaohlike, harden their hearts with every Jewish accession to their unreasonable demands. They even scorned Israel's willingness, declared to the Palestine Concilation Commission, to admit 100,000 Arab refugees.

But what alternative is there to peace? A stalemate, hardening of the present irreconcilable situation? Or is a catastrophic eruption preferable to holding out the olive branch?

And what of the Arabs? Will they ever be reconciled to Israel's existence? Their responsible leaders no longer threaten to drive the Israelis into the sea. They now demand the acceptance of prior boundary conditions for the recognition of the new state. They reject Israel's proposal to meet face to face to resolve their mutual problems. Yet past experience argues in favor of a round table conference. Dr. Bunche, representing the U.N. at the Rhodes Island mediation sessions, succeeded in concluding an armistice agreement not only because of his tact and firmness but also because of his wise insistence on both parties dealing directly with each other. The Palestine Conciliation Commission, comprised of U.S., French and Turkish representatives designated by the General Assembly, failed in their mission because they kept Arab and Israeli delegations apart.

The Arab situation is in constant flux. Next in intensity to their hate for Israel is their hate for one another. Despite the Arab League, fathered by Great Britain, they have no inherent unity. Their mutual jealousies and suspicions will not be eradicated by treaties, federations, unions or Arab-sponsored resolutions at the U.N. Were they not afraid of one another, some of the Arab states would negotiate a peace with Israel, as had been planned by Abdullah, grandfather of Jordan's King Hussein.

Who can foretell the destiny of the United Arab Republic consisting of Egypt-Syria with Yemen as an appendage? What assurance is there for the survival of this union when the federation of Iraq and Jordan was so short-lived? What of the independence of Lebanon and Jordan? Will Saudi Arabia merge her destiny with Nasser?

Logic dictates that peace negotiations with Israel will be initiated in the event of either of these alternatives: If there is a single Arab union, then the fears and jealousies of the individual states would no longer block direct conversations. If the Arab world becomes divided into two opposing forces, one or both of them, to bolster their own strength, might find it advisable to be relieved of the Israeli tensions. There are other alternatives as well: democracy replacing dictatorship with imperialist ambitions; the defeat of Nasserism by a new leadership in Africa; the defeat of Russia in the Middle East and above all the creation of a new climate through an end to the cold war.

If any of the above possibilities eventuate, then despite the present added threats to Israel from the new alignments in the Middle East it is conceivable that peace between Arabs and Israel would be brought appreciably nearer to realization.

However, should the cold war lead to a hot war, then nothing will matter. The Middle East may or may not be a direct target for devastation by one side or the other but it cannot remain unscathed, and the destiny of both Jews and Arabs will be in the balance. If the current tensions between East and West persist, Arab-Jewish relations will continue in an explosive state.

Concisely, this is the world outlook in relation to the Middle East: chaos and dissension in that area best serve the present Russian policy. Under the Bolshevik aegis, Russia has established a foothold in the Arab world where the czarist ambitions failed. French influence has reached the zero mark with worldwide Moslem antagonism resulting from her unsuccessful colonial operations in Africa. British activities in the area are suspected of being prompted by selfish interests.

The United States failed in the attempt to fill the vacuum left by England and France. Neither the grants in money nor arms have gained real friends for America among the Arab nations. Nor have the policies of the Western Powers succeeded in barring Russia from the Middle East.

Peace between the Arab states and Israel will be advanced only when East and West stop feuding in their maneuvers to make the Middle East their back yard. The great powers individually and the U.N. collectively must agree to guarantee the borders of Israel as well as those of the Arab states. The United States in cooperation with Russia, if the Kremlin is to be trusted, can help establish a secure peace between Israel and the Arab nations. But they cannot impose their will on either or both parties. When the powers decide what smaller nations should do without their consent, the results are likely to be disastrous.

A united East and West can help persuade disputant nations to engage in conversations leading to peace but cannot impose conditions of settlement on either or both parties. The first step, a round table conference between Arabs and Jews, can be undertaken only by sincere and selfless cooperation on the part of West and East in the area sacred to Jew, Christian and Moslem alike.

Despite the present turmoil, we may yet see the fulfillment of the long-deferred prophetic hope: "In that day shall there be a highway out of Egypt to Assyria, and the Assyrian shall come into Egypt and the Egyptian into Assyria. . . . In that day shall Israel be a third with Egypt and with Assyria, a blessing in the midst of the earth. . . . Blessed be Egypt My people and Assyria the work of My hands, and Israel Mine inheritance."

Glossary

Achdut Hoavodah—Poalai Zion	United Workers—Labor Zionist Party
Adam	Man
Adat Israel	Congregation of Israel
Adom	Red
Agudat Israel-Poalai Agudat Israel	Orthodox Party
Ain B'rerah	No Alternative
Aizel	National Military Organization
Aliyah	Immigration
Am Ha-aretz	Jewish Illiterate
Am Israel	The People of Israel
Am Olam	Everlasting People
Apikores (plural, Apikorsim)	Agnostic
Ashkenazi (plural, Ashkenazim)	A Follower of East European Jewish tradition
Banayich	Thy children
Bar Mitzvah	Age of assuming religious responsibilities
Bet Israel	House of Israel
B'ezrat Hashem	With God's Help
Bilu	Pre-Political Zionist movement
B'nai Israel	The Children of Israel
Bonayich	Thy builders
Dom	Blood
Gadna	Student military organization
Galut	Exile

Haganah	Self Defense
Halachah	Jewish traditional law
Halukah	Distribution of charitable funds in Palestine
Halutz (plural, Halutzim)	Pioneer
Haluziut	Pioneering
Hamashbir Hamerkazi	Central Purchasing Cooperative
Hapoel Hamizrachi—Mizrachi	Religious Party
Hapoel Hatzair	The Young Worker's Movement
Hasid (plural, Hasidim)	The Pious
Havlagah	Self Restraint
Herut	Freedom Party
Hesed	Act of kindness
Hevrat Ovdim	Workers' Cooperative Association
Hibat Zion (Hovave Zion—Lovers of Zion)	Love for Zion movement
Histadrut	General Federation of Labor
Hutz La-aretz	Beyond Israel's borders
Irgun	National Military Defense
Kashrut	Jewish dietary laws
Keren Hayesod	Foundation Fund
Keren Kayemet L'Yisrael	Jewish National Fund
K'hal Yisrael	Congregation of Israel
Kibbutz—(plural, Kibbutzim)	Collective Settlement
Kibbutz Hadali	Religious Collective Settlement
Knesset	Israel's Parliament
Knesset Israel	Community of Israel
Kohen	Of priestly descent
Kupat Holim	Sick Fund
Ma'barah (plural, Ma'barot)	Transition Camp
Malben	Organization Devoted to the Aid of Enfeebled Immigrants

Mapai	Socialist Labor Party
Mapam	United Labor Party
Maskil (plural, Maskilim)	Enlightened
Maskit	Agency to provide gainful home employment in the arts and crafts
Masorah	Jewish tradition
Mezuzah (plural, Mezuzot)	Parchment scroll attached to door post
Mitnagid (plural, Mitnagim)	Opponents
Moshav (plural, Moshavim)	Small Holders Settlement
Moshav Ovdim (plural, Moshve Ovdim)	Workers' Settlement
Moshav Shitufi—(plural, Moshuvim Shitufim)	Cooperative or Partnership Settlement
Moshava (plural, Moshavot)	Private Land Ownership Settlement
Nahal	Military Training Organization, with preparation for agricultural life
Negev	The southern section of Israel
Neturai Karta	Guardians of the City
Oleh (plural, Olim)	Immigrant
Poalai Zion	The Labor Zionist Party
Sabra	Native Israeli
Sanhedrin	Ancient Ecclesiastical and Judicial Tribunal
Sephardi (plural, Sephardim)	One following the Spanish Jewish tradition
Shekel	World Zionist Organization tax
Shomer (plural, Shomrim)	Watchman
Shulhan Aruch	Jewish Ritual Code
Solel Boneh	Federations Building Industry Cooperative
Talmud	The body of Jewish civil and canonical law (also lore) consisting of the combined Mishna, or text and Gemora, or commentary, or restrictedly, Gemora alone

Talmud Torah K'neged Kulom	Above all, learning
Tnuva	Cooperative for the sale and distribution of the produce of the land
Torah	Jewish Law and Lore; in the narrow sense, the Pentateuch or the Holy Scroll containing it
Tozeret Ha aretz	Produced in the land
Tzur Israel	Rock of Israel
Ulpan	Adult Extension School for the Study of Hebrew
Vaad Leumi	National Jewish Council in Palestine
Yeshiva (plural, Yeshivot)	Academy for sacred higher Jewish learning
Yishuv	The Jewish Settlement in Palestine
Yom Kippur	Day of Atonement
Youth Aliyah	Youth Immigration
Zahal	Israel's Defense Army
Zedakah	Charity

Table of Equivalents

1 Dunam	0.247 acre
1 IL (Israeli pound), exchange value	$.56
1 Kilogram	2.2046 ILS
1 Kilometer	.62137 mile
1 Liter	.908 dry quart, or 1.0567 liquid quarts

Index